D1571493

About Island Press

Island Press is the only nonprofit organization in the United States whose principal purpose is the publication of books on environmental issues and natural resource management. We provide solutions-oriented information to professionals, public officials, business and community leaders, and concerned citizens who are shaping responses to environmental problems.

In 1994, Island Press celebrated its tenth anniversary as the leading provider of timely and practical books that take a multidisciplinary approach to critical environmental concerns. Our growing list of titles reflects our commitment to bringing the best of an expanding body of literature to the environmental community throughout North America and the world.

Support for Island Press is provided by Apple Computer, Inc., The Bullitt Foundation, The Geraldine R. Dodge Foundation, The Energy Foundation, The Ford Foundation, The W. Alton Jones Foundation, The Lyndhurst Foundation, The John D. and Catherine T. MacArthur Foundation, The Andrew W. Mellon Foundation, The Joyce Mertz-Gilmore Foundation, The National Fish and Wildlife Foundation, The Pew Charitable Trusts, The Pew Global Stewardship Initiative, The Rockefeller Philanthropic Collaborative, Inc., and individual donors.

About The Student Conservation Association

The Student Conservation Association (SCA) fosters lifelong stewardship of the environment by offering opportunities for education, leadership, and personal and career development while providing the highest quality public service in natural resource management, environmental protection, and conservation. Since 1957, SCA has placed nearly 30,000 American high school and college student volunteers in more than 300 national parks and wilderness areas throughout the United States. Their essential conservation work includes preparation of American parks for the massive public use they receive, restoration of overused areas, maintenance of thousands of backcountry trails, and preservation and study of wildlife and wildlife habitats. In addition, the Association has offered international exchange programs with Russia, Estonia, Latvia, Mexico, and Canada. One of the extraordinary legacies of SCA is that thousands of the students previously involved in this program are now actively engaged in conservation careers.

THE
GUIDE TO
GRADUATE
ENVIRONMENTAL
PROGRAMS

THE
GUIDE TO
GRADUATE
ENVIRONMENTAL
PROGRAMS

The Student Conservation Association

ISLAND PRESS
Washington, D.C. ● Covelo, California

ISLAND PRESS is a trademark of The Center for Resource Economics.

Library of Congress Cataloging-in-Publication Data

The guide to graduate environmental programs / The Student Conservation
  Association
      p.   cm.
  Includes bibliographical references and index.
  ISBN 1-55963-339-5 (cloth). — ISBN 1-55963-340-9 (paper)
  1. Environmental sciences—Study and teaching (Higher)—United
States. 2. Universities and colleges—United States—Graduate work.
I. Student Conservation Association (U.S.)
GE80.G85   1997
363.7'0071'173—dc21   97-5603
                                                                CIP

Printed on recycled, acid-free paper ♲

Manufactured in the United States of America

10 9 8 7 6 5 4 3 2 1

CONTENTS

FOREWORD

In my twenty years at The Student Conservation Association (SCA), I have seen the quest for information about environmental volunteer and employment opportunities skyrocket. Every day we receive hundreds of telephone calls at our New Hampshire headquarters from people of all ages who want to conserve and preserve the natural resources that are so crucial to the quality of our lives. In the past these calls have focused on the volunteer opportunities that SCA provides natural resource management agencies and eager participants. Over the past several years, however, there has been a rapidly growing and enthusiastic interest, both among people who call SCA as well as among those I meet in my travels, in how to prepare to enter the environmental workforce as professionals. The diversity of interests and career goals of these individuals is striking. It indicates the surprisingly wide range of jobs and careers that characterizes environmental employment, including positions as environmental lawyers, waste management engineers, nonprofit development and public relations specialists, park rangers, "green" marketers, natural resource managers, foresters, and hundreds of other opportunities too numerous to list here.

In response to this growing interest SCA developed *Earth Work* magazine, a monthly periodical that provides employment postings as well as feature articles on jobs and careers in the environment and the people who hold them. In 1993, spurred on by the magazine's success, we published *Earth Work: A Resource Guide to Nationwide Green Jobs*—a compilation of articles selected from the magazine, as well as new, never before published information on how to prepare for green employment and where to find it.

With this guide to graduate environmental programs SCA takes another step along the path of providing accurate and comprehensive career information to young people, as well as jobseekers and career changers of all ages, whose interests lead them to graduate programs and degrees that will qualify them for fulfilling jobs and careers conserving, protecting, and restoring our natural resource heritage.

The Guide to Graduate Environmental Programs uses clear language and accurate, up-to-date facts to take you through the complicated process of identifying, applying to, entering, and matriculating at the graduate school of your choice. This book will help you to compare graduate schools by size, location, program focus, research facilities and opportunities, student mix, and academic reputation. You will learn from this guide, for instance, which graduate schools emphasize research, which provide fellowships, which have high and which have low student-faculty ratios, which focus on labs and fieldwork, and which encourage diversity. And, most importantly, you will have at your fingertips the most up-to-date admissions and program information on more than 150 graduate schools nationwide.

The Student Conservation Association is pleased to have this opportunity to provide you with this one-of-a-kind resource book that can guide your way to graduate study and, we hope, future work in the environment. On behalf of all of us, I wish you clarity, enthusiasm, and success as you prepare to become what our Earth needs so much: skilled, well-educated, and committed stewards. Good luck on your graduate school adventure!

SCOTT IZZO
SCA President, 1989–1996

HOW THIS BOOK CAME TO BE

The Guide to Graduate Environmental Programs is the product of several years of collaboration involving many individuals and institutions. As part of ongoing efforts to identify information needs, Island Press recognized in 1990 that prospective graduate students needed help in evaluating environmental programs. However, since several of the major programs were undergoing extensive changes at that time, a book seemed premature. Instead, Island Press editors monitored the progress of rapidly evolving graduate programs through its advisory board.

Two years later, Island Press received a proposal for a similar project from Diana Francis, a career counselor at the University of California, Santa Barbara (UCSB), who had noted that UCSB undergraduates needed guidance in selecting graduate environmental programs. Sensing that the time was now ripe to undertake the project, Island Press shared their ideas and research with her. With the assistance of UCSB career center staff, Ms. Francis generated a preliminary list of 412 environmental programs, departments, and schools at universities across the country. Upon leaving UCSB Ms. Francis contributed the results of her research to Island Press. Island Press then fleshed out the concept and engaged The Student Conservation Association (SCA), a nonprofit organization based in Charlestown, New Hampshire, as the project sponsor. With the enthusiastic support of SCA president Scott Izzo, Richard Wizansky agreed to oversee the development of the volume on SCA's behalf.

Working with SCA, and with the assistance of Dr. Stephen Kellert of the

Yale School of Forestry and Environmental Studies, Yale graduate students Kate Bickert and Harriet Honigfeld designed a survey, a copy of which is included as Appendix B of this volume. The survey was mailed to faculty representing each of the 412 programs; when the surveys were returned, Ms. Bickert and Ms. Honigfeld compiled the results. Elissa Wolfson and Kristy Manning then summarized and synthesized those results and added supplementary information to form the text of the book. Special thanks go to executive editor Barbara Dean and other Island Press staff who provided valuable guidance throughout the lengthy research and writing process.

INTRODUCTION

Congratulations on your decision to pursue entrance into a graduate environmental program. In many ways, there is no better time to embark upon such a worthwhile and valuable experience. Employment opportunities in the environmental field are on the rise, and graduate programs across the country are expanding their curricula. Environmental protection and the responsible management of natural resources have become top priorities among citizens, business leaders, and decision makers in this country, and in-depth knowledge of environmental processes and policies is now a highly valued asset.

Regardless of academic institution, disciplinary field, or type of degree pursued, a graduate education represents a major investment of time, money, and energy. In the environmental field, such an investment can reap a variety of benefits. First, careers such as environmental law, advanced scientific research, or teaching require the specialized training that comes with graduate work. Second, you may feel a particular subject to be of such great importance that you want to delve into it in depth, either to make it your life's work or for your own personal satisfaction. Finally, there may be more conventional payoffs; while jobs in environmental engineering and other technical professions may be attainable with just a bachelor's degree, a graduate degree may double your starting salary in such fields. In fact, for many professionals either anticipating or currently working in the environmental field, the lack of a graduate degree can be a major obstacle to entry or advancement.

Environmental problems and the strategies required to resolve them carry some very unique characteristics. Environmental issues do not respect geographic or political boundaries; for example, efforts to slow global climate change, to protect marine fisheries, or to mitigate acid rain require skills of diplomacy and international relations as well as familiarity with economics, policy, and scientific processes. Hence, the pursuit of a graduate education in the environment offers both the challenge and the opportunity of reconciling multiple disciplines, including biology, chemistry, economics, statistics, law, and philosophy, to name just a few. In an academic climate that often relegates seemingly related disciplines to separate departments and programs, structuring such an education can pose one of the biggest challenges of all.

This book is designed to help prospective graduate students navigate that process. As you may have already discovered, there is currently no other guide that focuses specifically on graduate environmental programs. You may also have found that, even after you have located a particular university with a program in your area of interest, it is difficult to know which department or person to contact—switchboard operators often do not know where to direct your call, especially if the word *environment* is not in the department's title (e.g., biology or public health). This guide provides the contact information needed to conduct a comprehensive yet targeted search for the graduate environmental program that best suits your individual goals.

Using This Guide

This book provides an overview of the process of researching and selecting graduate environmental programs, as well as in-depth profiles of the individual programs. Part I provides information on such important details as prerequisites, the application process, and opportunities for concurrent degrees and cross-registration; the final chapter of this part offers an overview of the various types of programs offering graduate environmental study. Part II, which constitutes the bulk of this volume, presents a series of profiles of graduate environmental programs from around the country. The format of the profiles is consistent throughout, facilitating direct comparison among programs or universities. The appendixes that make up Part III contain a listing of contact information for some programs not profiled in the book, a sample copy of the survey form used to gather information for the program profiles, and a listing of some related resources. And in Part IV profiles are indexed by state and program topic area.

Compiling the Profiles

To compile the profiles listed in Part II, The Student Conservation Association considered a preliminary list of 412 environmental programs, departments, and schools within universities across the country. That list was drawn up by the career center staff at the University of California, Santa Barbara, based upon a literature search, queries over the Internet, and contact with environmental professionals and associations. Certificate-only programs were not included. Selection preference was given to programs mentioned repeatedly by environmental professionals and to those drawing a more diverse student body. In recognition of the fact that people of color have long been under-represented within the environmental movement and over-represented among those most impacted by pollutants, special efforts were made to contact universities that are members of either the Hispanic Association of Colleges and Universities or the Historically Black Colleges and Universities to ensure their representation in this guidebook.

Postcards requesting information and course catalogues were sent to all 412 programs. Subsequently, a comprehensive survey designed by faculty and graduate students at the Yale School of Forestry and Environmental Studies was mailed to faculty representing each program (see Appendix B). Of the 412 graduate programs queried, 156 programs completed and returned their surveys, a response rate of 38 percent. Each of these surveys has been reworked into a profile. To supplement this information, and to ensure that all of the most noteworthy programs are included in this guide, additional profiles have been compiled for a select number of key programs that failed to return their surveys. These latter profiles were based on literature review and personal interviews. The absence of a particular profile, or segment of a profile, reflects no editorial judgment on the part of SCA. If you have additional information on other exemplary graduate environmental programs, please let us know so that we can send them a survey and include them in future editions of this guide.

While this guide presents the latest available information, derived directly from the universities themselves, bear in mind that there are an ever-expanding number of programs in the environmental field and that existing programs are constantly evolving. (In fact, survey results indicate that 37 percent of queried universities plan to make some changes, including adding faculty or expanding curricula, within their environmental programs over the next several years.) Most of the information provided was accurate as of November 1994—the date by which the surveys were completed—and some follow-up verification was conducted during the summer of 1996. You should expect to encounter changes in names, titles, and phone numbers as new programs are created, others merge, and still others strive to find their niches within their respective universities.

PART I

GRADUATE ENVIRONMENTAL STUDY: A ROAD MAP

CHAPTER 1

RESEARCHING GRADUATE ENVIRONMENTAL PROGRAMS

As the number of graduate environmental programs continues to increase, prospective students today have greater freedom than ever before to choose a program best suited to their needs and interests. With this freedom, however, comes the challenge of identifying the most appropriate program to meet your individual goals. In addition to the expansion of programs specifically geared toward environmental studies, there has been a steady increase in the number of interdepartmental, interdisciplinary, off-campus, and part-time graduate programs offered at universities throughout the country. Many universities have established combined-degree programs, enabling students to combine their master's and doctoral work or to mix academic and professional studies. Researching environmental programs requires careful consideration of all of these factors, and more.

Environmental Career Opportunities in the 1990s

As you begin your search, you will first need to decide which type of degree or program is most appropriate for you. If you have been out in the working world, you may have already experienced the "glass ceiling" in your career

3

advancement that can come with holding a bachelor's degree alone. Regardless of your professional background or lack thereof, the prospect of attaining certain career goals may influence your choice of a particular environmental discipline.

Those interested in an environmental career today are no longer limited to working as a park ranger or biologist—though talented professionals in such fields continue to play an important role in protecting our environment. In fact, today there are millions of people working in a wide variety of environmental professions. For example, an environmental manager may work for a consulting firm or large company to develop and implement pollution prevention strategies. Environmental engineers conduct technical analyses of water and air pollution controls or work in the bioremediation field, which uses bacteria to destroy chemicals. An ecological scientist may specialize in fish and wildlife management for the U.S. Forest Service, or in biodiversity research on behalf of The Nature Conservancy. And master's graduates who specialize in geographical information systems (GIS) are in great demand by public and private agencies: computerized GIS systems are increasingly used by national and state parks and forests, the U.S. Army Corps of Engineers, private companies, and tourist developments to analyze data on natural resources and land use.

For prospective graduate students less inclined toward the natural sciences, there is plenty of room within the environmental field for "generalists." In the nonprofit sector, fund raisers or public relations experts are in high demand; graduates with broad-based environmental knowledge and strong writing or communications skills are valuable assets for many organizations. Particularly in Washington, D.C., but also in state capitals all over the country, policy analysts—who may work for advocacy groups, public agencies, or legislative bodies—are coveted for their strong familiarity with environmental laws, economics, and the political process. Environmental educators are needed in K–12 classrooms and at colleges, nature centers, parks, zoos, and museums across the country. Environmental lawyers work for public agencies, corporations, private firms, insurance companies, and nonprofit think tanks and advocacy groups. And there are numerous opportunities to work in the field of environmental services or products, whether as an ecotourism guide or in the marketing department of a manufacturer of "green" products.

For additional information on environmental career opportunities, there are several guides currently available, many of which are listed in Appendix C of this book.

Since environmental issues cross such a range of disciplines, and with such a wide range of employment opportunities available, structuring a coherent and directed educational agenda can be a difficult task. Many employers are acknowledging this challenge by remaining flexible and opening their minds to a variety of hiring criteria. Indeed, the academic preparation of some of our most celebrated environmentalists ranges from the traditional to the alternative. Deceased scientist-writer Rachel Carson, who alerted the world to the dangers of pesticides with *Silent Spring*, earned a master's in zoology from Johns Hopkins. Wangari Maathai, who launched Kenya's Green Belt Movement—a women's grassroots project that has planted 10 million trees throughout Africa—was the first Kenyan woman to earn a Ph.D., in the study of anatomy at the University of Nairobi. Politician, author, and professor Dr. Barry Commoner, currently director of the Queens College Center for the Biology of Natural Systems, holds a Ph.D. in biology from Harvard University. And eco-entrepreneur Tom Chappell, president of Tom's of Maine, a line of natural body care products, earned an M.A. in theology from Harvard Divinity School.

Some students feel that it is important to know exactly what their career goals are before applying to graduate schools. Several years of working within a particular field may make your course work more meaningful when you finally do attend, providing a relevant context for a more directed course of study. However, others view graduate school primarily as a means to further clarify career goals. An illuminating class, a fulfilling internship, or participation in a community activity during graduate school can help focus the academic experience, inspiring enthusiasm for future career opportunities.

Choosing Your Degree

You will also need to decide which type of degree—master's or doctoral—to pursue. While master's degrees are indeed becoming a minimum requirement for many jobs beyond entry level, bear in mind that a Ph.D. may be considered too advanced, too specialized, or too esoteric for other positions; preference may be given to candidates with more practical job experience. Talking to people working in your chosen field may help you decide just how much education you want and need.

Finally, you should also consider whether to follow an "academic" or "professional" course of study. Recently, as the demand for graduate education—

and particularly for more flexible graduate education—has grown, the distinctions between academic and professional programs have become less clear. Because only a small portion of programs officially label themselves as either "academic" or "professional," in many cases it is necessary to review a variety of aspects of a program—course requirements, career counseling services, alumni career paths—to determine its orientation.

Generally, academic doctoral degrees, most often the Doctor of Philosophy, or Ph.D., require highly focused and original research in a chosen field; this is the degree students interested in "hard" sciences—such as environmental biology or chemistry—might pursue. Professional doctoral degrees include the Doctor of Medicine (M.D.), and Doctor of Jurisprudence (J.D.); a student interested in environmental law would pursue the latter. Master's degrees may be either academic or professional in orientation and are now offered in many fields. In professional fields such as environmental marketing (M.B.A.), public policy (M.P.P. or M.P.A.), and environmental engi-

---

After earning a master's in sociology from Texas Agricultural and Mechanical (Texas A&M) University, Gavin Smith went on to pursue a Ph.D. in urban and regional science, also at Texas A&M. His goal was to parlay the theoretical knowledge he had gained as a master's student into a more pragmatic and applied approach to resolving practical issues of environment and development. Concentrating in the areas of environmental planning and dispute resolution, Gavin took courses in wildlife and fisheries science, ecology, environmental policy, and political science before completing his thesis on growth management, environmental conflict, and the politics of development in a local watershed.

Gavin chose the field of environmental planning specifically for its practical approach. "Because I had already earned a graduate degree with a fairly theoretical focus, I was looking for an interdisciplinary Ph.D. program that would give me skills and tools that I could apply to real-world problems." Upon earning his doctorate, Gavin moved to North Carolina, where he was employed first with the Environmental Fund for North Carolina and later with a grassroots watershed protection group. He recently began working for the state of North Carolina in the area of emergency management planning, helping to implement the National Flood Insurance Program for communities in the coastal plain.

neering (M.S. or M.Eng.), a master's is often sufficient to find a good job. In general, the programs offering a professional degree tend to provide a broader and more interdisciplinary range of courses than most academic programs.

Beginning Your Search

To allow ample time for completing the application process, it is a good idea to begin gathering information on programs and universities up to a year and a half before your expected date of matriculation. If you are applying for national scholarships, or if your undergraduate school has an evaluation committee through which you are applying to a law school, you may need to begin the process two years before matriculation in order to meet the necessary deadlines.

A useful way to begin your research is to consult this guide to find out what environmental programs exist in your field of interest. As you scan the profiles in Part II, you will find the quick facts you need—such as which degrees are offered, areas of student and faculty specialization, program details, tuition costs, and financial aid availability—to come up with a preliminary, manageable list of programs suited to your interests and budget.

You may then want to compare similar programs by considering such questions as: How stringent are admissions and degree requirements? What are the academic abilities, demographic representation, and success levels of the students that have completed this program? What research, library, and computer facilities are available? What is the student-faculty ratio? What internships, assistantships, international study opportunities, and career counseling services are available to graduate students? The profiles in this guide address such questions as well.

To obtain the literature you need to conduct your research, contact the schools directly—a neatly typed or hand-printed postcard is all that is necessary. All materials requests should be addressed directly to the admissions office. In addition to your return address, most admissions offices are interested in knowing your intended matriculation date. Items to request include: an admissions application, information and applications for scholarships and financial aid, recommendation forms, program brochures or catalogues, faculty profiles and research interests, lists of student projects and papers, a student handbook, information on related institutions and research facilities, and a list of recent alumni employers. Also, always request the general graduate bulletin or catalogue, which may reveal additional programs of interest.

Continue your research by consulting professional associations and by requesting information via e-mail and the World Wide Web. (Most universities and many academic departments now sponsor Web sites; the profiles in Part II provide information on locating sites for almost every program.) As you hone in on the universities you really want to apply to, it is a good idea to become familiar with publications and professional journals that focus on the current issues in your field. Note which universities are on the journals' editorial boards—their inclusion reflects strength in that field. Article bylines will let you know who is publishing often in your field of interest, and where they are teaching.

Weighing Key Factors

As you delve deeper into your search, you will find that in addition to course requirements, tuition, and facilities there are a variety of less quantifiable factors that distinguish one program from another. These elements range from the size of the program (our survey indicates that program size ranges from a minimum of 5 students to a maximum of 550, with the average being 72 students) to whether the program is heavily structured or highly flexible. Some of these aspects can only be determined through discussions with students or faculty; others are buried within course catalogues or promotional brochures. And many elements of a program can only be appreciated through the "gut reaction" that comes with a campus visit. In the following pages, we describe some of the most fundamental factors that can set one program apart from another.

Cross-Registration and Concurrent Degrees. As testimony to the highly interdisciplinary nature of environmental studies, 92 percent of the universities we surveyed allow students to cross-register with other departments, and 40 percent offer joint degrees with other schools or programs within the university. This latter option, also known as the combined or concurrent degree program, allows the student to enroll in two separate programs and earn two separate degrees (e.g., an M.S. and an M.B.A.) at once. Students pursuing a concurrent degree find that a well-organized program can result in a tremendous amount of synergy, not only programmatically but also in terms of the opportunity it provides for interacting with classmates who hold diverse perspectives on environmental issues.

At Duke University, Kristine Anastasio pursued a concurrent degree program in environmental management and public policy through dual enrollment in the School of Forestry and Environmental Studies (now the Nicholas School of the Environment) and the Graduate Program in Public Policy (now the Sanford Institute of Public Policy). After five semesters of course work, two summers of internships, and one combined master's project, she earned a Master of Environmental Management and a Master of Public Policy. "Due to a very high level of administrative and academic coordination between the two programs, I was able to obtain two master's degrees for little more than the price of one. Even though the two programs are entirely self-sufficient, there is a great spirit of information exchange at Duke that enables—and often requires—all students to delve into disciplines offered in other departments and schools. In addition to the two programs in which I was enrolled, I took courses at the Duke Law School, the University of North Carolina, and North Carolina State University. And while I was required to submit two separate versions of my combined master's project, my various advisors were all on the same page."

Among the universities surveyed, the most popular joint degree programs combine environment with business (17 percent), law (12 percent), education (10 percent), public policy (5 percent), and public health (5 percent). It is also possible to obtain joint degrees in such fields as international relations, engineering, landscape planning/architecture, and the physical sciences. Completion of a concurrent degree program can take anywhere from a semester to several years longer than an individual degree, but it almost always requires significantly less time and money than the separate completion of two individual programs.

Recognizing the value of information sharing in addressing environmental problems, as well as the relative strengths and weaknesses of individual programs, many schools are forming research and educational partnerships involving "team teaching" and cross-registration among universities. In this way, students enrolled in a school that is lacking in certain disciplines—for example, forestry or coastal zone management—can benefit from course offerings and instruction at neighboring institutions.

International Opportunities. As environmental issues become increasingly international in nature, the proliferation of global treaties and new markets in other countries will continue to create new job opportunities abroad. Recognizing the growing importance of such issues, as well as the increasing demand for professionals with practical international experience, 36 of the universities profiled in this guide offer programs focusing on international environmental issues. In addition to sponsoring research and outreach in such regions as Central America, Africa, China, and South America, many schools offer fellowships, field trips, discussion groups, and internships focused on international work. Twenty-two percent of schools report having alumni who are working internationally. If you are interested in pursuing international study or work, you may wish to consider schools that have a higher percentage of international students and that have faculty conducting research abroad.

Career Counseling Services. Since many environmental graduate students enroll specifically to prepare for a career in the environmental field, one-on-one career counseling can be a tremendous asset to a graduate program. Sixty-nine percent of the universities we surveyed offer career counseling programs, and most universities report that over 80 percent of their students find work within six months of graduation. In addition to maintaining databases of career opportunities and advising students on resumé preparation, cover letters, and interview techniques, many career counselors offer guidance on obtaining fellowships and summer internships. Most schools can provide prospective students with a general overview of the types of organizations employing recent alumni, if not a list of employers' names, specific positions, and salary ranges. Such career information can also provide some interesting insights into the culture of the graduate program itself; a program that places the majority of its graduates with environmental consulting firms and large government agencies may offer a completely different educational experience and learning climate than one whose graduates gravitate toward outdoor recreation and natural resources management.

Tuition, Financial Aid, Assistantships, and Loans. While the amount of tuition required to enroll in a graduate environmental program varies widely from one program to the next, enrollment in a graduate program in the 1990s is a major financial investment. Even given the accessibility of federally subsidized lending programs, it is not uncommon for students to discover that their available funding simply cannot cover the high cost of tuition plus living expenses and textbooks. Those who do obtain the maximum loan amount can find themselves saddled with significant debt upon graduation—a burden that can seem particularly heavy in a field that, at least compared to business, law, or medicine, is not known for its high salaries.

Fortunately, many schools offer a variety of financial aid benefits to help ease this load. Such assistance can range from a reduction in tuition—usually based on need—to special fellowships rewarding scholarly or service-oriented merit. And several institutions offer graduate work-study assistantships that can pay up to several thousand dollars per semester. Assistantships, which at some institutions are offered to all students and at others to only a select few, typically require 10 to 20 hours per week of research or clerical work in the office or lab of departmental staff or faculty. Most programs also sponsor teaching assistant (TA) positions, usually offered to the top students in a class; TAs may be asked to assist with class preparation and the grading of problem sets and exams or, in some cases, to lead class discussion on a regular basis.

Information on financial aid is not always spelled out clearly in a program's literature; the admissions office of each program can provide further detail on the range of available opportunities.

Walking the Talk: Environmental Literacy and the "Shadow Curriculum." While environmental programs are offered at hundreds of universities around the country, it is surprising how few of them make a point of practicing what they preach in their daily operations. In recent years, numerous campaigns have been launched to make university practices more environmentally friendly. Many of these programs are driven almost entirely by student initiative, almost in grassroots fashion. At the other end of the spectrum, high-level educators from around the world have joined to form the Association of University Leaders for a Sustainable Future (ULSF), which is working to promote "environmental literacy," the internalization of ecological principles and ethics into educational programs. At the heart of this concept is what ULSF terms the "shadow curriculum," linking environmental literacy with institutional environmental performance.[1] In short, how does a university's own environmental performance—its solid waste practices, transportation policies, and impact on the local community—mesh with its educational mission?

---

[1]Thomas Kelly, Learning from the "Shadow Curriculum." *The Declaration.* Medford, MA: Association of University Leaders for a Sustainable Future, May–August 1996.

Several universities have begun to take these concepts to heart by insti-
tutionalizing a range of environmental initiatives. For example, the Center
for Regenerative Studies at California State Polytechnic University Pomona,
currently under construction, will employ solar energy and natural sewage
treatment to support housing, classroom, and research facilities for 90 students, faculty, and staff. The University of Virginia's Solar Resource Center
will use photovoltaic cells to power a new building wing that will employ energy-efficient technology and design. Through campus "environmental au-
dits," the University of South Carolina, University of Pennsylvania, Brown
University, and many others are examining the environmental impacts of
university operations in solid waste, water, energy, and transportation. Most

With 47,000 students and 17,500 faculty, Rutgers University generates
a large amount of solid waste. A New Jersey state university, in 1988
Rutgers established its Environmental Procurement Program to meet a
state requirement that all public institutions divert a minimum of 60
percent of their waste stream by 1995. In 1992, student advocates
convinced the university to institute operational policies to encourage
recycling and source reduction through a series of educational programs and a major push to revamp university purchasing practices.

The "command center" responsible for implementing these strategies is the University Procurement Department, which manages all university purchasing contracts. As director of purchasing, Kevin Lyons
has instituted an initiative to evaluate the environmental impact of all
incoming purchases and outgoing waste. In the process, he has involved university vendors in a public awareness campaign to educate
students, faculty, and staff on source reduction practices. As a condition of each service contract, Lyons requires that all service providers
participate actively in implementing the Rutgers Environmental Public
Awareness Program by placing educational advertisements in newspapers, recommending strategies to increase campus participation in the
program, providing case studies of successful programs at other
schools, and helping Rutgers develop further waste reduction strategies. Finally, Lyons also actively encourages student projects, many of
them undertaken for course credit, that generate useful data and recommendations for further source reduction initiatives by the University
Procurement Department.

of these projects involve the close collaboration of students, faculty, administrators, and other staff.

Some programs are working to instill environmental literacy by using course work involving "service learning" through hands-on projects in local communities. Brown's Community Environmental Service Initiative provides technical assistance to community residents, organizations, and public agencies; for example, the Partnerships to Prevent Lead Poisoning initiative combines research, community education, and public outreach to identify and reduce the risk of childhood lead poisoning in the Elmwood neighborhood of Providence.

Ethnic Diversity. With most programs consisting almost entirely (90–100 percent) of Caucasian students, there is an unfortunate lack of ethnic diversity in all but a few schools profiled in this guide. This discrepancy is reflected throughout the environmental movement as well. A number of domestic environmental organizations are attempting to address this issue via task forces and active recruiting of minorities. The National Park Service has organized programs to attract college students of color to work as seasonal rangers. Some universities are following suit. Each summer, Virginia Polytechnic Institute and State University hosts three days of a career camp held by Virginia's George Washington National Forest; the professors teach urban and ethnically diverse students about careers in natural resources. The profiles listed in Part II contain information about the ethnic makeup of each program.

Institutional and Faculty Prestige. For better or for worse, the prestige of a university or program can play a major role in influencing the applicant's selection process, the employer's hiring decision, and society's perception of an individual's credentials. When the quality of a program fails to live up to its name, the relative weight of this factor can be a source of great frustration for some students—especially if that program is an expensive one. For some, this frustration is dispelled when they enter the job market, where many employers seek out graduates of "name" schools. In a field where excellent programs exist at schools of all sizes and levels of national recognition, but where many good programs remain unknown due to the fledgling nature of the entire field, balancing prestige with other important factors can be a very delicate process.

At the graduate level, in some fields it is actually considered more important to study under a preeminent faculty member than it is to study at a prestigious university. Graduate research funds are often funneled to the faculty members in charge of favored projects, and a graduate department's reputation often depends largely upon the reputation of its faculty. For Ph.D. candidates pursuing a future in research or academia, one's faculty advisor can be an extremely important credential.

Hence, it is a good idea to learn as much as you can about the faculty members at the universities that interest you most, particularly since most Ph.D. candidates, as well as academically oriented master's degree candidates, must select their own advisors, often early on in their studies. In researching the faculties of various universities, consider their academic backgrounds, the research they are currently conducting, and their interaction with colleagues within their own and other departments. Do not underestimate the relative importance of their teaching skills, accessibility, and concern with student development; a relatively unknown faculty member whose office door is always open may be preferable to a prestigious advisor who is overburdened with travel, research, and publishing commitments (as is often that case at major research universities). If you visit the school, sit in on some classes and schedule appointments with those faculty who interest you most. Graduate students and recent alumni can also provide you with valuable (and often highly candid) perspectives on individual professors as well as the program as a whole.

Personal Preferences and "Lifestyle" Factors. In evaluating the many elements that constitute a graduate education, do not be afraid to give your own personal traits and preferences considerable weight. For students accustomed to being a "big fish in a small pond," a smaller school may provide a welcome feeling of security or greater opportunity to excel; conversely, the anonymity of a large department or university could provide a much-needed change for those who have attended smaller undergraduate institutions. The structure of a program and its level of flexibility are also important factors to consider; some students appreciate the programmatic guidance and standardized performance evaluation that a highly structured program provides, while others may thrive in a program offering a great deal of freedom and opportunities to follow one's own initiative.

And don't discount issues of lifestyle; for many prospective students, graduate school offers a rare (and even luxurious, to those tied to a specific location) opportunity to relocate to a new town or region of the country and to experience something completely new. Because the daily requirements of a graduate program can be stress-inducing, some students make a point of choosing a program in a highly "livable" community. Such factors as housing affordability, climate, an urban or rural setting, and proximity to natural and cultural amenities can play a major role in shaping the graduate experience.

Finally, remember that where you go to school could later influence your employment options; our study shows that most alumni end up working in the same region of the country as the universities they attended. In addition to the regional bias that some employers practice in their hiring, logistically it can simply be easier to find a job in the area in which one lives. Because many graduate programs allow and even require participation in local activities—whether through a paid internship, volunteer program, or research project—your educational experience may place you in close contact with local employers. In sum, then, where you attend school could very well be where you choose to remain upon receiving your degree.

Visiting the School

If at all possible, visit the universities that interest you most. Such a visit may or may not include your admissions interview (described in Chapter 2); if it does, try to schedule your interview toward the latter part of your visit so that you will have had a chance to get a feel for the campus and to formulate some questions. Be sure to write or call the admissions office several weeks in advance to give them a chance to arrange a campus tour and set up appointments with faculty members and students. Request a campus map and suggestions for accommodations; in many cases the admissions office can make arrangements for you to stay with a student, providing a prime opportunity for questions and a firsthand glimpse into the culture of the program.

If a campus visit is impossible, try to obtain a promotional video, now available from most universities. But remember that such videos—like the course catalogues and bulletins—are produced by the institutions themselves; it is obviously in their interest to show themselves in the best possible light. Visiting a campus in person will enable you to sit in on some classes, check out the library, read the student newspaper and alumni magazine, peruse bulletin boards for extracurricular activities, take a walk around the surrounding town—in short, to really get an intuitive feel for the university and see if it is a good match with your own needs.

CHAPTER 2

THE APPLICATION PROCESS

Although it seems wise to refrain from putting all your eggs in one basket, it is surprising how many prospective students apply to only one or two schools. For those applicants who are determined to enroll in one specific program, there may be no need to apply to a variety of schools; if you are not accepted into your one choice the first time around, you can always apply again. However, if you do intend to matriculate as soon as possible and at all costs, be sure to apply to at least one program into which you are confident of being accepted. Sixty percent of the universities we surveyed report changes in the size of their master's applicant pools; of those, 88 percent report increases. And of the 30 percent of Ph.D. programs reporting changes in size, 93 percent report increases. In short, competition for admission is increasing at all levels.

Meeting Your Deadline

Application deadlines can range from one full year prior to matriculation for some early decision programs to just a few months before matriculation for programs with rolling admissions (in which there is no deadline, and admissions decisions are made as applications are submitted). The majority of deadlines for August/September entry will fall between January and March of the year of matriculation.

Many schools often encourage and act upon early applications. Applying early to such universities is much more likely to work to your advantage than to your disadvantage, as applicants are not usually rejected early unless their qualifications are clearly not up to par for that university. Early application demonstrates your strong motivation to attend a particular university, and it gives admissions committees ample time to consider those aspects of your application that are more open to interpretation (such as your application essay).

Perhaps, in your case, an application deadline is unusually early, or you have made a last-minute decision to attend graduate school. If it is not possible for you to meet a deadline, contact the university and/or department to find out if they will consider a late application. In some cases, a space may become available at the last minute.

Prerequisites: Course Work and the GRE

Application requirements vary widely from one program to another and from one university to another. An early start may be critical, as fulfilling the missing prerequisites for programs you are interested in may require evening, weekend, or summer classes. The profiles in this guide, under the subhead "Admission to the Program," will inform you of these prerequisites, including required courses, degrees, and Graduate Record Examination (GRE) scores.

As a condition of enrollment, many graduate programs require the successful completion of introductory course work in such areas as economics, calculus, biology, chemistry, ecology, or statistics. Try not to let that criterion deter you from applying to a specific program; in some cases, specific prerequisites are not necessarily required for admission but rather must be taken prior to enrolling in certain classes. Some schools may advise you to take a course during the summer preceding the first semester; others may simply require that you take your prerequisite at the university prior to enrolling in the specific course to which the prerequisite applies. In retrospect, some graduates of master's programs have regretted not having pursued a specific area of concentration, particularly one heavily grounded in science, simply due to the daunting level of unfulfilled prerequisites, or to a general feeling of "science intimidation." Others have been relieved to find programs that do not require intensive preparation in the sciences. If you are intimidated by science, it is possible to find programs with minimal science prerequisites; however, you may discover that taking an introductory course (for example, at a local community college) in ecology or statistics may provide just the refresher you need to prepare for a rigorous graduate program.

The GRE, a multiple choice test designed to measure the verbal, mathematical, and analytical skills you have developed during your academic career, is required by nearly three-quarters of the graduate schools profiled in this guide. In addition, departments within universities sometimes have their own requirements for scores in certain subject areas. Some schools require a minimum GRE score as a condition of enrollment, while others consider scores on a case-by-case basis. The profiles listed in Part II provide information on GRE requirements and average scores for some programs.

Registering for and taking the GRE well in advance of your application process will give you the chance to take the exam again if you need to improve your scores. Taking a preparatory course, or working with a guidebook that includes model exams with each question answered and explained, can help better prepare you for your first GRE. Appendix C provides references for several recommended guidebooks.

Since GREs are the only standardized measurement available to admissions committees, some universities give them considerable weight. But at most universities, grades and recommendations by known faculty are considered to be somewhat more important than GRE scores. Before you go to the trouble of taking your GREs, be certain that you wish to matriculate in the near future; many programs do not accept scores that are more than five years old.

Some graduate schools also require your alma mater to send your official transcripts directly to them; to have this done, you will need to contact your college registrar. While your grades are important, other factors on your transcript are taken into consideration as well. These include your course load, the difficulty level of the courses you have taken, and the reputation of your undergraduate institution.

The Application Essay

For many students, writing an essay, or personal statement, is the most difficult part of the application process. While specific requirements vary widely, an application essay should basically be a clear, succinct statement of your background, ideas, and goals. Some programs require only a few paragraphs about why you want to attend graduate school, while others— particularly business schools—may request half a dozen separate essays asking you to expand upon your strengths, weaknesses, and achievements, or to solve complex hypothetical problems.

The information a university may be trying to glean from your essay often falls into three areas: background information, such as your interests, education, research, or work experience; future-oriented expectations, such as your reasons for deciding to pursue graduate education in this particular field and at this particular university, your expectations of the program and career opportunities within the field, and your short- and long-term goals; and personality factors, such as characteristics that differentiate you from your peers and would add diversity to the student body, your enthusiasm about and commitment to your field of study, and your level of maturity. A very unique and creative piece of writing may help you stand out among the multitudes of applicants at highly competitive schools.

If you are given a choice, there are any number of subjects to discuss. Being the leader of a project or initiative looks good, as do publishing outside of school and press coverage of anything you have accomplished. Do your professional and extracurricular activities relate to your academic and career plans? A consistent, directed profile sets you apart by showing the extent and depth of your commitment to your field. You should have something that you stuck with and succeeded in to show your capacity for follow-through, perseverance, and dedication—mastery of a field will serve you better than dabbling in a series of unconnected endeavors.

Upon completion of your essay, circulate it among your professors, advisors, employers, or other trusted acquaintances for critiquing, editing, and proofing. Be absolutely sure that the final draft of your essay, and your entire application, contains no spelling or grammatical errors, that there are no blank spaces on your application, and that the print is clear and easy to read. If you want to use an essay for more than one school, be sure that it truly fits the topics called for, without sounding forced; although this advice may seem obvious, be sure to proofread carefully to ensure that all mentions of the previous school's name are deleted and replaced by the next school's.

Letters of Recommendation

Most graduate schools also require several letters of recommendation. If you will not be going to graduate school immediately after graduation from college, but if you are planning to pursue further education sometime in the future, consider opening a credentials file with your undergraduate college, if it offers this service. Forms with the university's letterhead are usually provided, and the recommendation letters written on these forms are kept on file for you until you begin the application process. Alternately, some graduate schools will provide their own forms for your references to complete, in which case you will need to wait until you receive the application packet to begin gathering your recommendations.

Selecting people to write recommendations for you is not always simple. You may get a clue from the recommendation forms provided by the schools: Do the questions lean more heavily toward academic abilities or personality traits? Recommendations from faculty members may be essential for academically oriented programs, while for professional programs recommendations from employers in the field may be equally valid. Identify likely potential references from among professors whose classes you have done well in, supervisors of extracurricular activities, and employers in your field with whom you have had a good working relationship. Consider whether certain faculty, employers, or acquaintances either are connected with the school to which you are applying or specialize in an academic area or profession that is central to that school's mission.

Once you have lined up your references, make it as easy as possible for them to write their letter. If possible, arrange a time to meet with them to provide them with any necessary recommendation forms, stamped and pre-addressed envelopes, and ample supporting materials—such as transcripts, a resumé, and basic information about the programs you are applying to and the course of study you are pursuing. For admission to many programs the delayed submission of a recommendation letter can hold up the review of an entire application—a source of great consternation to anxious applicants. A polite way to follow up is to drop your references a thank-you note about a week before the deadline date—this will remind those who have forgotten and show your appreciation to those who have remembered.

Should you retain the right to see the letter of recommendation? The answer will lie in part with each writer. Some references will prefer to write a letter they know will be confidential; they may feel less limited in expressing their thoughts on your qualifications, or they may simply believe—often accurately so—that a confidential letter will have increased validity and carry more weight as part of your application.

If you are returning to school after several years of employment, have not established a credentials file, and are having difficulty obtaining letters of recommendation from your former undergraduate professors, check with each graduate school you are applying to regarding requirements for faculty recommendations. Their policies may vary considerably; they may waive the requirement of letters of recommendation altogether, or allow you to substitute letters from employers. And at some undergraduate institutions, the dean's office can produce a generic letter testifying to your overall college performance.

Additional Application Materials

Once you have your recommendations in hand, consider potential research, thesis, or dissertation subjects, as some applications will ask you to include a tentative research proposal. It is often useful to include an up-to-date resumé with your application, and if nothing else, this exercise will help you to organize and articulate your skills and experience. Also gather writing samples, published work, and any other relevant material you may wish to include with your application.

Filing Your Applications

Graduate schools often have different application procedures, so take careful note of the most crucial points—particularly the deadlines for submitting test scores, transcripts, and the application itself, as well as whether each deadline represents when these materials should be postmarked or received. Some particularly competitive programs have a two-step application process: If a preliminary application is deemed up to par, the applicant is then invited to submit a second application. Some universities may require all application materials to be sent along in one package; others may request that letters of recommendation and/or transcripts be sent separately. Application fees are usually required for each application you submit. However, if you can demonstrate financial hardship, these application fees may be waived. An individual school's procedures for obtaining fee waivers are often specified on its application form; if not, check with the financial aid office.

If you are applying for financial aid, your financial aid forms are often due along with your application. One question that often comes to a student's mind is whether applying for financial aid will hurt their chances for admission—and unfortunately, the answer is "maybe." With cutbacks in federal aid to education, some universities have had to turn away from "need-blind" admissions policies. But even though you may need to consider tuition costs and financial aid availability, do not base your university selection on these factors. Many expensive universities have generous financial aid budgets. Apply to your ideal programs first, and then think about financing. Get a good, comprehensive guidebook to financial aid, as the field is vast, complicated, and beyond the scope of this book.

If you are applying for an academic program, most universities will require you to send your application materials to their graduate school office, which in turn will forward your complete file to the appropriate department. The department chair, a faculty committee, or both working together will then make a recommendation, usually to the graduate dean or vice president responsible for admissions decisions. However, students applying to a professional school within a university will usually submit their materials directly to that school. Make a copy of your entire application before mailing it, so that you can refer back to your application responses prior to your interview. Also, if your application is lost, as occasionally happens, you'll be able to quickly submit another. Mail it certified delivery—the extra cost is worth the guaranteed receipt.

The Interview

Some university programs, and almost invariably law and business schools, require applicants to come in for an interview. This is an excellent opportunity for you to show an admissions office that you would be an asset to their program. Think of the interview as an information exchange rather than an inquisition. Interviewers are looking to assess your critical thinking and problem-solving skills; they are more likely to ask you a controversial question, or present you with a hypothetical problem to solve, than to test your knowledge of obscure facts. You may be asked to expand upon the same subjects you wrote about in your essay: your interests, academic training, job experiences and research interests, why you want to pursue graduate study, and how you plan to use your degree to further your career aspirations.

Bring along a list of questions to ask, copies of your GRE scores and transcripts, interview confirmation letter, and any course catalogues, brochures, directions, or maps that the school has sent you. For certain fields you may also have to bring along a portfolio of your work to present at the time of your interview. Such a portfolio should include pieces that are most closely related to your proposed area of specialization and that best demonstrate your skills and experience in that area. If, for example, you are interested in specializing in environmental architecture, and are applying to architecture schools, include any ideas, floor plans, or blueprints you may have developed for energy-efficient or nontoxic buildings. If you are considering specializing in environmental journalism, include any articles or papers you may have had published in environmental journals or newspapers.

You can prepare yourself for a graduate school interview by thoroughly reading the university's literature, anticipating the questions you are likely to be asked, and practicing your responses. If you are interviewing with more than one school, try to arrange it so that your first-choice school is your last interview. Prior interviews will help you build your confidence and present yourself more smoothly. During the interview, have some insightful questions of your own to ask, but avoid asking questions that can be answered by reading the literature. If a question requires careful construction, do not be afraid to pause and collect your thoughts. And, of course, be well-groomed, neatly dressed, and on time.

At the conclusion of the interview, ask for a business card, to ensure that you have the correct title and spelling of your interviewer's name. Be sure to write a thank-you note to your interviewer within the next few days.

Final Decisions

The importance assigned to specific aspects of your application will vary from university to university and from program to program. While it is difficult to gauge which criteria are most relevant, and while decisions are generally made on an individualized, case-by-case basis, your grades are probably the single most important criterion in the admissions decision. Letters of recommendation and GRE scores often carry weight with admissions committees, and the reputation of your undergraduate school, the rigor of your course work, the quality of your application essay, and how well you did in your interview are also taken into account.

If you are not accepted into your top-choice school, don't despair. Remember that if you are unhappy with the program you finally choose, there is always the possibility of transferring later on. In fact, 66 percent of the universities we surveyed accept transfer students, and 68 percent accept incoming students at the beginning of any term. If you would like to re-apply to a program, make an appointment with an admissions counselor, dean, or faculty member for an informational interview. Ask what would strengthen your application if you were to apply again. Often, time and experience will remedy the weaknesses in an application. If you have attended an undergraduate program that is not well known nationally, it may help to volunteer, intern, or work for a well-known and long-established organization. Or you may be academically strong but lacking in professional experience.

In fact, some schools are reluctant to accept students straight out of college; many admissions committees are finding that older students with professional experience add diversity to the student body and interesting perspectives to class discussions. For those graduate programs that prefer more mature applicants, obtaining work experience will provide you with practical skills, increase your ability to apply your knowledge, and focus and/or generate career and research interests to such a degree that you may be accepted on the next go-round.

Having to choose among the schools that have accepted you can be a welcome dilemma. If possible, take your time in making a choice. Visit the campuses again and talk to as many students, faculty, and alumni as you can. As an accepted applicant, you may have many new questions. Then list your bottom-line considerations, such as cost, prestige, academic quality, and location. Think about which school will best help you realize your own career goals, and consider which programs best suit your own personal academic style and personal preferences.

CHAPTER 3

AN OVERVIEW OF GRADUATE PROGRAMS

Graduate environmental programs come in all shapes and sizes, and sifting through the wide variety of options can be an intimidating and confusing process. Some of the more exciting programs promote group projects, hands-on problem solving, and fieldwork. Others rely heavily on lectures, seminars, and lab work. And each program organizes its course offerings under different disciplinary headings and according to different areas of specialization. For example, according to the SCA survey, the largest areas of student specialization are: 50 percent in Applied Quantitative Ecology; 33 percent in Earth Systems Science; 30 percent in Resource Policy, Administration, and Planning; 27 percent in Environmental Quality and Public Health; and 27 percent in Environmental Science. In the highly interdisciplinary environmental field, such categories are often difficult to define, and programs in Environmental Science or Earth Systems can vary considerably from one school to the next.

The individual profiles provided in Part II are intended to help clarify the range of programs offered on university campuses throughout the United States. To provide a context for the individual programs profiled in Part II, and to help focus your search, in the following pages we describe several of the more popular types of programs available. Please bear in mind that the following examples represent only a sampling of the many programs offered, and their inclusion does not imply any preference or editorial judgment on the part of SCA.

Comprehensive Environmental Studies Programs

In pursuing a graduate degree in "environmental studies" or "environmental science," a student generally enrolls in one program or department and is expected to undertake a structured course of study, usually in three areas: (1) "core" courses providing an introduction to certain important concepts or topics—perhaps an introductory ecology course, applied statistics, environmental or natural resource economics, soil science, or environmental policy; (2) a series of electives or advanced classes in a specialized area of concentration, for example, water or forest resources, economics and policy, or resource ecology; and (3) an independent research project resulting in a paper, thesis, or dissertation. Each environmental studies program is carefully designed to provide an interdisciplinary foundation in the basics of environmental processes while allowing enough flexibility to accommodate individual interests. The most comprehensive programs offer instruction drawing from biology, chemistry, botany, ecology, economics, policy, law, and ethics—all without having to leave the department.

One of the oldest, and perhaps the best known, programs of this model is the Yale University School of Forestry and Environmental Studies. Founded as the Yale Forest School in 1900 by Gifford Pinchot and Henry S. Graves, in 1972 the program was renamed to reflect a broad commitment to the study of ecosystem management and environmental processes. Candidates for the Master of Environmental Studies degree take a series of core multidisciplinary courses, including natural resource economics and applied statistics, before concentrating in a specific Advanced Study Area—either Ecosystem Science and Management, Conservation Biology, Coastal and Watershed Systems, Environmental Policy and Management, or Social Ecology and Community Development. Yale also offers a Master of Forestry for students interested in the management or administration of forest lands, a Master of Forest Science intended primarily for students pursuing a research career and doctoral study, and several programs at the doctoral level.

The Nicholas School of the Environment at Duke University offers a program that is similar in organization to Yale's, although the Nicholas School provides a wider selection of courses in the area of "environmental quality," including ecotoxicology and water and air quality. Originally established in 1938 as the School of Forestry, the program became the School of Forestry and Environmental Studies in 1974 and the School of the Environment in

1991. In 1996, as the result of a $20 million gift from a university trustee, the program was renamed the Nicholas School of the Environment. This chain of events is less a sign of confused institutional identity than testimony to the rapid evolution of environmental studies as both a discipline and a priority for Duke University. In 1994, the program moved from cramped quarters to its spacious home in the new Levine Science Research Center, and the school's Marine Laboratory, located in Beaufort, North Carolina, will soon have a new building with state-of-the-art research facilities. One of the Nicholas School's best assets is its close relationship with other universities in the Raleigh–Durham–Chapel Hill region, which include the University of North Carolina at Chapel Hill and North Carolina State University. The Nicholas School encourages cross-registration with these institutions as well as with other departments within Duke, including public policy, law, business (all offering concurrent degrees), economics, and geology.

Rounding out what many easterners have come to know as the "triumvirate" of major environmental studies institutions is The University of Michigan's School of Natural Resources & Environment. Like Yale and Duke, Michigan offers a structured hierarchy of core courses, concentration areas, and specialized fields of study. Prospective students may apply in one of three concentrations: Resource Policy and Behavior, Resource Ecology and Management, or Landscape Architecture. In the first year, all students take a course entitled "Integrative Problem Solving: Case Studies," which provides the analytic framework and skills necessary for resolving environmental dilemmas from a truly interdisciplinary perspective. Also unique to Michigan is its program concentration in Advocacy, Behavior, and Environmental Education, which draws from the disciplines of sociology, psychology, communication, education, and political science.

While the Yale, Duke, and Michigan programs offer excellent facilities, well-known faculty, and a strong reputation among potential employers (particularly in the eastern United States), they are somewhat pricey (tuition at Yale was about $17,000 in 1996–1997), the programs are relatively large (Duke's enrollment is up from about 130 in 1990 to over 200 in 1995), and competition for admission continues to increase. These factors, combined with research and tenure pressures that at times can render faculty inaccessible, can be daunting to those seeking a more intimate or collegial learning environment.

As described in the profiles in Part II, there are numerous environmental studies programs throughout the country ranging widely in size, expense, and programmatic scope. At the University of Wisconsin–Madison, the Institute for Environmental Studies offers graduate degrees in Conservation Biology and Sustainable Development, Environmental Monitoring, Land

Resources, and Water Resources Management. At about $4,000 per year for in-state residents and $8,000 for nonresidents, the State University of New York (SUNY) College of Environmental Science and Forestry offers M.S. and Ph.D. degrees through the Faculties of Environmental and Forest Biology, Environmental Studies, and Environmental and Resource Engineering, among others. And with only 35 full-time students, the Graduate School of Environmental Studies at Bard College sponsors a Master of Science in Environmental Studies that is earned over three consecutive summer sessions and requires the successful completion of a series of core courses and a master's thesis.

"Experiential" Programs

For those prospective students who do not thrive in a traditional classroom environment or who wish to pursue fields with a heavy "experiential" focus, there are a variety of alternative graduate programs throughout the country that break the mold of the traditional university curriculum. Some offer extensive "field" experience; others emphasize the practicum or independent study. Most provide an opportunity to develop a personalized course of study as well as an intimate learning environment offering close interaction with faculty and fellow students. Such programs are particularly suited to students who tend to feel lost in large lecture programs, or who may appreciate the chance to structure their own schedule—a level of flexibility that can actually require a great deal of self-discipline.

For example, the Audubon Expedition Institute offers a master's program in which students travel the country on school buses, conducting field research and visiting practitioners representing a diversity of interests and professions related to natural resources and the environment. At Evergreen State College, rather than enroll in a series of separate courses, each quarter students study one comprehensive topic, which they examine from a variety of disciplinary perspectives. Faculty members provide in-depth letters of evaluation instead of grades.

Recognizing the importance of hands-on experience in a field where most students intend to pursue a professional career, many institutions place a heavy emphasis on the "practicum," which may take the form of an internship, hands-on project, or job. In some cases, the practicum becomes the defining element of the student's graduate work; in others, it provides a unique opportunity to conduct research or to acquire certain practical skills that cannot be conveyed in a lecture or seminar.

Antioch New England requires that all students participate in seminars designed to help them establish professional goals and identify the skills and activities necessary to achieve them. The school sponsors a practicum orientation program and an annual practicum fair. In the final semesters of the program, under close supervision by site supervisors and advisors, students complete two four-credit practica in a school or organizational setting. At Prescott College, study proceeds in three stages: Theory, Practicum, and Thesis. In close consultation with a faculty advisor, students design a highly personalized plan of study combining reading, library and field research, practical experience, and, if so desired, course work. Every three weeks, students submit a "study packet" summarizing their progress, and twice a semester they present their work at weekend colloquia involving students and faculty. Similarly, Goddard College and its partner institution, the Institute of Social Ecology, sponsor a Master of Arts in Social Ecology based heavily on participation in a series of intensive colloquia, workshops, and seminars, as well as ongoing independent study, a practicum, and final project.

Management of Natural Resources

With their mission of providing an in-depth overview of environmental processes and policies, most of the more comprehensive programs described above tend to produce graduates who can "speak the language" of environment with great fluency—a skill that is particularly useful for careers in environmental consulting, government, the nonprofit sector, and the policy arena. For those pursuing careers in the management of natural resources—for example, forestry, fisheries or wildlife management, or marine science—there are hundreds of programs offering a solid grounding in scientific processes and natural resource policy combined with hands-on training in research and management techniques. Many of the most successful programs in this area are offered by "land grant" and "sea grant" schools. In exchange for partial government funding, these institutions are required to provide the public with educational programs, usually through "cooperative extension," in the areas of agriculture, human ecology, and natural resource management. This mandated interaction with the public on "real-world" issues provides students with opportunities to investigate and influence resource management issues firsthand.

With graduate programs offered in four departments of its College of Forestry, Oregon State University also offers advanced degrees in rangeland resources, fisheries and wildlife, marine resource management, and oceanic and atmospheric sciences. Students interested in pursuing a career in forest resources may choose from master's programs in forest engineering, forest products, forest sciences, and forest resources. Louisiana State University (LSU) and North Carolina State University (NCSU) also offer comprehensive programs in natural resource management—LSU through its Department of Forestry, Wildlife, and Fisheries, and NCSU through the College of Agriculture and Life Sciences and the College of Forest Resources. As the "birthplace of watershed science," the Colorado State University College of Natural Resources offers programs in watershed science, forestry, wildlife biology, and fishery biology. Other schools with strong programs in natural resource management include the Auburn School of Forestry, Clemson College of Forest and Recreation Resources, and Virginia Polytechnic and State University's College of Forestry and Wildlife Resources.

In the area of marine science, the University of Alaska–Fairbanks School of Fisheries and Ocean Sciences has over 50 graduate students in the areas of fisheries, marine biology, and oceanography. The University of Miami Rosenstiel School of Marine and Atmospheric Science offers programs in marine biology and fisheries, marine and atmospheric chemistry, and applied marine physics, among others. The Moss Landing Marine Laboratories in Monterey, California, is operated by a consortium of six campuses of the California State University.

Ecology, Evolutionary Biology, and Conservation Biology

Despite its multidisciplinary focus, the study of environmental processes is grounded in the biological sciences. Focused research and scientific discovery in this field has provided modern society with an encyclopedia of knowledge that has fueled the progress of the environmental movement. For those students committed to academic research and scholarly achievement in conservation biology, evolutionary biology, population ecology, or other aspects of the ecological sciences, there are a variety of research-oriented programs available at the master's and doctoral levels.

Not surprisingly, some of the most well-respected programs of this category are located within prestigious universities that are widely recognized for their strength in the natural sciences. For example, Stanford University and Harvard University were ranked number one (in a three-way tie with the Massachusetts Institute of Technology) in *U.S. News & World Report*'s 1996

As a "science advisor" for a U.S. federal agency, Christine Bergmark oversees the monitoring of the environmental programs of the agency-supported International Agriculture, Forestry, and Fisheries Research Centers, among other responsibilities. Christine received her doctorate in plant physiology and plant ecology from North Carolina State University in 1990. She launched her government career four years ago via a fellowship offered by the American Association for the Advancement of Science that is available only to candidates with a Ph.D.

According to Christine, "I didn't feel that any one academic program can realistically fill all of one's needs in an interdisciplinary field, so I chose a dual path. I placed my academic studies into focused, in-depth areas, to learn the intricacies of research and science in a few select areas, while choosing life experiences to fill in the breadth. These life experiences included many different kinds of employment and volunteer work including the Peace Corps, teaching environmental science courses at several different universities, and participating in community activities and environmental groups. I do think there is merit in delving into at least one area in depth as a part of one's academic program. I felt that I could broaden into other areas as much as I desired later in life, but that I might not always have the discipline to focus so narrowly and intensely on just one area."

survey of the top Ph.D. programs in the biological sciences.[1] Stanford's Department of Biological Sciences is home to some of the country's most respected ecological scientists, including Paul Ehrlich, author of *The Population Bomb;* and noted author, educator, and scientist Edward O. Wilson is at Harvard. Princeton University's Department of Ecology and Evolutionary Biology is known for its doctoral programs in evolutionary ecology, conservation biology, and population and community ecology, among others. Recent Princeton graduates hold senior positions at organizations like the Environmental Defense Fund and the Smithsonian Institution, not to mention teaching positions at major universities around the world.

---

[1]*U.S. News & World Report.* Ph.D. Rankings. *America's Best Graduate Schools.* Washington, D.C.: *U.S. News & World Report,* 1996, p. 65.

Environmental Law

As the fastest growing legal specialty, environmental law is becoming a popular area of study at schools throughout the country. While many law schools offer at least one course on the topic, several institutions have designed more comprehensive programs that combine a variety of course offerings, special seminars, and even specialized degrees. At Vermont Law School, tied for first with Lewis and Clark in the *U.S. News & World Report* ranking of environmental law programs,[2] students have the choice of pursuing the Master of Studies in Environmental Law (M.S.E.L.) or the joint J.D.-M.S.E.L. degree. Recent graduates of the M.S.E.L. program have found positions as policy analysts, legislative associates, and environmental consultants, while graduates of the joint degree program generally specialize in environmental law in the private, public, or nonprofit sectors.

The Chicago–Kent College of Law, Illinois Institute of Technology offers a Program in Environmental and Energy Law that requires a series of six environmental courses and seminars taken in the second and third years of J.D. study. Chicago–Kent's Environmental Law Society works with public interest groups, government agencies, and law clinics to address local environmental issues; the society has provided legal assistance to neighborhood groups concerned with hazardous waste disposal. With over 140 participating students, the program is co-directed by Stuart Deutsch and Dan Tarlock, both national experts in environmental law; Fred P. Bosselman, well known for his contributions to land use law, is also on the faculty.

There are many other law schools throughout the country that, whether or not they offer extensive course work related to the environment, do provide opportunities to study environmental law. Many universities, including Duke and Yale, offer concurrent degree programs in which students design a study plan consisting of courses from both the law and environmental studies programs. Several law schools have founded special "centers" focused on research and study in environmental law. For example, the University of Colorado School of Law is home to the Natural Resources Law Center, which sponsors seminars, workshops, and other public education programs in the areas of public lands, water law, and tribal natural resource issues, among others. At these institutions, even if the J.D. program does not offer a wide range of environmental law courses, students have the opportunity to interact with noted leaders in environmental law. Finally, many law schools encourage faculty- or student-run initiatives, such as environmental law societies, that sponsor brown bag lunches, guest lecture series, or com-

---

[2]Ibid., p. 23.

munity projects. At the Pace University School of Law, which offers a comprehensive environmental law program, Robert F. Kennedy, Jr., oversees an Environmental Litigation Clinic that gives student interns the opportunity to address local and regional environmental issues.

Other universities known for their environmental law programs include Tulane University, George Washington University, and the University of California, Berkeley.

City and Regional Planning, Architecture, and Design

As urban sprawl, traffic congestion, and other land use issues increasingly dominate public concern and debate, the role of the planner is taking on greater relevance, particularly at the local level. At the University of North Carolina (UNC) at Chapel Hill, students pursuing a Master of Regional Planning may specialize in land use and growth management, environmental planning, coastal management, or transportation. Faculty members of

In the field of sustainable community development, the city of Chattanooga, Tennessee, is widely recognized as an environmental "success story." Over the past two decades, Chattanooga has cleaned up its air and riverfront, instituted one of the country's most successful affordable housing programs, and revitalized its downtown area. While these successes can be credited to a variety of individuals, partnerships, organizations, and extensive community participation, much of the city's land use planning and downtown economic successes have been guided by RiverValley Partners and its Riverfront/Downtown Planning and Design Center.

The Planning and Design Center was founded in 1981 in response to a sentiment among local architects that architecture students from the University of Tennessee at Knoxville (UTK) represented an energetic and valuable source of planning and design expertise. In 1981, the Lyndhurst Foundation provided funding for a student laboratory focusing on urban design issues in Chattanooga. Today, that laboratory is housed in the Riverfront/Downtown Planning and Design Center, where UTK architecture students have helped design such projects as Ross' Landing Park and Plaza, the Miller Park District Urban Design Guidelines, and other nationally acclaimed planning initiatives.

UNC's Department of City & Regional Planning are often requested to advise state and local officials on planning issues, and students have the opportunity to examine and influence local planning efforts through case studies and research projects. For example, as part of a seminar on sustainable development, a group of students has advised the town of Chapel Hill on strategies for balancing economic growth, responsible land use planning, and environmental protection. The University of California, Berkeley, also offers a top-notch program in city and regional planning, as do the Massachusetts Institute of Technology and Cornell University.

Architecture, landscape architecture, and design are also increasingly relevant to efforts to manage growth and the environment, and many universities are acknowledging this trend by shifting their curricula toward greater recognition of environmental and ecological processes. At the University of Virginia's (UVA) School of Architecture, Dean William McDonough, an international expert in ecologically friendly architecture, has launched the Institute for Sustainable Design. Together with his colleagues in the Department of Urban and Environmental Planning, over the past several years Dean McDonough has helped position UVA at the forefront of environmental architecture programs.

Other Program Areas

Again, the above list of program areas is not intended to be all-inclusive; rather, we hope it has served as a useful navigational aid to help guide your thinking as you conduct your search. In fact, there are as many additional specialized areas of study as there are schools that offer them. The following profiles describe programs in environmental education, environmental health sciences, park and recreation management, and environmental engineering, among others. To help focus your search, Part IV includes a list of programs cross-referenced by environmental resource or topic area.

PART II

PROGRAM PROFILES

Explanation of Profile Format and Content

The majority of profiles listed in the following pages were generated from in-formation provided through the surveys submitted in late 1994. As de-scribed in the Introduction to this volume, the authors conducted extensive follow-up research to verify and update data in the summer of 1996. We have also provided profiles of several important programs for which we did not receive completed surveys. To the fullest extent possible, we have main-tained a consistency of format among profiles such that you can easily com-pare one program to another. However, the sheer number and range of pro-grams necessitate some degree of flexibility; thus, you may detect some variability among profile format and content.

While the information presented in the profiles is self-explanatory, there are a few points that may benefit from some initial clarification. They in-clude:

University vs. Program Information. The profiles are listed in alphabetical order according to the university through which they are offered. Each uni-versity heading includes a brief description of the school's history and loca-tion, followed by a profile for a specific environmental program offered through that university. In some cases we have provided profiles for more than one environmental program at a university; in such situations, the first program profile is usually more complete than the additional descriptions in order to avoid repetition of "generic" information like tuition and admissions contacts (described below). Finally, to the greatest extent possible, we have included contact information for additional programs that did not receive or fill out a survey. These programs can be found at the end of the university profile under the heading "Other graduate environmental programs (no pro-files available)."

Contact Information. In almost every profile we have provided information for two categories of contacts: "Faculty" and "Admissions." The faculty con-tact is generally the chair or director of the profiled program; this would be the person whom prospective applicants might contact to discuss substan-tive and some specific administrative aspects of the targeted program. The admissions contact is usually the graduate studies or admissions office of the university through which the program is offered. The applicant would contact this office to receive a graduate bulletin, application forms, and other general information about the university. In most cases, the admissions office will be able to provide literature describing the specific program in question; however, there may be some programs (for example, interdepartmental "institutes" of environmental studies or research) that produce extensive promotional literature that cannot be obtained through the "admissions" contact. In sum, the admissions contact can provide general overview information about departments, programs, and curricula offered at the university, while a follow-up call to the faculty contact may yield additional, more detailed information.

In cases where we have included more than one program profile under a university heading, we have only listed the admissions contact once—in the first program profile—unless that information varies from program to program.

Areas of Specialization. As shown in the sample survey provided in Appendix B, the presentation of "areas of specialization" in the profiles was dictated by our own delineation of subject categories; rather than providing their own information about areas of concentration, most respondents filled out our survey according to our own categories. This process provides the continuity necessary to make comparisons among programs; however, literature obtained directly from each program may provide alternative and potentially more useful categories. In a few profiles we have provided specialization lists that were generated by the respondents themselves or that came straight from the program's own literature. In such cases we have indicated the source of the alternative list of categories.

ALABAMA AGRICULTURAL
AND MECHANICAL (A&M) UNIVERSITY

Established in 1875, Alabama Agricultural and Mechanical (A&M) University has a total enrollment of 5,400, over 1,200 of whom are graduate students. Situated on an 850-acre campus in the city of Huntsville (population 170,000), Alabama A&M is a state land-grant institution and belongs to the Historically Black Colleges and Universities.

☜ Plant and Soil Science Program

FACULTY CONTACT:

Govind C. Sharma
Plant and Soil Science Program
School of Agricultural and
  Environmental Sciences
Alabama A&M University
Normal, AL 35762

ADMISSIONS CONTACT:

School of Graduate Studies
Alabama A&M University
Normal, AL 35762

Phone: 205-851-5462
Fax: 205-851-5429
E-mail: gsharma@asnaam.aamu.edu

Plant and Soil Science Program Web site: http://saes.aamu.edu/pscd.htm

Quick Facts About the Plant and Soil Science Program
- Year established: 1890
- Enrollment: 30 master's students / 15 doctoral students
- Graduate degrees conferred: Master of Science, doctorate
- Master's degree requirements include: for thesis option, 24 semester hours of course work, 6 hours research, thesis; for non-thesis option, 32 semester hours course work and 4 hours master's report
- Doctoral degree requirements include: required courses, dissertation, qualifying exam, oral exam, one semester of teaching participation
- Faculty/Advisee ratio: 1:3

Areas of Specialization
Applied and Quantitative Ecology (40% of students)
Environmental Geography (20%)

Botany (15%)
Solid Waste Management (5%)
Environmental Chemistry (5%)

Special Program Features

A department of the School of Agricultural and Environmental Sciences, this program is best known for its emphasis on soil/environmental sciences, plant science, remote sensing/GIS, and plant molecular biology. Graduate students can cross-register for courses within other departments. International program experiences include student exchanges and research at field stations in Africa. As a land-grant institution, Alabama A&M sponsors cooperative extension programs in agriculture and natural resources, community development, and other service areas in 12 counties in northern Alabama.

Admission to the Program

- Admission requirements for master's applicants include: 4 semesters of chemistry, 2 of biology, 1 of calculus, 2 of natural science, 2 of physical science. Average GRE scores: 550 verbal/550 math
- Admission requirements for doctoral applicants include: master's degree. Average GRE scores: 550 verbal/550 math
- Master's students accepted each year (on average): 10% of 50 applicants
- Doctoral students accepted each year (on average): 25% of 20 applicants
- Students may matriculate at the start of any term; transfer students are accepted.

About the Students

There are 38 male and 7 female graduate students enrolled in this program; all are full-time; 15 are international and 30 domestic; 25% are Caucasian, 45% Black, and 10% Asian. Graduate students range in age from 22 to 40, with a median age of 25. About half of the students are master's students and the other half are doctoral candidates.

About the Faculty

There are 26 faculty affiliated with this program. The average faculty member teaches 2 courses and advises 3 master's and 1 doctoral student per year. Advisors are assigned to and chosen by students. Faculty research is currently being conducted both domestically and internationally. Ten faculty specialize in Applied and Quantitative Ecology, 4 in Botany, 4 in Environmental Geography, 1 in Environmental Law, 2 in Environmental Quality and Public Health, 1 in Environmental Chemistry, 5 in Forestry, and 1 in Resource Policy and Planning.

Tuition and Financial Aid

Tuition in 1996 was $103 per semester hour for state residents and $216 per semester hour for nonresidents. Research and teaching assistantships are available to qualifying students.

Facilities

Computer facilities include 15 IBM/clones, 2 Sun workstations, mini VAX, and access to Internet and E-mail. The school also owns 500 acres of field research space on campus and at the Winfred Thomas Agricultural Experiment Station, which includes a greenhouse, crop museum, lake, tree nursery, and weather station.

Career Counseling and Job Placement

This program offers student internships or educational opportunities both within the local commmunity and nationwide. Career counseling and job placement services include job placement counselors, on-campus interviews, job books, and job fairs. Alumni work within the government sector, for semi-governmental organizations, and in science or academia. Thirty percent of alumni work in Alabama, and 50% work in the Southeast. Eighty percent of the students find work within six months of graduation.

☞ Other graduate environmental programs at Alabama A&M (no profiles available):

Master of Urban and Regional Planning. No contact information available. School of Agricultural and Environmental Sciences. *Phone:* 205-851-5783.

ANTIOCH NEW ENGLAND GRADUATE SCHOOL

With a total enrollment of over 1,400 graduate students, Antioch New England Graduate School is located in the small city of Keene, in the Mt. Monadnock region of southern New Hampshire. Founded in 1964, it was the first major "satellite" learning center established by Antioch College, which itself was founded in 1852 in Yellow Springs, Ohio, as an alternative to the traditional college experience.

☜ Department of Environmental Studies

FACULTY CONTACT:
Mitchell Thomashow, Co-Chair
Dept. of Environmental Studies
Antioch New England
   Graduate School
40 Avon Street
Keene, NH 03431

Phone: 603-357-3122
TDD: 603-357-7254
E-mail: admissions@antiochne.edu

ADMISSIONS CONTACT:
Carolyn Bassett
Co-Director of Admissions
Antioch New England
   Graduate School
40 Avon Street
Keene, NH 03431-3516

Phone: 603-357-3122

Antioch New England Web site: http://www.antiochne.edu/

Quick Facts About the Department of Environmental Studies

- Year established: 1972
- Enrollment: Over 325 master's and doctoral candidates
- Graduate degrees conferred: Master of Science, doctorate
- Degree requirements for master's students include: required courses, internship or practicum, master's project
- Degree requirements for doctoral candidates include: required courses, independent study and research, practicum, dissertation
- Faculty/Advisee ratio: 1:20

Areas of Specialization

Environmental Education—Teacher certification offered (50% of students)
Resource Policy and Planning (30%)
Environmental Science (20%)

Special Program Features

Known for its "practioner-oriented" educational approach, Antioch New England is also recognized for its programs in environmental education and resource management. All students are required to complete two supervised internships or practica in a school or organizational setting; professional seminars in the first two semesters provide the training necessary for defining career goals and for identifying and successfully completing practica. Graduate students can cross-register for courses within other departments, but joint degree programs are not offered. International program opportunities include research positions, internships, and student exchanges in South America.

Admission to the Program

- GRE scores are not required.
- Admissions decisions are made on a rolling basis.
- Master's students accepted each year: 60% of 150 applicants
- Students may matriculate at the start of any term; transfer students are accepted.

About the Students

There are 135 male and 190 female graduate students enrolled in this program; all 325 are full-time. There are 5 international and 320 domestic graduate students ranging from age 25 to 60, with a median age of 30; 97% of the graduate students are Caucasian, 1% Black, 1% Hispanic, and 1% Asian.

About the Faculty

There are 12 faculty affiliated with this program. The average full-time faculty member teaches 4–8 courses and advises 5–8 master's students per year. Advisors are both chosen by and assigned to students. Faculty research is currently being conducted both domestically and internationally. There are 6 faculty specializing in Applied and Quantitative Ecology, 2 in Conservation Biology, 1 in Earth Science, 6 in Environmental Education, 1 in Environmental Law, 2 in Environmental Quality and Public Health, 1 in Environmental Science, 3 in Environmental Studies, and 2 in Resource Policy and Planning.

Tuition and Financial Aid

Tuition for the 1995–96 fiscal year ranged from $17,150 to $19,075 for the total degree program. Over 60% of the graduate students in this program receive financial aid, primarily in the form of loans for tuition and work-study. No fellowships, scholarships, or assistantships are available at present.

Facilities

Computer facilities include 20 Macintoshes, computer labs, and Internet and E-mail access. Free or low-cost computer training is available. One building, 28 classrooms, 2 laboratories, 1 library, and various museum collections are available to graduate students. These facilities are handicapped accessible. The school also owns environmental education and land management facilities that can be used for student research.

Career Counseling and Job Placement

Antioch New England offers student internships and educational opportunities within the local commmunity. Career counseling and job placement services include job books, an alumni database, and active advising. Ten percent of alumni work within the government sector, 5% for semi-governmental organizations, 60% for nonprofits, 10% for private small business, 5% for corporations or industries, and 10% in science or academia. Eighty percent of alumni work in the Northeast, and 80% of the students find work within six months of graduation.

ARIZONA STATE UNIVERSITY

Established in 1885, Arizona State University has a total enrollment of 45,000 students on two campuses; graduate enrollment is approximately 11,000. The University's 330-acre main campus is located in Tempe, a sunny, mid-sized urban city. This school belongs to the Hispanic Association of Colleges and Universities.

☜ Department of Botany

FACULTY CONTACT:

J. Kenneth Hoober
Department Chair
Department of Botany
Arizona State University
Box 871601
Tempe, AZ 85287-1601

Phone: 602-965-3414

ADMISSIONS CONTACT:

Bart A. Chafe
Graduate Secretary
Department of Botany
Arizona State University
Box 871601
Tempe, AZ 85287-1601

Phone: 602-965-7730

Department of Botany Web site: http://www.asu.edu/lsvl.la.asu.edu/botany/

Quick Facts About the Department of Botany

- Enrollment: 31 master's students / 33 doctoral students
- Graduate degrees conferred: Master of Science, doctorate
- Degree requirements for master's students include: 30 semester hours of credit, including 6 hours of research and thesis credit; master's thesis; seminar presentation; oral examination
- Degree requirements for doctoral students include: 50 credit hours of research and dissertation, 30 hours of course work, 4 hours of seminar; dissertation; oral and written examination
- Faculty/Advisee ratio: 1:3

Areas of Specialization

Botany (42% of students)
Applied and Quantitative Ecology (30%)
Molecular Biology (27%)

Special Program Features

This program is best known for its Center for Early Events in Photosynthesis and Center for Environmental Studies. Graduate students can cross-register for courses within other departments. Joint degree programs and international program experiences are not offered. In addition to course and lab work, the Department sponsors a weekly seminar series featuring guest lecturers as well as faculty and students.

Admission to the Program

- Admission requirements for master's applicants include: 4 semesters of chemistry, 2 of biology, 2 of calculus, 2 of physical science. Average GRE scores: 584 verbal/664 math
- Admission requirements for doctoral applicants include: average GRE scores: 556 verbal/629 math
- Students may matriculate at the start of any term; transfer students are accepted.

About the Students

There are 35 male and 29 female graduate students currently enrolled in this program; 56 are full-time and 8 part-time; 17 are international and 47

domestic; 80% of the graduate students are Caucasian, 5% Black, 6% Hispanic, and 9% Asian. They range from age 21 to 69, with a median age of 34.

About the Faculty

There are 20 faculty affiliated with this program. The average full-time faculty member teaches 2 courses and advises 8 master's and 4 doctoral students per year. Students choose their faculty advisors. Faculty research is currently being conducted both domestically and internationally. There are 2 faculty specializing in Applied and Quantitative Ecology, and 16 in Botany.

Tuition and Financial Aid

Tuition in 1996–97 was $102 per semester hour for state residents and $346 per semester hour for nonresidents. Over 60% of the graduate students in this program receive financial aid. All are supported through teaching or research assistantships, with several fellowships offered to the best-qualified graduate students. Graduate assistantships average about $11,000 per academic year.

Facilities

Computer facilities include 5 IBM/clones, 2 Macintoshes, 1 terminal per 13 students, and Internet and E-mail access. Free or low-cost computer training is available. There are 4 buildings, 22 classrooms, 18 laboratories, and 3 libraries available to graduate students. All facilities are handicapped accessible. The Department recently moved into a new building with modern laboratories and greenhouse facilities. Field research is conducted at the ASU Horticultural Resource Center. The school also owns Camp Tontozona, a pine tree altitude exosystem, and Sierra Anches, a Sonoran desert ecosystem. Housing, facilities, and equipment are available on each site for student research.

Career Counseling and Job Placement

No career counseling or job placement services are offered. Fifteen percent of alumni work within the government sector, 12% for nonprofits, 15% for private small business, and 36% in science or academia.

☜ Department of Zoology

FACULTY CONTACT:

James Collins
Department Chair
Department of Zoology
Arizona State University
Tempe, AZ 85287-1501

Phone: 602-965-0386

Department of Zoology Web site:
http://www.asu.edu/lsvl.la.asu.edu/zoology/

ADMISSIONS CONTACT:

Administrative Assistant
Graduate Programs
Department of Zoology
Arizona State University
Tempe, AZ 85287-1501

Quick Facts About the Department of Zoology

- Year established: 1962
- Enrollment: 25 master's students / 44 doctoral students
- Graduate degrees conferred: Master of Science, Master of Natural Sciences, doctorate
- Degree requirements for master's students include: required courses, master's thesis, master's project
- Degree requirements for doctoral students include: required courses, dissertation, oral exam
- Faculty/Advisee ratio: 1:3

Special Program Features

This program is best known for its emphasis on stream ecology, conservation, and endangered species. Students may concentrate in any of the following subject areas: Behavior, Biology Education, Cell Biology and Developmental Biology, Ecological Genetics, History of Biology, Morphology and Systematics, and Physiology. Joint degree programs are offered. International program experiences include research opportunities and field stations in South and Central America, China, Mexico, and Canada.

Admission to the Program

- GRE scores are required of all graduate applicants, with good scores in biology and analytic.

- Students may matriculate only in the fall; transfer students are sometimes accepted.

About the Faculty

There are 41 faculty members and research scientists affiliated with the Department of Zoology.

Tuition and Financial Aid

Over 60% of the graduate students receive financial aid; stipends in 1996 were $10,430 for master's students and $13,000 for doctoral candidates.

Career Counseling and Job Placement

Career counseling and job placement services include active alumni contact, on-campus interviews, job books, an alumni database, job fairs, and travel funding. Ten percent of alumni work within the government sector, 5% for corporations or industries, and 80% in science or academia. Ninety-eight percent of the students find work within six months of graduation.

☚ School of Planning and Landscape Architecture

CONTACT:

School of Planning & Landscape Architecture
College of Architecture and Environmental Design
Arizona State University
Tempe, AZ 85287-2005

Phone: 602-965-7167
Fax: 602-965-9656

College of Architecture and Environmental Design Web site:
http://www.asu.edu/lsvl.la.asu.edu/caed/

Quick Facts About the School of Planning and Landscape Architecture

- Year established: 1973
- Enrollment: 110 master's students
- Graduate degrees conferred: Master of Science in Environmental Resources, Master of Environmental Planning
- Degree requirements for master's students include: required courses, master's thesis

Special Program Features

An academic unit of the College of Architecture and Environmental Design, the School of Planning and Landscape Architecture offers a professional Master of Environmental Planning degree as well as a Master of Science in Environmental Resources. Students pursuing the Master of Environmental Planning may specialize in one of three areas: landscape ecological planning, urban and regional development, or urban design.

The Environmental Resources Program is best known for its emphasis on environmental planning, and wildlife habitat and management. Students enrolled in the Environmental Resources program may specialize in either natural resources management or range ecology. Future plans include expanding the landscape ecology and planning departments. Joint degree programs are not offered. International program experiences include student exchanges in Western Europe.

Admission to the Program

- GRE scores are not required.
- Students may matriculate at the start of any term; transfer students are sometimes accepted.

About the Students

Sixty graduate students are enrolled in planning and landscape architecture degree programs. There are about 30 graduate students enrolled in the Environmental Resources Program.

About the Faculty

There are 12 faculty affiliated with planning and landscape architecture instruction. The Environmental Resources Program has 5 additional faculty.

Career Counseling and Job Placement

The Environmental Resources Program offers student internships, but there are no career counseling or job placement services available. Fifty percent of alumni work within the government sector, 10% for semi-governmental organizations, 10% for private small business, 20% for corporations or industries, and 10% in science or academia. Fifty percent of alumni work in the western United States, and 60% of the students find work within six months of graduation.

☞ **Other graduate environmental programs at Arizona State University (no profiles available):**

Ph.D. in Environmental Design and Planning, a new joint program of the School of Planning and Landscape Architecture and the School of Architecture. *Contact:* School of Planning & Landscape Architecture. *Phone:* 602-965-7167.

AUBURN UNIVERSITY

Established in 1856, Auburn University has a total enrollment of 22,000 students, 3,000 of whom are graduate students. The University is located on a 1,871-acre campus in the city of Auburn, Alabama, population 33,000. As the land-grant university of Alabama, Auburn owns a demonstration forest and environmental preserve near campus, the Solon Dixon Forestry Education Center near Andalusia, and forest lands at several university agricultural experiment stations statewide.

☞ Department of Zoology and Wildlife Science

FACULTY CONTACT:

Christine Sundermann
Graduate Program Officer
331 Funchess Hall
Auburn University, AL 36849-5414

Phone: 334-844-4850
Fax: 334-844-4348

GRADUATE SCHOOL CONTACT:

John F. Pritchett
Dean of the Graduate School
Hargis Hall
Auburn University, AL 36849-5122

Phone: 334-844-4700

Zoology Web site:
http://www.auburn.edu/Student_info/bulletin_graduate/courses/zy.html

Graduate School Web site: http://www.grad.auburn.edu

Quick Facts About the Department of Zoology and Wildlife Science

- Year established: 1930s
- Enrollment: 60 master's students / 15 doctoral students
- Graduate degrees conferred: Master of Science, doctorate
- Degree requirements for master's students include: 30 hours of course work, master's thesis

- Degree requirements for doctoral students include: 60–80 hours of course work, dissertation, qualifying exam, oral exam
- Faculty/Advisee ratio: 1:3

Areas of Specialization

Applied and Quantitative Ecology (55% of students)
Botany (10%)
Conservation Biology (10%)

Special Program Features

This program is best known for its emphasis on wildlife ecology, and evolutionary biology/systematics. In addition to the M.S. and Ph.D. in Zoology, the M.S. in Wildlife, and the Ph.D. in Wildlife Science and Zoology, it offers a Master of Arts in College Teaching, a non-thesis degree for students interested in teaching at community or junior college. The Master of Zoological Studies, also a non-thesis degree, emphasizes in-depth academic course work in the zoological sciences. Graduate students can cross-register for courses within other departments. Joint degree programs are not offered. International program experiences include research opportunities and field stations in Central America.

Admission to the Program

- Admission requirements for master's applicants include: 3 quarters of chemistry, 6 of biology, 1 of calculus, 1 of physical science. Minimum GRE scores: 500 verbal/500 math
- Admission requirements for doctoral applicants include minimum GRE scores: 500 verbal/500 math
- Master's students accepted each year: 40% of 60 applicants
- Doctoral students accepted each year: 40% of 20 applicants
- Transfer students are accepted.

About the Students

There are 50 male and 25 female graduate students currently enrolled in this program; 70 are full-time and 5 part-time; 5 are international, and 70 domestic; 90% are Caucasian, 5% Hispanic, and 5% Asian. Graduate students range from age 21 to 42, with a median age of 25.

About the Faculty

There are 25 faculty affiliated with this program. The average faculty member teaches 2 courses and advises 3 master's and less than 1 doctoral student per year. Students choose their faculty advisors. Faculty research is currently being conducted both domestically and internationally. There are 14 faculty specializing in Applied and Quantitative Ecology, and 2 in Botany.

Tuition and Financial Aid

Tuition in 1996 was $2,250 per year for state residents and $6,750 per year for nonresidents. Over 60% of the graduate students in this program receive financial aid. All master's and doctoral students are awarded either teaching or research assistantships.

Facilities

Computer facilities include 35 IBM/clones, 5 Macintoshes, mainframe satellite labs, and access to Internet and E-mail. There are 5 buildings, 30 laboratories, 1 library, and various museum collections available to graduate students. Some facilities are handicapped accessible. For teaching and research purposes, the program provides access to the Alabama Agricultural Experiment Station, the Paleo-Herp Laboratory, and the Wildlife Research Facility.

Career Counseling and Job Placement

No career counseling or job placement services are offered. Twenty percent of alumni work within the government sector, 5% for private small business, 10% for corporations or industries, and 65% in science or academia. Ninety-five percent of the students find work within six months of graduation.

☂ School of Forestry

CONTACT:

George Bengtson
Associate Dean for Educational Programs
School of Forestry
108 M. White Smith Hall
Auburn University, AL 36849-5418

Phone: 334-844-1006
Fax: 334-844-1084

School of Forestry Web site: http://www.forestry.auburn.edu/

Quick Facts About the School of Forestry

- Year established: 1946
- Enrollment: 35 master's students / 10 doctoral students
- Graduate degrees conferred: Master of Science, Master of Forestry, doctorate
- Degree requirements for master's students include: required courses, master's thesis for M.S., master's project and summer practicum for M.F.
- Degree requirements for doctoral students include: required courses, dissertation, qualifying exam, oral exam
- Faculty/Advisee ratio: 1:2

Areas of Specialization (according to program literature)

Forest Biology and Ecology
Forest Economics, Management and Policy
Forest Biometrics
Forest Engineering/Forest Harvesting
Forest Products and Wood Science

Special Program Features

The Auburn School of Forestry sponsors a comprehensive and relatively "traditional" forestry program that is increasingly emphasizing the environmental implications of forest management. The program is best known for its emphasis on forest regeneration, wetlands ecology, and resource policy and law. Its Forest Engineering/Forest Harvesting program is the largest in the South, and the School recently instituted a Center for Southern Forest Engineering that conducts research on best management practices in collaboration with the Department of Agricultural Engineering and the U.S. Forest Service. Future plans for the School of Forestry include augmenting faculty strengths in integrated forest protection and urban forestry.

Joint degree programs are offered with the colleges of Agriculture and Engineering, and international program experiences include research opportunities, internships, and education exchanges in South America and China. In addition to the Solon Dixon Forestry Education Center near Andalusia, Alabama, the program provides GIS facilities and a Forest Products Laboratory for research in forest products and wood science.

Admission to the Program

- Admission requirements for master's applicants include course work in chemistry, biology, calculus, and economics; average GRE scores are 550 verbal and 650 math.
- Average GRE scores for doctoral applicants are 600 verbal and 700 math.
- Students may matriculate at the start of any term, but transfer students are not accepted.

Career Counseling and Job Placement

The School of Forestry offers student internships and cooperative educational opportunities with Habitat for Humanity, and workshops for Project Learning Tree facilitators. Career counseling and job placement services include job placement counselors, active alumni contact, on-campus interviews, an alumni database, job fairs, and interview skills development. Ten percent of alumni work within the government sector, 5% for semi-governmental organizations, 5% for nonprofits, 25% for private small business, 35% for corporations or industries, and 20% in science or academia. Thirty-five percent of alumni work in the Southeast, 5% in Washington, D.C., and 40% in international locations. Ninety-five percent of the students find work within six months of graduation.

☎ Other graduate environmental programs at Auburn University (no profiles available):

Department of Fisheries and Allied Aquacultures, Auburn University, Auburn, AL 36849-5419. *Phone:* 334-844-4786. *Fax:* 334-844-9208.

AUDUBON EXPEDITION INSTITUTE

The only accredited college and graduate school affiliated with a national environmental organization, the Audubon Expedition Institute (AEI) is jointly sponsored by the National Audubon Society, the Lesley College Graduate School of Arts and Social Sciences, and the Institute for Expedition Education. AEI was established in 1969 and has a total enrollment of approximately 100 students (50 of them graduate students) who travel the country in converted schoolbuses to gain firsthand experience in environmental education and problem solving.

🎓 Graduate Program in Environmental Education

CONTACT:

Sanna McKim
Outreach Director
Audubon Expedition Institute
P.O. Box 365
Belfast, ME 04915

Phone: 207-338-5859
Fax: 207-338-1037

Web site: Applicants may request a catalogue and admissions information through the National Audubon Society Web site at http://www.audubon.org/audubon/aeiform.html

Quick Facts About the Audubon Expedition Institute

- Enrollment: 50 master's students
- Graduate degree conferred: Master of Science
- Master's degree requirements include: required courses, master's thesis or 1 semester internship, 2 semesters of travel in the United States, 1 semester of bioregional study; graduate credits come through Lesley College in Massachusetts, of which this is an off-campus program
- Faculty/Advisee ratio: 1:6

Admission to the Program

- Bachelor's degree, academic initiative, leadership qualities, environmental and community committment required for master's program; GRE scores are not required.
- Students may matriculate only in the fall; transfer students are sometimes accepted.

Special Program Features

This program is best known for its emphasis on deep ecology and environmental leadership skills. All students specialize in Environmental Education, which includes Conservation Biology, Environmental Studies, Parks and Recreation Management, and Social Ecology; graduate students can cross-register for courses within other departments. Joint degree programs are offered with the Lesley School of Education. International program experiences are not offered.

About the Students

There are 24 male and 26 female graduate students currently enrolled in this program; all are full-time; 2 are international and 48 domestic; 97% are Caucasian, 1% Black, 1% Hispanic, and 1% Asian. Graduate students range from age 24 to 56, with a median age of 29.

About the Faculty

There are 20 faculty affiliated with this program. The average faculty member teaches 4 courses and advises 12 master's students per year. Students work with teams of advisors. Faculty research is currently being conducted domestically. All faculty specialize in Environmental Education, Environmental Studies, and Social Ecology.

Tuition and Financial Aid

Tuition in 1996–97 was $31,368 for the full degree program, which includes food and travel while on the bus. Students are responsible for personal camping gear and transportation to and from the bus. Limited tuition grants are available.

Facilities

Computer facilities include several laptops on each bus and at headquarters. Computer training is not available. There are various buildings, museums, and libraries available to graduate students at universities and other "stops" across the country. Some of these facilities are handicapped accessible.

Career Counseling and Job Placement

This program offers internships, chosen and designed by students, which range from teaching in the classroom, to lobbying in Washington, D.C., to running Green City projects. Career counseling and job placement services include job placement counselors (at Lesley College), active alumni contact, job books, and an alumni database. Ten percent of alumni work within the government sector, 5% for semi-governmental organizations, 10% for non-profits, 10% for private small business, 5% for corporations or industries, and 50% in science or academia. Ninety percent of alumni work in New England and throughout the West, 5% in Washington, D.C., and 5% in international locations. Most students find work within six months of graduation.

BALL STATE UNIVERSITY

Established in 1918, Ball State University has a total enrollment of 9,500 students. It is located on a 955-acre urban campus in Muncie, Indiana.

☛ Department of Natural Resources & Environmental Management

FACULTY CONTACT:

Dr. Charles Mortensen, Chairperson
Dept. of Natural Resources and
  Environmental Management
Room 110; West Quadrangle
Ball State University
Muncie, IN 47306-0495

Phone: 317-285-5781

ADMISSIONS CONTACT:

Graduate School
Ball State University
2100 W. Riverside
Muncie, IN 47306

Phone: 317-285-1297

Ball State University Web site: http://www.bsu.edu

Quick Facts About the Department of Natural Resources & Environmental Management

- Year established: 1970
- Enrollment: 10 master's students
- Graduate degrees conferred: Master of Arts, Master of Science

- Degree requirements for master's students include: required courses, master's thesis or master's project
- Faculty/Advisee ratio: 1:1

Areas of Specialization

Environmental Quality and Public Health (50% of students)
Parks and Recreation Management (25%)
Applied and Quantitative Ecology (10%)
Earth Science (10%)
Environmental Law (5%)

Special Program Features

This program is best known for its emphasis on (1) environmental science, and (2) outdoor recreation. Graduate students can cross-register for courses within other departments. Joint degree programs are not offered. International program experiences include field stations and field study courses in Central America and Europe.

Admission to the Program

- Admission requirements for master's applicants include: average GRE scores: 450 verbal/450 math
- Students may matriculate at the start of any term; transfer students are accepted.

About the Students

There are 7 male and 3 female graduate students currently enrolled in this program; 5 are full-time and 5 part-time; none are international; all are Caucasian. Graduate students range from age 22 to 40, with a median age of 25.

About the Faculty

There are 10 faculty affiliated with this program. The average faculty member teaches 6 courses and advises 1 master's student per year. Advisors are assigned to students for course work; students choose advisors for research. Faculty research is currently being conducted both domestically and internationally. There are 3 faculty specializing in Applied and Quantitative Ecology, 2 in Earth Science, 1 in Environmental Education, 2 in Environmental Quality and Public Health, and 2 in Parks and Recreation Management.

Tuition and Financial Aid

Tuition in 1996 was $3,048 per year for state residents and $7,824 for nonresidents. Under 20% of the graduate students in this program receive financial aid; 30% are awarded teaching assistantships.

Facilities

Computer facilities include 10 IBM/clones, 1 Macintosh, a variety of computer labs, and access to Internet and E-mail. Free or low-cost computer training is available. One building, 6 classrooms, and 3 laboratories are available to graduate students. All facilities are handicapped accessible. The school also owns a former private farm, now devoted to teaching, research, and public service. Research plots and nature trails are available for student research. Other natural reseach areas include an arboretum, an aquatic wildlife preserve, the Ginn-Nixon Woods, and the Cooper Wildlife Preserve.

Career Counseling and Job Placement

This program offers student internships or educational opportunities with local commmunity health departments, environmental advocacy groups, environmental agencies, and industries. Job placement counselors are available. Fifty percent of alumni work within the government sector, 5% for semi-governmental organizations, 5% for nonprofits, 20% for private small business, 20% for corporations or industries. Sixty percent of alumni work in Indiana.

☚ Other graduate environmental programs at Ball State University (no profiles available):

Master of Urban and Regional Planning (Department of Architecture). *Contact:* J. Paul Mitchell. *Phone:* 317-285-1963. *Fax:* 317-285-2648.

Master of Architecture, Master of Science in Historic Preservation (Department of Architecture). *Contact:* Marvin E. Rosenman. *Phone:* 317-285-1900. *Fax:* 317-285-2648.

Master of Landscape Architecture (Department of Landscape Architecture). *Contact:* David Ferguson. *Phone:* 317-285-1900. *Fax:* 317-285-1765.

BARD COLLEGE

Established in 1860, Bard College has a total enrollment of 1,100 students. Bard's 700-acre campus is situated in the Hudson River Valley between the 1,400-acre Tivoli Bays Wildlife Management Area and the Montgomery Place historic restoration.

🎓 Graduate School of Environmental Studies

FACULTY CONTACT:

Jane Wolfson, Director
Graduate School of
   Environmental Studies
Bard College
Post Office Box 5000
Annandale-on-Hudson, NY
   12504-5000

Phone: 914-758-6822

ADMISSIONS CONTACT:

Graduate School of
   Environmental Studies
Bard College
Post Office Box 5000
Annandale-on-Hudson, NY
   12504-5000

Phone: 914-758-7483

Graduate School of Environmental Studies Web site:
http://www.bard.edu/graduate/gses/index.htm

Quick Facts About the Graduate School of Environmental Studies

- Year established: 1988
- Enrollment: 47 master's students
- Graduate degree conferred: Master of Science in Environmental Studies
- Degree requirements for master's students include: 36 credits, including required courses, master's thesis, research practicum
- Faculty/Advisee ratio: 1:7

Areas of Specialization

Applied and Quantitative Ecology (60% of students)
Resource Policy and Planning (25%)
Environmental Quality and Public Health (5%)
Environmental Science (5%)
Environmental Studies (5%)

Special Program Features

This program is best known for its emphasis on being interdisciplinary; students do not major in a specific area. Graduate students cannot cross-register for courses within other departments, as there are no other relevant departments at the school; however, students can take courses at other graduate institutions. Joint degree programs and international program experiences are not offered. The program averages three years in length; course work is completed over 2 or 3 summers (two 4-week terms are offered each summer), and students conduct independent research throughout the remainder of each year. The program sponsors a required weekly "Environmental Issues" seminar with invited guest speakers. Other requirements include a field course and tutorial.

Admission to the Program

- Admission requirements for master's applicants include: 2 semesters of chemistry, 2 of biology, 1 of calculus, 1 of economics, 2 of social science; GRE scores not required.
- Master's students accepted each year: 50% of 50 applicants.
- Students may matriculate only in the summer; transfer students are accepted.

About the Students

There are 19 male and 28 female graduate students currently enrolled in this program; 40 are full-time and 7 part-time; none are international; 96% are Caucasian, 2% Hispanic, and 2% Asian. Graduate students range from age 23 to 62, with a median age of 34.

About the Faculty

There are 18 faculty affiliated with this program. The average faculty member teaches 1 course and advises 3.5 master's students per year. Advisors are initially assigned to students; they can be changed at a later date. Faculty research is currently being conducted both domestically and internationally. There are 7 faculty specializing in Applied and Quantitative Ecology, 2 in Botany, 1 in Conservation Biology, 1 in Earth Science, 1 in Environmental Geography, 2 in Environmental Law, 1 in Environmental Quality and Public Health, 2 in Environmental Studies, 2 in Resource Policy and Planning, and 2 in Social Ecology.

Tuition and Financial Aid

Tuition in 1996 was $5,750 for the summer session and $460 per credit of independent study. Over 60% of the graduate students in this program receive financial aid; 4% of the students are awarded fellowships, and 82% are awarded scholarships.

Facilities

Computer facilities include 60 IBM/clones, 5 Macintoshes, 65 terminals, and access to Internet and E-mail. Free or low-cost computer training is available. There are 3 libraries and various museum collections available to graduate students. Facilities are handicapped accessible. The school owns a 40-acre secondary forest and a 23-acre old field parcel. The campus's 600 acres of fields and forests can also be used for student research. The Bard College Ecology Station on the Hudson River includes classroom, laboratory, and computer facilities, as well as a library and herbarium, and the new David Rose Science Research Laboratory is the only professional research station on the Hudson River.

Career Counseling and Job Placement

Career counseling and job placement services include active alumni and past-faculty contact and job books. Ninety percent of alumni work for nonprofits; 85% work in the Mid-Atlantic region.

BAYLOR UNIVERSITY

With a total enrollment of 12,000 students, Baylor University was established in 1845 and is located on a 400-acre campus in the mid-sized city of Waco, Texas.

🐦 Department of Environmental Studies

FACULTY CONTACT:
Dudley J. Burton
Director of Graduate Studies

ADMISSIONS CONTACT:
Graduate Admissions
Baylor University

The Department of
  Environmental Studies
Glasscock Energy Research Center
Baylor University
P.O. Box 97266
Waco, TX 76798-7266

P.O. Box 97264
Waco, TX 76798

Phone: 817-755-3405
Fax: 817-755-3409

Phone: 817-755-3584

Department of Environmental Studies Web site:
http://www.baylor.edu/baylor/Grad_catalog/EnvSt.htm/

Quick Facts About the Department of Environmental Studies

- Year established: 1969

- Enrollment: 27 master's students

- Graduate degrees conferred: Master of Science in Environmental Studies, Master of Environmental Studies

- Degree requirements for master's students include: 30 semester hours of graduate courses, including 6 hours of research and thesis; oral examination

- Faculty/Advisee ratio: 1:10

Areas of Specialization

Environmental Quality and Public Health (30% of students)
Earth Science (25%)
Resource Policy andPlanning (15%)
Conservation Biology (10%)
Environmental Studies (10%)
Applied and Quantitative Ecology (5%)
Environmental Education (5%)

Special Program Features

This program is best known for its emphasis on wastewater treatment, solid waste management, and renewable energy. Current research interests include environmental planning, hazardous and toxic materials management, and sustainable agriculture, among others. Graduate students can cross-register for courses within other departments. Joint degree programs are not offered. International program experiences include field stations for research in Africa and Central America.

Admission to the Program

- Admission requirements for master's applicants include: average GRE scores: 500 verbal/500 math
- Master's students accepted each year: 10% of 240 applicants
- Students may matriculate at the start of any term; transfer students are accepted.

About the Students

There are 15 male and 12 female graduate students currently enrolled in this program; 24 are full-time and 3 part-time; 7 are international and 20 domestic; 75% are Caucasian and 25% Asian.

About the Faculty

There are 7 faculty affiliated with this program. The average faculty member teaches 6 courses and advises 10 master's students per year. Advisors are assigned to students. Faculty research is currently being conducted both domestically and internationally. There are 2 faculty specializing in Applied and Quantitative Ecology, 1 in Conservation Biology, 3 in Earth Science, 3 in Environmental Quality and Public Health, 3 in Environmental Studies, and 3 in Resource Policy and Planning.

Tuition and Financial Aid

Tuition in 1996 was $6,192 per year. Over 60% of the graduate students in this program receive financial aid. All are awarded teaching or research assistantships.

Facilities

Computer facilities include 1 terminal per 15 students and access to Internet and E-mail. Free or low-cost computer training is available. One building, 1 classroom, 2 laboratories, 3 libraries, and various museum collections are available to graduate students. The Department also has access to the

Glasscock Energy Research Center, which is used for meteorological and solar research as well as ecological and waste management experiments. Facilities are not handicapped accessible.

Career Counseling and Job Placement

This program offers student internships or educational opportunities within the local community. Career counseling and job placement services are not available. Thirty percent of alumni work within the government sector, 10% for nonprofits, 25% for private small business, 10% for corporations or industries, and 25% in science or academia. Seventy-five percent of the students find work within six months of graduation.

☞ Program in Environmental Economics

CONTACT:

W. James Truitt, Chair
Department of Economics
Baylor University
Waco, TX 76798

Phone: 817-755-4785

Department of Economics Web site:
http://www.baylor.edu/baylor/Grad_catalog/Economics.html

Quick Facts About the Program in Environmental Economics

• Year established: 1978
• Enrollment: 6 master's students
• Graduate degree conferred: Master of Science in Environmental Economics
• Degree requirements for master's students include: required courses, master's thesis
• Faculty/Advisee ratio: 1:1

Special Program Features

This program offers a Master of Science in Environmental Economics that requires 18 hours of economics courses, 6 hours of environmental studies courses, and 6 hours of environmental problem-solving research. The results of this research are expected to be submitted for publication in an approved journal. A Master of Arts and Master of Science in International Economics are also offered. Joint degree and international program experiences are not offered.

Admission to the Program

- Master's candidates in the Program in Environmental Economics have average GRE scores of 525 verbal and 525 math.
- Students may matriculate at the start of any term; transfer students are accepted.

Tuition and Financial Aid

Some 41–60% of the graduate students in this program receive financial aid; 50% are awarded research assistantships.

Career Counseling and Job Placement

Career counseling and job placement services include job placement counselors, on-campus interviews, job books, and job fairs. All students find work within six months of graduation.

☜ Other graduate environmental programs at Baylor University (no profiles available):

Department of Biology. *Contact:* O. Lind, Chair. *Phone:* 817-755-2911.

BEMIDJI STATE UNIVERSITY

Established in 1921, Bemidji State University has a total enrollment of 5,400. Its setting is an 83-acre lakeside campus in a small town.

☜ Center for Environmental Studies

FACULTY CONTACT:
S. A. Spigarelli, Director
Center for Environmental Studies

ADMISSIONS CONTACT:
Graduate Studies
Bemidji State University

Bemidji State University
1500 Birchmont Drive, NE
Bemidji, MN 56601-2699

102 Deputy Hall
1500 Birchmont Drive NE
Bemidji, MN 56601-2699

Phone: 218-755-2910
Fax: 218-755-4048

Phone: 218-755-2027

Bemidji State University Web site: http://bsuweb.bemidji.msus.edu/

Quick Facts About the Center for Environmental Studies

- Year established: 1969
- Enrollment: 27 master's students
- Graduate degrees conferred: Master of Science
- Degree requirements for master's students include: 50 credits of course work (25 credits of core courses, 25 in field of emphasis), proficiency in statistics, written comprehensive exam, oral thesis defense
- Faculty/Advisee ratio: 1:8

Areas of Specialization

Applied and Quantitative Ecology (20% of students)
Earth Science (20%)
Environmental Quality and Public Health (20%)
Environmental Science (20%)
Environmental Education (10%)
Environmental Geography (10%)

Special Program Features

Students may choose among a variety of fields of emphasis, including environmental chemistry, ecology, policy and planning, and geohydrology. Each student also conducts an independent research project and submits a thesis. Graduate students can cross-register for courses within other departments. Joint degree programs and international program experiences are not offered.

Admission to the Program

- Admission requirements for master's applicants include: average GRE scores: 550 verbal/600 math

- Masters students accepted each year: 60% of 25 applicants
- Students may matriculate at the start of any term; transfer students are accepted.

About the Students

There are 20 male and 7 female graduate students currently enrolled in this program; 23 are full-time and 4 part-time; 4 are international and 23 domestic; 86% are Caucasian, 3% Black, and 11% Asian. Graduate students range from age 22 to 46, with a median age of 25.

About the Faculty

There are 2 full-time and 25 associate faculty affiliated with this program. The average faculty member teaches 4 courses and advises 6 master's students per year. Students choose their faculty advisors. Faculty research is currently being conducted domestically. There are 2 faculty specializing in Applied and Quantitative Ecology, 1 in Botany, 2 in Conservation Biology, 2 in Earth Science, 1 in Environmental Education, 2 in Environmental Geography, 1 in Environmental Law, 2 in Environmental Quality and Public Health, 2 in Environmental Science, and 1 in Environmental Studies.

Tuition and Financial Aid

Tuition in 1996 was $76 per credit for state residents and $120 for nonresidents. Over 60% of the graduate students in this program receive financial aid; 75% are awarded teaching or research assistantships.

Facilities

Computer facilities include 2 IBM/clones, 8 Macintoshes, 1 terminal per 2.7 students, and access to Internet and E-mail. Free or low-cost computer training is available. One building and one library are available to graduate students. Facilities are handicapped accessible. The school also owns Hobson Forest, which includes native forest, bog, and pond areas. The campus is located on Lake Bemidji, the site of many student research projects.

Career Counseling and Job Placement

This program offers student internships or educational opportunities within the local commmunity. Career counseling and job placement services include job placement counselors, active alumni contact, and job books. Fifty percent of alumni work within the government sector, 5% for semi-governmental organizations, 20% for private small business, 5% for corporations or industries, and 20% in science or academia.

BOSTON UNIVERSITY

Located on a 45-acre campus along the Charles River in the city of Boston, Massachusetts, Boston University was established in 1847 and has a total enrollment of 29,000.

☝ Center for Energy and Environmental Studies

FACULTY CONTACT:
Xiannuan Lin
Director of Graduate Studies
Center for Energy and
    Environmental Studies
Boston University
675 Commonwealth Avenue
Boston, MA 02215

ADMISSIONS CONTACT:
Graduate School
Boston University
705 Commonwealth Avenue
Room 112
Boston, MA 02215

Phone: 617-353-3083
E-mail: cees@bu.edu

Center for Energy and Environmental Studies Web site:
http://cees-server.bu.edu/

Quick Facts About the Center for Energy and Environmental Studies

- Year established: 1979

- Enrollment: 64 master's students

- Graduate degrees conferred: (1) Master of Arts in Energy and Environmental Analysis, (2) Master of Arts in Environmental Remote Sensing and Geographic Information Systems (ERS/GIS), and (3) Master of Arts in International Relations and Resource and Environmental Management (IRREM)

- Degree requirements for master's students include: required courses; policy paper required for joint degree students in International Relations and Environmental Management

- Faculty/Advisee ratio: 1:12

Areas of Specialization

Environmental Law (40% of students)
Earth Science (38%)
Resource Policy and Planning (7%)
Environmental Geography (5%)
Environmental Quality and Public Health (5%)
Applied and Quantitative Ecology (2%)
Conservation Biology (3%)

Admission to the Program

- Admission requirements for master's applicants include: 1 semester of calculus, 1 of economics, 2 of natural science; and proficiency in a foreign language. Average GRE scores are 570 verbal/650 math

- Master's students accepted each year: 32% of 180 applicants

- Students may matriculate only in the fall; transfer students are accepted.

Special Program Features

This program is best known for its emphasis on ecological economics, energy analysis, and environmental modeling. The Master of Arts in Energy and Environmental Analysis places a heavy emphasis on computer modeling. The Master of Arts in ERS/GIS requires extensive background in calculus and statistics as a condition of enrollment. And the Master of Arts in IRREM is a joint program of the Center for Energy and Environmental Studies and the Department of International Relations. Graduate students can cross-register for courses within other departments. Joint degree programs are offered with the School of International Relations. International program experiences are not offered. Future plans include additional professionally oriented M.A. programs.

About the Students

There are 30 male and 34 female graduate students currently enrolled in this program; 10 are international and 54 domestic; 75% are Caucasian, 5% Black, 10% Hispanic, and 10% Asian. Graduate students range from age 22 to 40, with a median age of 24.

About the Faculty

There are 9 faculty affiliated with this program. The average faculty member teaches 4 courses and advises 7 master's and 2 doctoral students per year. Students choose their faculty advisors. Faculty research is currently being conducted both domestically and internationally. There are 7 faculty specializing in Applied and Quantitative Ecology, 1 in Conservation Biology, 1 in Corporate Environmental Management, 7 in Earth Science, 6 in Environmental Geography, 6 in Environmental Law, 3 in Environmental Quality and Public Health, and 2 in Resource Policy and Planning.

Tuition and Financial Aid

Tuition in 1996 was $19,420 per year. Some 21–40% of the graduate students in this program receive financial aid; 2% are awarded scholarships; and 27% are awarded teaching or research assistantships.

Facilities

Computer facilities are extensive, and include access to Internet and E-mail. Free or low-cost computer training is available. One building, 2 classrooms, 3 laboratories and 7 libraries are available to graduate students. All facilities are handicapped accessible.

Career Counseling and Job Placement

Student internships can count in lieu of a class toward the degree; they are highly recommended, but not automatically provided. Career counseling and job placement services include active alumni contact, job books, and an alumni database. Ten percent of alumni work within the government sector, 20% for semi-governmental organizations, 5% for nonprofits, 60% for private small business, and 5% in science or academia. Ninety percent of the students find work within six months of graduation.

☛ Other graduate environmental programs at Boston University (no profiles available):

Department of Geography. *Contact:* Curtis Woodcock. *Phone:* 617-353-2092.

Program in Ecology, Behavior, & Evolution. *Contact:* Robert Hausman. *Phone:* 617-353-2432.

BRIGHAM YOUNG UNIVERSITY

With a total enrollment of 32,300 students, Brigham Young University is located on an urban campus in the mid-sized city of Provo, Utah.

✿ Department of Botany & Range Science

CONTACT:

Kimball Harper
Graduate Coordinator
Department of Botany & Range Science
489 WIDB
P.O. Box 25181
Provo, UT 84602-5181

Phone: 801-378-2129

Department of Botany & Range Science Web site:
http://www.byu/edu/newhome.html

Quick Facts About the Department of Botany & Range Science

• Year established: 1993

• Enrollment: 32 master's students / 8 doctoral students

• Graduate degrees conferred: Master of Arts, Master of Science, doctorate

• Degree requirements for master's students include: course work (24 hours), master's thesis (6 hours), oral exam and defense

• Degree requirements for doctoral students include: required courses (24 hours), dissertation (18 hours), work experience, qualifying exam, oral exam

• Faculty/Advisee ratio: 1:10

Areas of Specialization

Applied and Quantitative Ecology (20% of students)
Conservation Biology (15%)
Environmental Geography (15%)
Botany (10%)
Environmental Law (10%)
Environmental Quality and Public Health (10%)

Environmental Science (10%)
Environmental Studies (5%)
Resource Policy and Planning (5%)

Special Program Features

This program is best known for its emphasis on restoration ecology, wildlife
biology, and conservation biology. It offers six degress: Biological Science
Education M.S., Botany M.S., Range Science M.S., Wildlife and Range Re-
sources M.S., Botany Ph.D., and Wildlife and Range Resources Ph.D.
Within each degree are a wide variety of possible areas of specialization.
Graduate students can cross-register for courses within other departments.
Joint degree programs are offered with the Law School and the School of
Public Policy. International program experiences include research opportu-
nities and field stations in South America and the South Pacific.

Admission to the Program

- Admission requirements for master's applicants include: 4 semesters of
  chemistry, 5 of biology, 1 of calculus, 1 of economics, 2 of natural science, 1 of physical science, 2 of social science; average GRE scores: 550
  verbal/550 math
- Admission requirements for doctoral applicants include: average GRE
  scores: 550 verbal/600 math
- Master's students accepted each year: 25% of 80 applicants
- Doctoral students accepted each year: 10% of 50 applicants
- Students may matriculate only in the fall; transfer students are accepted.

About the Students

In 1994 there were 19 male and 10 female graduate students enrolled in
this program; all were full-time; none international; 96% were Caucasian
and 4% Asian. Graduate students range from age 21 to 47, with a median
age of 26.

About the Faculty

There are 17 faculty affiliated with this program. The average faculty member teaches 3.5 courses and advises 1.5 master's and less than 1 doctoral
students per year. Students choose their faculty advisors. Faculty research is

currently being conducted both domestically and internationally. Six faculty specialize in Applied and Quantitative Ecology, 7 in Botany, 3 in Conservation Biology, and 1 in Environmental Quality and Public Health.

Tuition and Financial Aid

Tuition in 1996 was $2,870 per year for state residents and $4,304 for non-residents. Some 41–60% of the graduate students in this program receive financial aid. Four percent of the master's students are awarded fellowships, 20% are awarded scholarships, and 65% are awarded teaching or research assistantships. Twenty-five percent of the doctoral students are awarded fellowships and 75% are awarded teaching or research assistantships.

Facilities

Computer facilities include 15 IBM/clones, 8 Macintoshes, 23 terminals, a main frame, and access to Internet and E-mail. Free or low-cost computer training is available. There are 3 buildings, 7 classrooms, 15 laboratories, libraries, and various museum collections available to graduate students. All facilities are handicapped accessible. The school also owns a natural area, with a laboratory and living quarters, at the northern edge of the Mohave Desert.

Career Counseling and Job Placement

This program offers student internships and educational opportunities with the U.S. Forest Service, Bureau of Land Management, and Utah Division of Wildlife Management. Career counseling and job placement services include job placement counselors, active alumni contact, on-campus interviews, and job fairs. Seventy percent of alumni work within the government sector, 10% for private small business, 10% for corporations or industries, and 10% in science or academia; 16% of alumni work in the Intermountain West region, 2% in Washington, D.C., and 2% in international locations. Ninety percent of the students find work within six months of graduation.

BROWN UNIVERSITY

Established in 1764, this Ivy League University has a total enrollment of 6,700 students. Its setting is a 133-acre campus in Providence, Rhode Island.

☟ Center for Environmental Studies

FACULTY CONTACT:

Harold Ward, Director
Center for Environmental Studies
Brown University
Box 1943
Providence, RI 02912

ADMISSIONS CONTACT:

Graduate School
Brown University
Box 1867
Providence, RI 02912

Phone: 401-863-3449
Fax: 401-863-3503
E-mail: EnvStu@brown.edu

E-mail:
    Graduate Admissions@brown.edu

Center for Environmental Studies Web site:
http://www.brown.edu/Departments/Environmental_Studies/

Quick Facts About the Center for Environmental Studies

• Year established: 1986

• Enrollment: 14 master's students

• Graduate degree conferred: Master of Arts in Environmental Studies

• Degree requirements for master's students include: required courses, master's thesis

• Faculty/Advisee ratio: 2:7

Areas of Specialization (no statistics available)

Applied and Quantitative Ecology
Corporate Environmental Management
Environmental Quality and Public Health (Environmental Tobacco Smoke)
Environmental Studies
Resource Policy and Planning

Special Program Features

This program is best known for its emphasis on urban environmental issues and on "active learning." Its small size offers extensive opportunity for informal interaction between students and faculty. Graduate students can cross-register for courses within other departments. Joint degree programs and international program experiences are not offered. Future program plans include faculty additions and expanded course offerings.

Admission to the Program

- GRE scores are not required.
- Master's students accepted each year: 25% of 20 applicants
- Students may matriculate at the start of any term; transfer students are not accepted.

About the Students

There are 7 male and 7 female graduate students currently enrolled in this program; 4 are full-time and 10 part-time; 3 are international and 11 domestic; 93% are Caucasian and 7% Asian. Graduate students range from age 22 to 45, with a median age of 30.

About the Faculty

There are 4 faculty affiliated with this program. The average faculty member teaches 2 courses and advises 3 to 4 master's students per year. Students choose their own team of faculty advisors. Faculty research is currently being conducted domestically. Three faculty specialize in Applied and Quantitative Ecology, 1 in Conservation Biology, 1 in Earth Science, 1 in Environmental Education, 2 in Environmental Quality and Public Health, 1 in Environmental Studies, and 1 in Environmental Sociology.

Tuition and Financial Aid

Tuition in 1996 was $20,608 per year. Under 20% of the graduate students in this program receive financial aid; 15% are awarded teaching assistantships.

Facilities

Computer facilities include 7 IBM/clones, 2 Macintoshes, 1 terminal per 4 students, 250 networked microcomputers, and access to Internet and E-mail. Free or low-cost computer training is available. One building, 1 classroom, 6 libraries, and various museum collections are available to graduate students. Facilities are handicapped accessible.

Career Counseling and Job Placement

Student internships are not offered. Career counseling and job placement services include active alumni contact, job books, and an alumni database.

Thirty percent of alumni work within the government sector, 20% for non-profits, 20% for private small business, and 30% in science or academia. Ninety percent of the students find work within six months of graduation.

CALIFORNIA POLYTECHNIC STATE UNIVERSITY, SAN LUIS OBISPO

With a total enrollment of 15,440 students, California Polytechnic State University, San Luis Obispo—also known as Cal Poly or Cal Tech—was established in 1900. It is located on a 5,000-acre campus on the northern edge of San Luis Obispo, population 42,000, on California's central coast between Monterey and Santa Barbara.

☞ Architecture Department

FACULTY CONTACT:

Jens Pohl, Professor
Architecture Department
Architecture and Environmental
   Design Building 05
Room 212A
California Polytechnic State University
San Luis Obispo, CA 93407

Phone: 805-756-2841
Fax: 805-756-1500
E-mail: dp141@oasis.calpoly.edu

ADMISSIONS CONTACT:

James Maraviglia
Director of Admissions
Cal Poly State University
San Luis Obispo, CA 93407

Phone: 805-756-2311

Architecture Department Web site: http://www.calpoly.edu/~arch/

Quick Facts About the Architecture Department

- Year established: 1976
- Enrollment: 50 master's students
- Graduate degree conferred: Master of Science in Architecture
- Degree requirements for master's students include: required courses, master's project
- Faculty/Advisee ratio: varies from 1:4 to 1:15

Areas of Specialization

Energy Studies (50% of students)
Applied and Quantitative Ecology (25%)
Decision Support Systems (25%)

Special Program Features

Housed within the College of Architecture & Environmental Design, the Architecture Program is best known for its emphasis on computer-assisted design, architectural science, and facilities management. Graduate students can cross-register for courses within other departments. Joint degree programs are offered with the Business School. International program experiences are not offered. Future program plans include greater focus on support systems for complex problem situations.

Admission to the Program

- GRE scores are not required.
- Master's students accepted each year: 50% of 40 applicants
- Students may matriculate at the start of any term; transfer students are accepted.

About the Students

There are 26 male and 24 female graduate students currently enrolled in this program; 12 are full-time and 38 part-time; 12 are international and 38 domestic; 80% are Caucasian, 2% Black, 8% Hispanic, and 4% Asian. Graduate students range from age 21 to 67, with a median age of 25.

About the Faculty

There are 4 faculty affiliated with this program. The average faculty member teaches 6 courses and advises 5 master's students per year. Students choose their faculty advisors. Faculty research is currently being conducted domestically; 1.5 faculty specialize in Applied and Quantitative Ecology, 2 in Energy Studies, and 2 in Decision Support Systems.

Tuition and Financial Aid

Tuition in 1996 was $0 per year (plus fees) for state residents and $164 per unit for nonresidents. Over 60% of the graduate students in this program receive financial aid; 10% are awarded scholarships; and 35% are awarded teaching or research assistantships.

Facilities

Computer facilities include 4 IBM/clones, about 300 stations, and access to Internet and E-mail. Free or low-cost computer training is available. One classroom, 2 laboratories, and 1 library are available to graduate students. Facilities are handicapped accessible. The school also owns an experimental building site, and about 9,000 acres of farm/range land and crop land, available for student research.

Career Counseling and Job Placement

This program offers neither student internships nor career counseling and job placement services. Ten percent of alumni work within the government sector, 80% for corporations or industries, and 10% go on to Ph.D. programs. Eighty percent of the students find work within six months of graduation.

☞ College of Agriculture

CONTACT:

Del Dingus
Graduate Coordinator
College of Agriculture
California Polytechnic State University
San Luis Obispo, CA 93407

Phone: 805-756-2753
Fax: 805-756-6577

College of Agriculture Web site: http://www.calpoly.edu/~cagr/

Quick Facts About the College of Agriculture

- Year established: 1965

- Enrollment: 85 master's students

- Graduate degrees conferred: Master of Science

- Degree requirements for master's students include: required courses, master's thesis

- Faculty/Advisee ratio: 1:3

Areas of Specialization

Applied and Quantitative Ecology (14% of students)
Forestry (4%)
Additional areas of specialization are listed below.

Special Program Features

This program is best known for its emphasis on food science and nutrition, and irrigation. Students pursuing the Master of Science in Agriculture may specialize in the following areas: General Agriculture, Food Science and Nutrition, Dairy Products Technology, International Agricultural Development, Agricultural Engineering Technology, or Soil Science. Graduate students can cross-register for courses within other departments. Joint degree programs are not offered. International program experiences include research opportunities, internships, and student exchanges in Central America, Japan, and Africa. Future program plans include the addition of new specializations.

Admission to the Program

- Admission requirements for master's applicants include: 2 semesters of chemistry, 2 of biology, 2 of calculus, 2 of natural science, 2 of physical science; average GRE scores: 610 verbal/520 math.
- Master's students accepted each year: 50% of 120 applicants
- Students may matriculate at the start of any term; transfer students are accepted.

About the Students

There are 48 male and 47 female graduate students currently enrolled in this program; 50 are full-time and 35 part-time; 85% are Caucasian, 10% Hispanic, and 5% Asian.

About the Faculty

Eighty-five faculty are affiliated with this program.

Tuition and Financial Aid

Tuition in 1994 was $700 for state residents and $1,700 for nonresidents. Some 21–40% of the graduate students in this program receive financial aid;

6% of the master's students are awarded fellowships and 6% are awarded scholarships.

Career Counseling and Job Placement

This program offers student internships. Career counseling and job placement services include job placement counselors, on-campus interviews, and job fairs. Ten percent of alumni work within the government sector, 70% for private small business, 10% for corporations or industries, and 10% in science or academia; 82% of alumni work in California. Ninety percent of the students find work within six months of graduation.

☛ Other graduate environmental programs at California Polytechnic State University, San Luis Obispo (no profiles available):

Department of City and Regional Planning. *Contact:* Michael Smith-Hermer. *Phone:* 805-756-2496.

CALIFORNIA STATE UNIVERSITY, CHICO

Established in 1887, California State University, Chico, has a total enrollment of 14,232 students. Its setting is a scenic campus along the banks of the Big Chico Creek in the small city of Chico, population 79,000. Chico lies at the foot of the western slope of the Sierra Nevada; the 2,400-acre Bidwell Park adjoins the campus.

☛ Department of Recreation & Parks Management

FACULTY CONTACT:
David E. Simcox
Graduate Coordinator
Department of Recreation
  & Parks Management
Tehama Hall 413
California State University, Chico
Chico, CA 95929-0560

ADMISSIONS CONTACT:
Graduate School
California State University, Chico
Chico, CA 95929-0875

Phone: 916-898-6408

Phone: 916-898-5391

Department of Recreation & Parks Management Web site:
http://www.csuchico.edu/cwis/catalog/recr/catrecr.html

Quick Facts About the Department of Recreation and Parks Management

- Year established: 1968
- Enrollment: 39 master's students
- Graduate degree conferred: Master of Arts in Recreation Administration
- Degree requirements for master's students include: 30 units required courses, either master's thesis or master's project
- Faculty/Advisee ratio: 1:3

Areas of Specialization

Parks and Recreation Management (63% of students)
Environmental Education (18%)
Resource Policy and Planning (12%)

Special Program Features

This program is best known for its emphasis on environmental education, interpretation, and social science in natural resource management. Graduate students can cross-register for courses within other departments. Joint degree programs and international program experiences are not offered. Future program plans include curriculum changes toward ecosystem management and more rigor in research.

Admission to the Program

- Admission requirements for master's applicants include: average GRE scores: 480 verbal/420 math
- Master's students accepted each year: 60% of 12 applicants
- Students may matriculate at the start of any term; transfer students are accepted.

About the Students

There are 20 male and 19 female graduate students currently enrolled in this program; all are full-time; 2 are international and 37 domestic; 89% are

Caucasian, 8% Asian, and 3% Native American. Graduate students range from age 24 to 53, with a median age of 28.

About the Faculty

There are 16 faculty affiliated with this program. The average faculty member teaches 6 courses and advises 2 master's students per year. Students choose their faculty advisors. Faculty research is currently being conducted both domestically and internationally. Three faculty specialize in Applied and Quantitative Ecology, 1 in Environmental Law, 10 in Parks and Recreation Management, and 2 in Resource Policy and Planning.

Tuition and Financial Aid

Tuition in 1996 was $0 (plus fees) per year for state residents and $246 per unit for nonresidents. Some 41–60% of the graduate students in this program receive financial aid; 15% are awarded teaching or research assistantships.

Facilities

Computer facilities include 2 Macintosh labs, 1 terminal per 2 students, 2 GIS computers, and access to Internet and E-mail. Free or low-cost computer training is available. One building, 5 classrooms, 2 laboratories and 1 library are available to graduate students. All facilities are handicapped accessible.

Career Counseling and Job Placement

This program offers cooperative educational opportunities with federal agencies (NPS, USFS, BLM), and with local parks and recreation agencies. Career counseling and job placement services include job placement counselors and active alumni contact. Sixty-five percent of alumni work within the government sector, 20% for private small business, and 15% in science or academia; 80% of alumni work in California, and 10% work in international locations. Ninety percent of the students find work within six months of graduation.

☃ Department of Geography and Planning

CONTACT FOR M.A.   CONTACT FOR MASTER OF RURAL
   IN GEOGRAPHY: AND TOWN PLANNING:

Dr. Guy King   Dr. William Collins
Butte 515   Butte 507
California State University, Chico   California State University, Chico
Chico, CA 95929   Chico, CA 95929

Phone: 916-898-5285   *Phone:* 916-898-5285

Department of Geography and Planning Web site:
http://www.csuchico.edu/geop/

Quick Facts About the Department of Geography and Planning

- Year established:
- Enrollment: 38 master's students
- Graduate degrees conferred: Master of Arts in Geography, Master of Rural and Town Planning
- Degree requirements for master's students include: course work, master's thesis

Special Program Features

The Master of Rural and Town Planning requires 36 units of course work, successful completion of an internship, and the completion and final approval of a thesis and planning project and oral defense. The Master of Geography requires 30 units of course work, completion and approval of a thesis, and completion of a public defense of that thesis. Graduate students cannot cross-register for courses within other departments, and joint degree programs and international program experiences are not offered.

Admission to the Program

- GRE scores are required for admission.
- Master's students accepted each year: 50% of 20 applicants
- Transfer students are not accepted.

About the Students

Ninety percent of the students are Caucasian and 10% Asian. The median student age is 28.

About the Faculty

There are 12 faculty affiliated with this program; advisors are assigned to students.

Tuition and Financial Aid

Some 21–40% of the graduate students in this program receive financial aid.

Career Counseling and Job Placement

This program offers student internships but no career counseling and job placement services. Sixty percent of alumni work within the government sector, 20% for private small business, 10% for corporations or industries, and 10% in science or academia.

CALIFORNIA STATE UNIVERSITY, FULLERTON

With a total enrollment of 22,097 students, California State University, Fullerton, was established in 1957. It is located in the small city of Fullerton and serves the Orange County area.

☜ Environmental Studies Program

FACULTY CONTACT:

Stewart Long, Director
Environmental Studies Program
LH-717
California State University,
 Fullerton
Fullerton, CA 92634-9480

Phone: 714-773-2243

ADMISSIONS CONTACT:

Office of Admissions and Records
LH-109
California State University,
 Fullerton
Fullerton, CA 92634-9480

Phone: 714-773-2300

University Web site: http://www.fullerton.edu/

Quick Facts About the Environmental Studies Program

• Year established: 1970
• Enrollment: 100+ master's students

- Graduate degree conferred: Master of Science
- Degree requirements include: 36 units of course work, including a master's thesis or master's project
- Faculty/Advisee ratio: 1:3

Areas of Specialization

Resource Policy and Planning (60% of students)
Environmental Science (30%)
Environmental Education (10%)

Special Program Features

Graduate students in the Environmental Studies Program may concentrate in any one of the following areas: (1) Environmental Sciences, (2) Environmental Policy & Planning, or (3) Environmental Education and Communication. Graduate students can cross-register for courses within other departments. Joint degree programs and international program experiences are not offered.

Admission to the Program

- Admission requirements include: ecology and statistics courses; GRE scores not required.
- Master's students accepted each year: 35% of 85 applicants
- Students may matriculate only in the fall; transfer students are sometimes accepted.

About the Students

There are 10 international and 90+ domestic graduate students currently enrolled in this program. Most are in their 30's.

About the Faculty

There are 32 faculty affiliated with this program. The average faculty member advises less than 1 master's student per year. Students choose their faculty advisors. Faculty research is currently being conducted both domestically and internationally. Faculty specialize in Applied and Quantitative Ecology, Conservation Biology, Earth Science, Environmental Education, Environmental Geography, Environmental Law, Environmental Quality and

Public Health, Environmental Science, Environmental Studies, Resource Policy and Planning, and Social Ecology.

Tuition and Financial Aid

Tution in 1996 was $0 (plus fees) per year for state residents and $246 per unit for nonresidents. No financial aid information is available.

Facilities

Computer facilities include IBM/clones, Macintoshes, and access to Internet and E-mail. Free or low-cost computer training, and free accounts to students are available. Facilities are handicapped accessible. The school also owns the Tucker Wildlife and Desert Studies Center, available for student research.

Career Counseling and Job Placement

This program offers student internships or educational opportunities within the local commmunity. Career counseling and job placement services include a center on campus with job placement counselors. Sixty percent of alumni work within the government sector, 30% for private small business, 10% for corporations or industries. Most students are already employed prior to graduation.

CALIFORNIA STATE UNIVERSITY, HAYWARD

Located on an urban campus of a mid-sized city overlooking San Francisco Bay, California State University, Hayward, was established in 1957. It has a total enrollment of 12,567 students.

☎ Environmental Education Specialization

FACULTY CONTACT:
Dr. Esther Railton-Rice
Department of Teacher Education
25800 Carlos Bee Drive
California State University, Hayward
Hayward, CA 94542-3077

ADMISSIONS CONTACT:
Admissions and Records
California State University, Hayward
Hayward, CA 94542

Phone: 510-885-3057   *Phone:* 510-881-3811

University Web site: http://www.mcs.csuhayward.edu/~morgan/esmond/

Quick Facts About the Environmental Education Specialization

- Year established: 1972
- Enrollment: 30 master's students
- Graduate degrees conferred: Master of Science
- Faculty/Advisee ratio: 1:18

Areas of Specialization

Environmental Education and Communications (100%)

Special Program Features

All students in this program specialize in Environmental Education and Communications, but electives are available in other areas. Students take a sampling of environmental education courses designed to build outdoor leadership skills and an understanding of environmental issues, and related electives. Graduate students can cross-register for courses within other departments. Joint degree programs are offered with the School of Education. International program experiences are not offered. This program is best known for its emphasis on teacher education, curriculum development, and field training for nonformal educators.

Admission to the Program

- GRE scores not required; applicants are usually teachers
- Master's students accepted each year: 90% of 15 applicants
- Students may matriculate at the start of any term; transfer students are accepted.

About the Students

There are both male and female, and both international and domestic graduate students currently enrolled in this program; most are part-time.

About the Faculty

There are 23 faculty affiliated with this program. The average faculty member teaches 16–18 courses and advises 18 master's students per year. Advisors are both assigned to and chosen by students. Faculty research is currently being conducted domestically. Three faculty specialize in Environmental Education.

Tuition and Financial Aid

Tuition in 1996 was $0 (plus fees) per year for state residents and $164 per unit for nonresidents. Under 20% of the graduate students in this program receive financial aid.

Facilities

Computer facilities include 30 IBM/clones, 30 Macintoshes, computer labs, and access to Internet and E-mail. Free or low-cost computer training is available. There are three libraries and various museum collections available to graduate students. All facilities are handicapped accessible. The school also owns a 40-acre undeveloped camp on one end of campus, available for student research.

Career Counseling and Job Placement

This program offers field work assignments (usually classroom teaching), but nonformal programs, such as science camps, are also available. Career counseling and job placement services include job placement counselors, active alumni contact, on-campus interviews, job books, an alumni database, job fairs, and placement offers for the certificate program. Two percent of alumni work within the government sector, 22% for nonprofits, 5% for private small business, 1% for corporations or industries, and 70% in science or academia; 95% of alumni work in California. Most students already have jobs, but often get reassignments upon graduation.

☂ Department of Geological Sciences

FACULTY CONTACT: ADMISSIONS CONTACT:
Alexis Moiseyev   Admissions and Records

Graduate Coordinator   California State University, Hayward
Department of Geological Sciences   Hayward, CA 94542
California State University, Hayward
Hayward, CA 94542-3088

Phone: 510-885-3438

Quick Facts About the Department of Geological Sciences

- Year established: 1968
- Enrollment: 25 master's students
- Graduate degrees conferred: Master of Science
- Degree requirements for master's students include: required courses, master's thesis
- Faculty/Advisee ratio: 1:10

Areas of Specialization

Earth Science (100%)

Special Program Features

This program is best known for its emphasis on sediment petrology/stratigraphy, oceanography, and hydrogeology. Graduate students can cross-register for courses within other departments. Joint degree programs and international program experiences are not offered.

Admission to the Program

- GRE scores not required.
- Master's students accepted each year: 80% of 5 applicants
- Students may matriculate at the start of any term; transfer students are accepted.

Tuition and Financial Aid

Under 20% of the graduate students in this program receive financial aid; 5% are awarded research assistantships.

Career Counseling and Job Placement

This program offers a listing of student internships or educational opportunities within the local commmunity. Career counseling and job placement services include job placement counselors, active alumni contact, and job fairs. Twenty-five percent of alumni work within the government sector, 75% for private small business; 85% of alumni work in the San Francisco Bay area.

CALIFORNIA STATE UNIVERSITY, LONG BEACH

Established in 1949, California State University, Long Beach, has a total enrollment of 26,277 students. It is located on a suburban campus in a mid-sized city, about one mile from the Pacific Ocean.

🎓 Department of Geological Sciences

FACULTY CONTACT:

James Sample, Associate Professor
Department of Geological Sciences
California State University, Long Beach
1250 Bellflower Blvd.
Long Beach, CA 90840-3902

Phone: 310-985-4809

University Web site: http://www.csulb.edu

Quick Facts About the Department of Geological Science

- Year established: 1949
- Enrollment: 35 master's students
- Graduate degrees conferred: Master of Science

- Degree requirements for master's students include: required courses, master's thesis, master's project
- Faculty/Advisee ratio: 1:4

Areas of Specialization
Earth Science (100% of students)

Special Program Features
All students specialize in Earth Science; graduate students can cross-register for courses within other departments. Joint degree programs and international program experiences are not offered. This program is best known for its emphasis on tectonics, geophysics, and hydrogeology. Future program plans include more focus on environmental geochemistry.

Admission to the Program
- Admission requirements for master's applicants include: 2 semesters of chemistry, 1 of biology, 2 of calculus; average GRE scores are in the 45th percentile
- Master's students accepted each year: 80% of 10 applicants
- Students may matriculate at the start of any term; transfer students are accepted.

About the Students
There are 27 male and 8 female graduate students currently enrolled in this program; 8 are full-time and 27 part-time; none are international; 77% are Caucasian, 10% Hispanic, 10% Asian, and 3% Native American. Graduate students range from age 25 to 55, with a median age of 30.

About the Faculty
There are 11 faculty affiliated with this program. The average faculty member teaches 4 courses and advises under 4 master's students per year. Students choose their faculty advisors. Faculty research is currently being conducted both domestically and internationally; 8 faculty specialize in Earth Science and 1 in Environmental Science.

Tuition and Financial Aid

Tuition in 1996 was $0 (plus fees) per year for state residents and $246 per unit for nonresidents. Some 21–40% of the graduate students in this program receive financial aid; 40% are awarded teaching or administrative assistantships.

Facilities

Computer facilities include 8 IBM/clones, 2 Macintoshes, 1 terminal per 3 students, 4 SUN workstations, and access to Internet and E-mail. Free or low-cost computer training is available. One building, 4 classrooms, 4 laboratories, and various libraries are available to graduate students. All facilities are handicapped accessible.

Career Counseling and Job Placement

Student internships are not offered. Job placement services include active alumni contact. Ten percent of alumni work within the government sector, 60% for private small business, 20% for corporations or industries, and 10% in science or academia; 95% of alumni work in the western United States. Ninety-five percent of the students find work within six months of graduation.

CALIFORNIA STATE UNIVERSITY, NORTHRIDGE

Located on a large suburban campus northeast of Los Angeles, California State University, Northridge, was established in 1956. It has a total enrollment of 24,310 students.

☜ Department of Geological Sciences

FACULTY CONTACT:

Eugene Fritsche, Graduate Adviser
Department of Geological Sciences
California State University,
    Northridge
18111 Nordhoff Street
Northridge, CA 91330-8266

ADMISSIONS CONTACT:

Admissions and Records
California State University,
    Northridge
18111 Nordhoff Street
Northridge, California 91330

Phone: 818-885-3541   *Phone:* 818-885-3700
Fax: 818-885-2820

University Web site: http://www.csun.edu/

Quick Facts About the Department of Geological Sciences

- Year established: 1975
- Enrollment: 29 master's students
- Graduate degree conferred: Master of Science
- Degree requirements for master's students include: required courses, master's thesis
- Faculty/Advisee ratio: 1:3

Areas of Specialization

Geology (100%)

Special Program Features

All students specialize in geology; graduate students can cross-register for courses within other departments. Joint degree programs and international program experiences are not offered. This program is best known for its emphasis on geological field studies and sedimentology.

Admission to the Program

- Admission requirements for master's applicants include: 2 semesters of chemistry, 1 of calculus, 8 of physical science; GRE scores are required
- Master's students accepted each year: 50% of 22 applicants
- Students may matriculate at the start of any term; transfer students are accepted.

About the Students

There are 23 male and 6 female graduate students currently enrolled in this program; 90% are Caucasian, and 10% Asian. Graduate students range from age 21 to 55, with a median age of 30.

About the Faculty

There are 12 faculty affiliated with this program. The average faculty member teaches 6 courses and advises 1 master's student per year. Students choose their faculty advisors. Faculty research is currently being conducted domestically. All faculty specialize in Earth Science.

Tuition and Financial Aid

Tuition in 1996 was $0 (plus fees) per year for state residents and $246 per unit for nonresidents. Under 20% of the graduate students in this program receive financial aid; 6% are awarded teaching assistantships.

Facilities

Computer facilities include 100 IBM/clones, 100 Macintoshes, and access to Internet and E-mail. Free or low-cost computer training is available. There are 2 classrooms, 4 laboratories, libraries, and various museum collections available to graduate students. All facilities are handicapped accessible. The school also owns a Desert Studies Consortium, available for student research.

Career Counseling and Job Placement

This program posts offerings of student internships and educational opportunities within the local commmunity. Career counseling and job placement services include job placement counselors, active alumni contact, on-campus interviews, job books, and job fairs. All students find work within six months of graduation.

CALIFORNIA STATE UNIVERSITY, SACRAMENTO

Located on a wooded urban campus near the American River in California's capital city, California State University, Sacramento, has a total enrollment of 22,726 students (5,000 of them graduate students) and was established in 1950.

☝ Department of Recreation and Leisure Studies

FACULTY CONTACT:

Edilberto Cajucam
Graduate Coordinator
Department of Recreation
  and Leisure Studies
School of Health and
  Human Services
California State University,
  Sacramento
6000 J Street
Sacramento, CA 95819-6110

Phone: 916-278-6752

ADMISSIONS CONTACT:

Admissions Office
California State University,
  Sacramento
6000 J Street
Sacramento, CA 95819-6018

Quick Facts About the Department of Recreation and Leisure Studies

- Year established: 1968
- Enrollment: 25 master's students
- Graduate degrees conferred: Master of Science
- Degree requirements for master's students include: master's thesis, master's project
- Faculty/Advisee ratio: 1:4

Areas of Specialization

Parks and Recreation Management (99%)

Special Program Features

This program is best known for its emphasis on commercial recreation, therapeutic recreation, recreation resource management, and recreation program management. Ninety-nine percent of the students specialize in Parks and Recreation Management; graduate students can cross-register for courses within other departments. Joint degree programs are not offered. International program experiences include internships and student exchanges in Australia/New Zealand.

Admission to the Program

- GRE scores are not required.

- Master's students accepted each year: 75% of 15 applicants
- Students may matriculate at the start of any term; transfer students are accepted.

About the Students

There are 10 male and 15 female graduate students currently enrolled in this program; 5 are full-time and 20 part-time; 1 is international and 24 domestic; 50% are Caucasian, 30% Black, 10% Hispanic, and 10% Asian. Graduate students range from age 25 to 55, with a median age of 26.

About the Faculty

There are 13 faculty affiliated with this program. The average faculty member teaches 6 courses and advises 2.5 master's students per year. Advisors are assigned to students. Faculty research is currently being conducted both domestically and internationally; 7 faculty specialize in Parks and Recreation Management.

Tuition and Financial Aid

Tuition in 1996 was $0 (plus fees) per year for state residents and $246 per unit for nonresidents. Some 21–40% of the graduate students in this program receive financial aid; 5% are awarded teaching assistantships.

Facilities

Computer facilities include 30 Macintoshes, 1 terminal per 10 students, and access to Internet and E-mail. Free or low-cost computer training is available. One building, 10 classrooms, 4 laboratories, and 1 library are available to graduate students. All facilities are handicapped accessible.

Career Counseling and Job Placement

This program offers student internships and educational opportunities within the local commmunity for those who do not have field experience. Career counseling and job placement services include job placement counselors, active alumni contact, on-campus interviews, and job fairs. Ninety percent of alumni work within the government sector, 5% for nonprofits, and 5% for private small business; 90% of alumni work in California. Most students are already employed and study part-time.

☝ Biological Sciences Graduate Program

FACULTY CONTACT:

C. David Vanicek, Professor
Biological Sciences Graduate
   Program
California State University,
   Sacramento
6000 J Street
Sacramento, CA 95819-6077

Phone: 916-278-6535

ADMISSIONS CONTACT:

Admissions Office
California State University,
   Sacramento
6000 J Street
Sacramento, CA 95819-6018

Quick Facts About the Biological Sciences Graduate Program

- Year established: 1959
- Enrollment: 25 master's students
- Graduate degrees conferred: Master of Science
- Degree requirements for master's students include: required courses, master's thesis
- Faculty/Advisee ratio: 1:5

Areas of Specialization

Applied and Quantitative Ecology (100% of students)

Special Program Features

Graduate students can cross-register for courses within other departments. Joint degree programs and international program experiences are not offered. Future plans include changes in course offerings and requirements.

Admission to the Program

- Admission requirements for master's applicants include: 4 semesters of chemistry, 8 of biology, 1 of calculus, 2 of physical science, 1 of social science; GRE scores not required
- Master's students accepted each year: 50% of 12 applicants
- Students may matriculate at the start of any term; transfer students are accepted.

Tuition and Financial Aid

Under 20% of the graduate students in this program receive financial aid; 10% are awarded scholarships.

Career Counseling and Job Placement

This program offers student internships for academic credit. No career counseling or job placement services are offered. Sixty percent of alumni work within the government sector, 30% for private small business, and 10% in science or academia; 90% of alumni work in the West Coast region. Seventy-five percent of the students find work within six months of graduation.

☚ Other graduate environmental programs at California State University, Sacramento (no profiles available):

Environmental Studies Center. *Contact:* Valerie Anderson, Director. *Phone:* 916-278-7995.

CALIFORNIA STATE UNIVERSITY, STANISLAUS

This university has a total enrollment of 5,877 students and is located on 230 acres in the community of Turlock (population 40,000) in the Central Valley between San Francisco and Yosemite.

☚ Marine Science Program

FACULTY CONTACT:

Pamela Roe,
  Marine Science Advisor
Department of Biology
California State University,
  Stanislaus
Turlock, CA 95380

Phone: 209-667-3476

ADMISSIONS CONTACT:

Mary Coker, Coordinator
Office of Graduate Studies
California State University,
  Stanislaus
801 West Monte Vista Avenue
Turlock, CA 95382

Phone: 209-667-3151

Marine Science Program Web site: http://arnica.csustan.edu/mlml.html
California State University Web site: http://www.csustan.edu/

Quick Facts About the Marine Science Program
- Year established: 1982
- Enrollment: 25 master's students
- Graduate degrees conferred: Master of Science
- Degree requirements for master's students include: required courses, master's thesis
- Faculty/Advisee ratio: 1:15

Areas of Specialization

Applied and Quantitative Ecology (100% of students)

Special Program Features

A joint endeavor with the Moss Landing Marine Laboratories at Moss Landing, California, this program is best known for its emphasis on marine and coastal studies. (An additional five cooperating State Universities—Fresno, Hayward, Sacramento, San Francisco, and San Jose—also offer course work at Moss Landing.) All students specialize in Applied and Quantitative Ecology; graduate students cannot cross-register for courses within other departments. Joint degree programs and international program experiences are not offered. (Please see the profile of Moss Landing for additional information on the Laboratories.)

Admission to the Program
- Admission requirements for master's applicants include: 3 semesters of chemistry, 6+ of biology, 2 of physical science; average GRE scores: 700 verbal/600 math
- Master's students accepted each year: 50% of 18 applicants
- Students may matriculate at the start of any term; transfer students are accepted.

About the Students

All 25 graduate students currently enrolled in this program are full-time; 1 is international and 24 domestic; 96% are Caucasian and 4% Asian. Graduate students range from age 23 to 40, with a median age of 26.

About the Faculty

There are 8 faculty affiliated with this program. The average faculty member teaches 4 courses and advises 6 master's students per year. Advisors are assigned to students. Faculty research is currently being conducted both domestically and internationally. All faculty specialize in Applied and Quantitative Ecology.

Tuition and Financial Aid

Tuition in 1996 was $0 (plus fees) per year for state residents and $246 per unit for nonresidents. Over 60% of the graduate students in this program receive financial aid; 40% are awarded teaching or research assistantships.

Facilities

Computer facilities include 15 IBM/clones, 15 Macintoshes, 20 VAX terminals, and access to Internet and E-mail. Free or low-cost computer training is available. There are 3 classrooms, 8 laboratories and 1 library available to graduate students. Some facilities are handicapped accessible.

Career Counseling and Job Placement

This program does not offer student internships or career counseling and job placement services.

CHICAGO–KENT COLLEGE OF LAW
ILLINOIS INSTITUTE OF TECHNOLOGY

Established in 1940, Illinois Institute of Technology has a total enrollment 6,700 students; 1,200 are enrolled in the Chicago–Kent School of Law. The university is located on a 120-acre campus in the middle of the large city of Chicago.

☞ Program in Environmental and Energy Law

FACULTY CONTACT:
Stuart Deutsch, Co-Director

ADMISSIONS CONTACT:
Office of Admissions and Financial Aid

Program in Environmental
   and Energy Law
Chicago–Kent College of Law
Illinois Institute of Technology
565 West Adams Street
Chicago, IL 60661-3691

Chicago–Kent College of Law
Illinois Institute of Technology
565 West Adams Street
Chicago, IL 60661-3691

Phone: 312-906-5040
Fax: 312-906-5280
E-mail: admitQ@kentlaw.edu

Phone: 312-906-5020
TDD: 312-906-5230

Chicago-Kent College of Law Web site: http://www.kentlaw.edu/

Quick Facts About the Program in Environmental and Energy Law

• Year established: 1984
• Enrollment: 120 law school students
• Graduate degree conferred: Juris Doctorate
• Faculty/Advisee ratio: 1:30

Areas of Specialization

Environmental Law (100% of students)

Special Program Features

This program is best known for its emphasis on urban environmental issues, hazardous waste regulation, energy and environment, and international environmental law. All students specialize in Environmental Law; graduate students can cross-register for courses within other departments. Joint degree programs and international program experiences are not offered. Future program plans include expansion of clinical, practice, and internship opportunities.

About the Students

There are 70 male and 50 female graduate students currently enrolled in this program; 75 are full-time and 45 part-time; 5 are international and 115 domestic; 91% are Caucasian, 5% Black, 2% Hispanic, and 2% Asian. Graduate students range from age 23 to 50.

About the Faculty

There are 11 faculty affiliated with this program. The average faculty member teaches 4 courses. Advisors are assigned to students. Faculty research is currently being conducted both domestically and internationally; 4 faculty specialize in Environmental Law.

Tuition and Financial Aid

Tuition in 1995–96 was $17,950 for the academic year. Some 41–60% of the graduate students in this program receive financial aid.

Facilities

Computer facilities include 120 IBM/clones, 2 Macintoshes, 10 students per terminal, and access to Internet and E-mail. Free or low-cost computer training is available. One building, 26 classrooms, and 2 libraries are available to graduate students. All facilities are handicapped accessible.

Career Counseling and Job Placement

This program offers student internships and educational opportunities within the local commmunity. Career counseling and job placement services include job placement counselors, active alumni contact, on-campus interviews, job books, an alumni database, job fairs, and faculty contact with employers. Thirty-five percent of alumni work within the government sector, 5% for semi-governmental organizations, 10% for nonprofits, and 10% for corporations or industries; 90% of alumni work in the Midwest and 10% in Washington, D.C. Ninety-five percent of the students find work within six months of graduation.

CITY UNIVERSITY OF NEW YORK (CUNY)

Established in 1961, the City University of New York is located on an urban campus in the middle of Manhattan. The Graduate School and University Center has a total enrollment of approximately 4,000 graduate students.

☂ Doctoral Program in Environmental Psychology

STAFF CONTACT: ADMISSIONS CONTACT:

Judith Kubran,   Graduate Admissions Office
  Program Administrator   City University of New York

Ph.D. Program in   Graduate Center
  Environmental Psychology   33 West 42nd Street, Box 295
City University of New York   New York, NY 10036-8099
Graduate Center
33 West 42nd Street, Box 295
New York, NY 10036-8099

Phone: 212-642-2575   *Phone:* 212-642-2575

City University of New York Web site: http://www.cuny.edu/

Quick Facts About the Doctoral Program in Environmental Psychology

- Year established: 1968
- Enrollment: 70 doctoral students
- Graduate degree conferred: doctorate
- Degree requirements for doctoral students include: required courses, oral exam, dissertation
- Faculty/Advisee ratio: 1:6

Areas of Specialization

Resource Policy and Planning (30% of students)
Social Ecology (15%)
Applied and Quantitative Ecology (10%)
Corporate Environmental Management (10%)
Environmental Studies (10%)
Parks and Recreation Management (10%)
Environmental Quality and Public Health (5%)

Special Program Features

A subprogram of the Doctoral Program in Psychology, graduate training in environmental psychology relies on seminars, field research, and practicum experiences to explore the nexus between the behavior and the physical environment. The program collaborates extensively with the Program's Center for Human Environments, which conducts research, training, and public education pertaining to local, regional, and national environmental problems. Graduate students can cross-register for courses within other departments. Joint degree programs and international program experiences are not offered.

Admission to the Program

- Admission requirements for doctoral applicants include: 1 semester of statistics in social science; average GRE scores: 650 verbal/650 math; master's degree not required
- Doctoral students accepted each year: 40% of 30 applicants
- Students may matriculate only in the fall; transfer students are accepted.

About the Students

There are 31 male and 39 female graduate students currently enrolled in this program; 65 are full-time and 5 part-time; 12 are international and 58 domestic; 75% are Caucasian, 10% Black, 10% Hispanic, and 5% Asian. Graduate students range from age 22 to 65, with a median age of 27.

About the Faculty

There are 9 faculty affiliated with this program. The average faculty member teaches 4 courses and advises 2–3 doctoral students per year. Students choose their faculty advisors. Faculty research is currently being conducted both domestically and internationally. One faculty specializes in Applied and Quantitative Ecology, 1 in Corporate Environmental Management, 1 in Environmental Education, 3 in Environmental Geography, 2 in Environmental Quality and Public Health, and 1 in Parks and Recreation Management.

Tuition and Financial Aid

Tuition in 1996 averaged $4,000 per year for state residents and $7,500 per year for nonresidents. Under 20% of the graduate students in this program receive financial aid; 10% of the doctoral students are awarded fellowships; 20% are awarded research assistantships.

Facilities

Computer facilities include access to Internet and E-mail. Free or low-cost computer training is available. One building, 3 classrooms, and all of CUNY and NY Public Library systems are available to graduate students. Facilities are handicapped accessible.

Career Counseling and Job Placement

This program offers no student internships or educational opportunities within the local commmunity, but students do participate in field research. Career counseling and job placement services include active alumni contact, and an alumni database. Fifty percent of the students find work within six months of graduation.

☙ Other graduate environmental programs at City University of New York (no profiles available):

Earth and Environmental Studies Program. *Contact:* Daniel Habib. *Phone:* 212-642-2202.

Ph.D. Program in Biology. *Contact:* Richard Chappell, Acting Executive Officer. *Phone:* 212-642-2457.

CLARK UNIVERSITY

Established in 1887, Clark University has a total enrollment of 2,200 undergraduates and 730 graduate students. It is located on a 45-acre campus in Worcester, Massachusetts, a mid-sized city (population 160,000) 40 miles west of Boston.

☙ Program in International Development & Social Change

FACULTY CONTACT:

Richard Ford, Director
Program in International
   Development & Social Change
Clark University
950 Main Street
Worcester, MA 01610-1477

Phone: 508-793-7201

Fax: 508-793-8820

ADMISSIONS CONTACT:

Admissions House
Clark University
950 Main Street
Worcester, MA 01610

Phone: 508-793-7431
            or 800-GO-CLARK

Fax: 508-793-8821

Clark University Web site: http://www.clarku.edu/

Graduate School Web site:
http://www.clarku.edu/graduatefolder/graduate.html

Quick Facts About the Program in International Development & Social Change

- Year established: 1972
- Enrollment: 30 master's students
- Graduate degree conferred: Master of Arts
- Degree requirements for master's students include: required courses, master's thesis, master's project, work experience
- Faculty/Advisee ratio: varies

Areas of Specialization

Community Mobilization and Natural Resources Management (35% of students)
Gender and Natural Resources Management (35%)

Special Program Features

This program is best known for its emphasis on community participation and development, and gender analysis and development. Graduate students can cross-register for courses within other departments. Joint degree programs are offered with the Graduate School of Geography. International program experiences include research opportunities, internships, student exchanges, and field stations in Central America, India, Africa, the Middle East, and the Caribbean. Future program plans include a new M.A. in Geographic Information Systems (GIS) and Development.

Admission to the Program

- Admission requirements for master's applicants include: 3–5 years of work experience; GRE scores are not required
- Master's students accepted each year: 10% of 150 applicants
- Students may matriculate only in the fall; transfer students are not accepted.

About the Students

There are 15 male and 15 female graduate students currently enrolled in this program; all are full-time; 15 are international and 15 domestic; 30% are Caucasian, 30% Black, 5% Hispanic, and 30% Asian. Their median age is 30.

About the Faculty

There are 4 faculty affiliated with this program. The average faculty member teaches 4 courses and advises 8–10 master's students per year. Students choose their faculty advisors. Faculty research is currently being conducted internationally. Four faculty specialize in Applied and Quantitative Ecology, 1 in Conservation Biology, 2 in Earth Science, 2 in Environmental Geography, 3 in Environmental Quality and Public Health, 3 in Environmental Science, 1 in Parks and Recreation Management, and 2 in Resource Policy and Planning.

Tuition and Financial Aid

Tuition in 1996 was $18,700 per year. Over 60% of the graduate students in this program receive financial aid. Thirty percent of the master's students are awarded fellowships, 60% are awarded scholarships, and 60% are awarded teaching or research assistantships.

Facilities

Computer facilities include 15 IBM/clones, 1 terminal per 3 students, 25 GIS computers, and access to Internet and E-Mail. Free or low-cost computer training is available. One classroom and 2 libraries are available to graduate students. Facilities are handicapped accessible.

Career Counseling and Job Placement

This program offers student internships or educational opportunities with agencies working overseas, such as Catholic Relief Services. Career counseling and job placement services include active alumni contact, job books, and faculty assistance. Thirty percent of alumni work for semi-governmental organizations, 40% for nonprofits, 10% for private small business, and 20% in science or academia. All students find work within six months of graduation.

☞ Program in Environment, Technology, and Society

Contact:
Halina Brown
Chair, Graduate Admissions
Program in Environment, Technology, and Society
Clark University
950 Main Street
Worcester, MA 01610-1477

Phone: 508-793-7655

Quick Facts About the Program in Environment, Technology, and Society

- Enrollment: 20 master's students
- Graduate degree conferred: Master of Arts
- Degree requirements for master's students include: required courses, master's thesis
- Faculty/Advisee ratio: 1:5

Areas of Specialization

Environmental Quality and Public Health (50% of students)
Resource Policy and Planning (30%)
Corporate Environmental Management (10%)
Social Ecology (10%)

Special Program Features

This program is best known for its emphasis on environmental risk assessment and technological hazard management. Graduate students can cross-register for courses within other departments. Joint degree programs and international program experiences are not offered. Future program plans include enlarging the number of course offerings.

Admission to the Program

- GRE scores are required
- Masters students accepted each year: 30% of 40 applicants

• Students may matriculate only in the fall; transfer students are not accepted.

Tuition and Financial Aid

Over 60% of the graduate students in this program receive financial aid. All master's students are awarded scholarships; 40% are awarded teaching or research assistantships.

Career Counseling and Job Placement

Career counseling and job placement services include job placement counselors and active alumni contact. Ten percent of alumni work within the government sector, 10% for semi-governmental organizations, 20% for nonprofits, 20% for private small business, 10% for corporations or industries, 10% in science or academia, and 10% in their own consulting businesses. All students find work within six months of graduation.

☀ Other graduate environmental programs at Clark University (no profiles available):

Program in Geography. *Contact:* Susan Hanson, 508-793-7336. *Department of Geography Web site:* http://www.clarku.edu/departments/geography/grad/cover.html

CLEMSON UNIVERSITY

With a total enrollment of 17,600 students, Clemson University was established in 1889 and is located on a 1,400-acre campus in the town of Clemson, South Carolina.

☀ Department of Parks, Recreation & Tourism Management

FACULTY/ADMISSIONS CONTACT

Francis McGuire, Professor
Department of Parks, Recreation
  & Tourism Management

Clemson University
263 Lehotsky Hall
Clemson, SC 29634-1005

Phone: 803-656-2183

Clemson University Web site: http://www.clemson.edu/

Graduate School Web site: http://www.grad.clemson.edu/

Quick Facts About the Department of Parks, Recreation & Tourism Management

- Year established: 1967
- Enrollment: 35 master's students / 25 doctoral students
- Graduate degrees conferred: Master of Science; Master of Parks, Recreation, and Tourism Management; doctorate
- Degree requirements for master's students include: master's thesis (for M.S.), master's project (for M.PRTM)
- Degree requirements for doctoral students include: dissertation, qualifying exam, oral exam
- Faculty/Advisee ratio: 1:6

Areas of Specialization

Parks and Recreation Management (100% of students)

Special Program Features

This program is best known for its emphasis on recreation resource management and travel and tourism. All students specialize in Parks and Recreation Management; graduate students can cross-register for courses within other departments. Joint degree programs and international program experiences are not offered.

Admission to the Program

- Admission requirements for master's applicants include average GRE scores: 550 verbal/550 math
- Admission requirements for doctoral applicants include average GRE scores: 600 verbal/600 math

- Master's students accepted each year: 30% of 30 applicants
- Doctoral students accepted each year: 15% of 20 applicants
- Students may matriculate at the start of any term; transfer students are accepted.

About the Students

There are 30 male and 30 female graduate students currently enrolled in this program; 45 are full-time and 15 part-time; 10 are international and 50 domestic; 80% are Caucasian, 5% Black, and 15% Asian. Graduate students range from age 22 to 48, with a median age of 29.

About the Faculty

There are 23 faculty affiliated with this program. The average faculty member teaches 4 courses and advises 3 master's and 3 doctoral students per year. Students choose their faculty advisors. Faculty research is currently being conducted both domestically and internationally. Nineteen faculty specialize in Applied and Quantitative Ecology, and 1 in Forestry.

Tuition and Financial Aid

Tuition in 1996 was $2,922 per year for state residents and $5,844 per year for nonresidents. Over 60% of the graduate students in this program receive financial aid. Fifty percent of the master's students are awarded research assistantships, and 80% of the doctoral students are awarded teaching or research assistantships.

Facilities

Computer facilities include 40 IBM/clones, 5 Macintoshes, 3 GIS computers, and access to Internet and E-mail. Free or low-cost computer training is available. One building, 7 classrooms, 2 laboratories, and 1 library are available to graduate students. Some facilities are handicapped accessible. The school also owns Clemson Forest, Clemson Laboratory for Special Populations, and the Archibald Tropical Research Center (Island of Dominica), all available for student research.

Career Counseling and Job Placement

Career counseling and job placement services include active alumni contact and job fairs. Fifty percent of alumni work within the government sector, 20% for nonprofits, and 30% in science or academia.

☗ Department of Forest Resources

FACULTY/ADMISSIONS CONTACT:

Allan Marsinko, Graduate Coordinator
Department of Forest Resources
Clemson University
238 Lehotsky Hall
Box 341003
Clemson, SC 29634-1003

Phone: 803-656-4839
Fax: 803-656-3304

College of Agriculture, Forestry and Life Sciences Web site:
http://agweb.clemson.edu/

Quick Facts About the Forest Resources Program

- Enrollment: 42 master's students / 15 doctoral students
- Graduate degrees conferred: Master of Science, Master of Forest Resources, doctorate
- Master's degree requirements include: master's thesis for M.S.; master's project for M.F.R.; oral exam
- Doctoral degree requirements include: dissertation, qualifying exam, oral exam
- Faculty/Advisee ratio: 1:3

Special Program Features

Graduate students can cross-register for courses within other departments. Joint degree programs are not offered. International program experiences include research opportunities in China. Future program plans include evaluation of the M.F.R. program.

Admission to the Program

- GRE scores are required for all graduate applicants
- Admission requirements for M.S. applicants are individualized; for M.F.R. applicants they include the equivalent of a B.S. in Forestry
- A master's degree is required for doctoral applicants
- Students may matriculate at the start of any term; transfer students are accepted.

About the Students

There are 45 male and 12 female graduate students currently enrolled in this program; 6 are international and 51 domestic. Faculty members agree to serve as advisors for any given student.

Tuition and Financial Aid

Over 60% of the graduate students in this program receive financial aid. Ten percent of the master's assistantships awarded are for teaching and 90% for research; all of the doctoral assistantships awarded are for research.

Career Counseling and Job Placement

This program does not offer student internships. Career counseling and job placement services include on-campus interviews. Seventy percent of alumni work in the Southeast.

☞ Other graduate environmental programs at Clemson University (no profiles available):

Department of Aquaculture, Fisheries and Wildlife Biology. *Contact:* D. Lamar Robinette. *Phone:* 803-656-3117.

Department of Environmental Toxicology. *Contact:* Ronald Kendall, Director, Clemson University, 1 Tiwet Drive, P.O. Box 709, Pendleton, SC 29670. *Phone:* 803-646-2200. *Fax:* 803-646-2277.

COLLEGE OF THE ATLANTIC

With a total enrollment of only 250 students, the College of the Atlantic was established in 1969 and is located on a 25-acre campus in the coastal town of Bar Harbor, Maine.

☜ Human Ecology Program

FACULTY CONTACT:

Melville Coté, Administrative Dean
Human Ecology Program
College of the Atlantic
105 Eden Street
Bar Harbor, ME 04609-1105

Phone: 207-288-5015
Fax: 207-288-4126

ADMISSIONS CONTACT:

Admission Office
College of the Atlantic
105 Eden Street
Bar Harbor, ME 04609-1105

Phone: 1-800-528-0025
Fax: 207-288-4126

Quick Facts About the Human Ecology Program
- Year established: 1991
- Enrollment: 6 master's students
- Graduate degree conferred: Master of Philosophy
- Degree requirements for master's students include: required courses, master's thesis
- Faculty/Advisee ratio: 1:1

Special Program Features
Joint degree programs and international program experiences are not offered.

Admission to the Program
- GRE scores are not required. Each student program is individually designed and must have a faculty sponsor prior to admission.
- Master's students accepted each year: 30–60% of 10 applicants
- Students may matriculate only in the fall; transfer students are not accepted.

About the Students
There are 3 male and 3 female graduate students currently enrolled in this program; all 6 are full-time; 1 is international and 5 domestic; 95% are Caucasian and 5% Asian. Graduate students range from age 23 to 40, with a median age of 25.

About the Faculty

There are 12 faculty affiliated with this program. The average faculty member teaches 5 courses and advises 1 master's student per year.

Tuition and Financial Aid

Tuition in 1996 was $15,450 for the academic year. Over 60% of the graduate students in this program receive financial aid—only loans are made.

Facilities

Computer facilities include 10 IBM/clones, 5 Macintoshes, 4 GIS computers, and access to Internet and E-mail. Free or low-cost computer training is available. A library and various museum collections are available to graduate students. Some facilities are handicapped accessible. The school owns 20 acres of forest land; field research opportunities in Acadia National Park are also available.

Career Counseling and Job Placement

Career counseling and job placement services include job placement counselors and active alumni contact.

COLORADO STATE UNIVERSITY

Established in 1870, Colorado State University has a total enrollment of 20,970 and is located on an 833-acre campus in the mid-sized city of Fort Collins, Colorado.

☂ Doctoral Program in Environmental Politics and Policy

FACULTY CONTACT:

Alan Lamborn, Graduate
  Coordinator
Doctoral Program in
  Environmental Politics and Policy

ADMISSIONS CONTACT:

The Graduate School
208 Administration Annex
Colorado State University
Fort Collins, CO 80523

Colorado State University
Fort Collins, CO 80523

Phone: 970-491-5156   *Phone:* 970-491-6817

Colorado State University Web site: http://www.colostate.edu/

Graduate School Web site: http://www.ColoState.EDU/Depts/Grad/

Quick Facts About the Environmental Politics and Policy Program

- Year established: MA program, 1963; Ph.D. program, 1976
- Enrollment: 22 master's students / 33 doctoral students
- Graduate degrees conferred: Master of Arts, doctorate
- Degree requirements for master's students include: required courses, master's thesis or professional paper, qualifying exam and oral exam
- Degree requirements for doctoral students include: required courses, dissertation, qualifying exam, oral exam
- Faculty/Advisee ratio: 1:4

Areas of Specialization

Environmental Policy, Administration, and Planning (100% of students)

Special Program Features

This program is best known for its emphasis on American environmental politics and policy; comparative environmental politics and policy; and international environmental politics and policy. All students specialize in Environmental Policy, Administration, and Planning; graduate students can cross-register for courses within other departments. Joint degree programs and international program experiences are not offered.

Admission to the Program

- Admission requirements for master's applicants include: 2 semesters of social science; average GRE scores: 599 verbal/600 math
- Admission requirements for doctoral applicants include: master's degree; average GRE scores: 639 verbal/649 math
- Master's students accepted each year: 37% of 47 applicants

- Doctoral students accepted each year: 26% of 28 applicants
- Students may matriculate at the start of any term; transfer students are accepted.

About the Students

There are 40 male and 15 female graduate students currently enrolled in this program; 33 are full-time and 22 part-time; 3 are international and 52 domestic; 98% are Caucasian, 1% Black, and 1% Asian. Graduate students range from age 23 to 55, with a median age of 29.

About the Faculty

There are 17 faculty affiliated with this program. The average faculty member teaches 5 courses and advises 1 master's and 2.5 doctoral students per year. Students choose their faculty advisors. Faculty research is currently being conducted both domestically and internationally; 15 faculty specialize in Resource Policy and Planning.

Tuition and Financial Aid

Tuition in 1996 was $3,109 per year for Colorado residents and $9,767 for nonresidents. Some 21–40% of the graduate students in this program receive financial aid; 5% of the master's students are awarded fellowships; 45% of the doctoral students are awarded teaching assistantships.

Facilities

Computer facilities include 40 IBM/clones, a word processing lab, 20 GIS computers, and access to Internet and E-mail. Free or low-cost computer training is available. One library is available to graduate students. All facilities are handicapped accessible.

Career Counseling and Job Placement

Career counseling and job placement services include informal counseling with committee members. Fifty percent of alumni work within the government sector, 5% for nonprofits, 5% for private small business, 10% for corporations or industries, and 30% in science or academia; 50% of alumni work in the Rocky Mountain West region and 10% in Washington, D.C. Over 90% of the students find work within six months of graduation.

🎓 Department of Earth Resources

FACULTY CONTACT:

Donlad Doehring, Head
Department of Earth Resources
Colorado State University
Fort Collins, CO 80523

Phone: 970-491-5661
Fax: 970-491-6307
E-mail: dond@picea.cfnr.colostate.edu

Department of Earth Resources Web site:
http://www.cnr.colostate.edu/ER/intro.html

ADMISSIONS CONTACT:

The Graduate School
208 Administration Annex
Colorado State University
Fort Collins, CO 80523

Phone: 970-491-6817

Quick Facts About the Department of Earth Resources

- Year established: 1973
- Enrollment: 69 master's students / 9 doctoral students
- Graduate degrees conferred: Master of Science, doctorate
- Degree requirements for master's students include: 30 graduate credits, master's thesis
- Degree requirements for doctoral students include: 72 graduate credits, dissertation
- Faculty/Advisee ratio: 14:78

Areas of Specialization

Earth Science (100% of students)

Special Program Features

This program is best known for being the "birthplace of watershed science." Graduate students can cross-register for courses within other departments. Joint degree programs are not offered.

Admission to the Program

- GRE scores are required for all graduate students
- Master's students accepted each year: <10% of 120 applicants
- Doctoral students accepted each year: <5% of 20 applicants

- Students may matriculate at the start of any term; transfer students are accepted.

Tuition and Financial Aid

Over 60% of the graduate students in this program receive financial aid. Both master's and doctoral students are awarded teaching and research assistantships.

Career Counseling and Job Placement

This program offers student internships or educational opportunities with federal agencies and oil companies. Career counseling and job placement services include job placement counselors, active alumni contact, on-campus interviews, and job fairs. All students find work within six months of graduation.

☞ Other graduate environmental programs at Colorado State University (no profiles available):

Department of Agricultural and Resource Economics. *Contact:* Paul Huszar, Coordinator. *Phone:* 970-491-6948.

Department of Atmospheric Science. *Contact:* Jane Wilkins. *Phone:* 970-491-8360.

Department of Biology, Graduate Programs in Zoology. *Contact:* Bruce Wunder, Chair. *Phone:* 970-491-5949.

Programs in Ecology. *Contact:* Dean Jaros, Coordinator. *Phone:* 970-491-6817.

Department of Fishery and Wildlife Biology. *Contact:* Richard Knight. *Phone:* 970-491-6714.

Department of Forest Sciences. *Contact:* Daniel Binkley. *Phone:* 970-491-6519.

Department of Range Science. *Contact:* Tana Allshouse. *Phone:* 970-491-4994.

Department of Recreation Resources. *Contact:* Glenn Haas, Chair. *Phone:* 970-491-5126.

COLUMBIA UNIVERSITY COLLEGE OF PHYSICIANS & SURGEONS and SCHOOL OF PUBLIC HEALTH

Established in 1767, Columbia University College of Physicians and Surgeons has a total enrollment of 2,000. It is located on an urban campus in the uptown area of Manhattan.

🎓 Division of Environmental Sciences

FACULTY CONTACT:

Dr. Joseph Graziano, Head
Division of Environmental Sciences
Columbia University
College of Physicians
   & Surgeons and School
   of Public Health
603 West 168th Street
New York, NY 10032

Phone: 212-305-1678
Fax: 212-305-3857

ADMISSIONS CONTACT:

Office of Student Services
School of Public Health
Columbia University
600 West 168th Street
New York, NY 10032

Phone: 212-305-3927

School of Public Health Web site: http://cpmcnet.columbia.edu/dept/sph/

University Web site: http://www.columbia.edu/

Quick Facts About the Division of Environmental Sciences

- Year established: 1960
- Enrollment: 50 master's students / 12 doctoral students
- Graduate degrees conferred: Master of Public Health, Doctor of Public Health
- Degree requirements for master's students include: required courses, work experience
- Degree requirements for doctoral students include: required courses, dissertation, qualifying exam, oral exam
- Faculty/Advisee ratio: 1:4

Areas of Specialization

Environmental Quality and Public Health (60% of students)
Environmental Health Sciences (40%)

Special Program Features

This program is best known for its emphasis on environmental health sciences; carcinogenesis; molecular epidemiology; and heavy metal toxicology. Graduate students can cross-register for courses within other departments. Joint degree programs are offered with the School of International Policy. International program experiences include research opportunities in Europe. Future plans include adding a Ph.D. degree program.

Admission to the Program

- Admission requirements for master's applicants include: 4 semesters of chemistry, 2 of biology, 2 of calculus; average GRE scores: 560 verbal/680 math
- Admission requirements for doctoral applicants include: average GRE scores: 600 verbal/720 math
- Master's students accepted each year: 50% of 50 applicants
- Doctoral students accepted each year: 50% of 4 applicants
- Students may matriculate at the start of any term; transfer students are accepted.

About the Students

There are 30% international and 70% domestic graduate students currently enrolled in this program; 70% are Caucasian, 10% Black, and 20% Asian. Graduate students range from age 23 to 38, with a median age of 31.

About the Faculty

There are 22 faculty affiliated with this program. The average faculty member teaches 1 course and advises 2 master's and 2 doctoral students per year. Advisors are assigned to students. Faculty research is currently being conducted both domestically and internationally. Four faculty specialize in Toxicology, 4 in Environmental Health, 4 in Medical/Health Physics, 1 in Occupational Medicine, and 2 in Tropical Disease.

Tuition and Financial Aid

Tuition in 1996 was approximately $20,000 for the academic year. Over 60% of the graduate students in this program receive financial aid. Ten percent of the master's students are awarded fellowships; 80% are awarded teaching or research assistantships. All doctoral students are awarded teaching or research assistantships.

Facilities

Computer facilities include 2 large computer laboratories and access to Internet and E-mail. Free or low-cost computer training is available. There are 6 buildings, 30 classrooms, 16 laboratories, and campus-wide libraries available to graduate students. Facilities are handicapped accessible.

Career Counseling and Job Placement

This program does not offer student internships or educational opportunities within the local commmunity. Career counseling and job placement services include job placement counselors, active alumni contact, on-campus interviews, and visits to government agencies. Forty percent of alumni work within the government sector, 10% for nonprofits, 10% for private small business, 10% for corporations or industries, and 30% in science or academia. Ninety percent of the students find work within six months of graduation.

☙ Other graduate environmental programs at Columbia University (no profiles available):

The Center for Environmental Research and Conservation is offering a new doctoral program in Ecology and Evolutionary Biology. *Contact:* Office of Student Affairs, Graduate School for Arts & Sciences, 107 Low Memorial Library, Columbia University, New York, NY 10027. *Phone:* 212-854-4737. *Fax:* 212-854-2863. *Web site:* http://www.cu.cerc *or* http://www.cu.bulletin/apply.html.

CORNELL UNIVERSITY

With a total enrollment of 19,000 (about 6,000 of them graduate students), Cornell University was established in 1865. It is located in Ithaca, a cosmopolitan town in the scenic upstate Finger Lakes area of New York. A state land-grant institution, this school belongs to the Hispanic Association of Colleges and Universities.

🐄 College of Agriculture and Life Sciences
Graduate Field of Natural Resources

FACULTY CONTACT:

Ray Ogelsby, Professor
College of Agriculture
  and Life Sciences
Graduate Field of Natural
  Resources
Cornell University
16 Fernow Hall
Ithaca, NY 14853

Phone: 607-255-2823
Fax: 607-255-1816

ADMISSIONS CONTACT:

The Graduate School
Sage Graduate Center
Cornell University
Ithaca, NY 14853-6201

Phone: 607-255-4884

College of Agriculture and Life Sciences Web site:
http://www.cals.cornell.edu/calshomepage.html

Cornell University Web site: http://www.cornell.edu/

Quick Facts About the Graduate Field of Natural Resources

- Year established: 1946
- Enrollment: 26 master's students / 22 doctoral students
- Graduate degrees conferred: Master of Science, Master of Professional Studies, doctorate
- Degree requirements for master's students include: master's thesis, 2 semesters in-residence
- Degree requirements for doctoral students include: dissertation, admission to candidacy examination
- Faculty/Advisee ratio: 1:3

Areas of Specialization

Applied and Quantitative Ecology (43% of students)
Resource Policy and Planning (26%)
Forestry (9%)
Environmental Studies (6%)
Conservation Biology (4%)
Environmental Education (4%)
Environmental Science (4%)
Social Ecology (4%)

Special Program Features

This program is best known for its emphasis on applied ecology, human dimensions in natural resource management, and agroforestry. Graduate students can cross-register for courses within other departments. Joint degree programs are not offered. International program experiences include research opportunities and training grants in Central America. Future program plans include the addition of landscape or watershed ecology and management courses.

Admission to the Program

- Admission requirements for all graduate applicants include: average GRE scores: 627 verbal/677 math
- Master's students accepted each year: 10% of 75 applicants
- Doctoral students accepted each year: 5% of 50 applicants
- Students may matriculate at the start of any term; transfer students are accepted.

About the Students

There are 29 male and 19 female graduate students currently enrolled in this program; all are full-time; 94% are Caucasian, 2% Hispanic, and 4% Native American.

About the Faculty

There are 31 faculty affiliated with this program. The average faculty member teaches 1.5 courses and advises 1.4 master's and 1.4 doctoral students per year. Students choose their faculty advisors. Faculty research is currently being conducted both domestically and internationally. Sixteen faculty specialize in Applied and Quantitative Ecology, 0.5 in Earth Science, 4.5 in Environmental Science, 1 in Environmental Studies, 2 in Forestry, and 4 in Resource Policy and Planning.

Tuition and Financial Aid

Tuition in 1996 was $10,000 for the academic year. Over 60% of the graduate students in this program receive financial aid. Ten percent of the master's students are awarded fellowships; 90% are awarded teaching or research assistantships. Twenty percent of the doctoral students are awarded fellowships; 80% are awarded teaching or research assistantships.

Facilities

Computer facilities include mainframes, supercomputers, various clusters of microcomputers, and access to Internet and E-mail. Free or low-cost computer training is available. There are 17 libraries available to graduate students. Some facilities are handicapped accessible. The school also owns an experimental forest south of Ithaca; an aquatic/fishery science field facility on Oneida Lake; and an experimental sugar bush at Lake Placid, New York, all available for student research.

Career Counseling and Job Placement

Career counseling and job placement services include job placement counselors, on-campus interviews, job books, and job fairs. All students find work within six months of graduation.

☛ Other graduate environmental programs at Cornell University (no profiles available):

Education Department, Environmental Education Program. *Contact:* Joseph Novak. *Phone:* 607-255-3005.
Cornell Center for the Environment. *Contact:* Karen McNally. *Phone:* 607-255-9996.

DALHOUSIE UNIVERSITY

Established in 1818, Dalhousie University is located in Halifax, Nova Scotia, a mid-sized port city in eastern Canada.

☛ School for Resource and Environmental Studies

FACULTY CONTACT:
Ann Dwire
Academic Program Coordinator
School for Resource and
    Environmental Studies
Dalhousie University
1312 Robie Street

ADMISSIONS CONTACT:
Office of the Registrar
Dalhousie University
Halifax, Nova Scotia
Canada B3H 4H6

Halifax, Nova Scotia
Canada B3H 3E2

Phone: 902-494-3632   *Phone:* 902-494-2450
Fax: 902-494-2630

School for Resource and Environmental Studies Web site:
http://quasar.sba.dal.ca:2000/sres/sres.html

University Web site: http://www2.dal.ca/

Quick Facts About the School for Resource and Environmental Studies

- Year established: 1978
- Enrollment: 40 master's students
- Graduate degrees conferred: Master of Environmental Studies
- Degree requirements for master's students include: required courses, master's thesis

Areas of Specialization

Applied and Quantitative Ecology, Conservation Biology, Corporate Environmental Management, Environmental Education, Environmental Geography, Environmental Law, Environmental Quality and Public Health, Environmental Science, Environmental Studies, Forestry, Parks and Recreation Management, Resource Policy and Planning, and Social Ecology.

Special Program Features

This program is best known for its emphasis on environmental management and policy, and environmental impact assessment. Graduate students can cross-register for courses within other departments. Joint degree programs are not offered. International program experiences include research opportunities in China and Southeast Asia.

Admission to the Program

- Admission requirements for master's applicants include: an honors degree in a natural or social science program
- Master's students accepted each year: 5–10% of 200 applicants
- Students may matriculate at the start of any term; transfer students are not accepted.

About the Students

Some 98.5% of the graduate students currently enrolled in this program are Caucasian, 0.5% Black, and 1% Asian. Graduate students range from age 22 to 50.

About the Faculty

There are 34 faculty affiliated with this program. The average faculty member teaches 1–2 courses and advises 2–3 master's students per year. Advisors are assigned to students; students choose their faculty supervisors. One faculty member specializes in Applied and Quantitative Ecology, 2 in Environmental Quality and Public Health, and 1 in Social Ecology.

Tuition and Financial Aid

Tuition in 1994 was $3087 (plus $2,700 for non-Canadians) in Canadian dollars for the two-year master's program. Full scholarships and teaching assistantships are available.

Facilities

Computer facilities include 1 IBM/clone, 2 Macintoshes, and access to Internet and E-mail. There are 3 buildings, 1 classroom, 1 laboratory, and 2 libraries available to graduate students. Some facilities are handicapped accessible.

Career Counseling and Job Placement

This program does not offer student internships or career counseling and job placement services. Fifty percent of alumni work within the government sector, 20% for semi-governmental organizations, 5% for nonprofits, 10% for private small business, 5% for corporations or industries, and 10% in science or academia. All students find work within six months of graduation.

DARTMOUTH COLLEGE

Established in 1769, Dartmouth College has a total enrollment of 5,000 students. It is located in the small college town of Hanover, in scenic southern New Hampshire.

🎓 Earth, Ecosystem and Ecological Sciences Program (EEES)

FACULTY CONTACT:

Andrew J. Friedland,
   Associate Professor
Earth, Ecosystem and
   Ecological Sciences Program
Dartmouth College
6182 Steel Hall
Hanover, NH 03755-3577

Phone: 603-646-3609
Fax: 603-646-1682
E-mail: keely.boivin@dartmouth.edu

ADMISSIONS CONTACT:

Keely Boivin
EEES
Environmental Studies Program
Dartmouth College
6182 Steel Hall
Hanover, NH 03755-3577

Phone: 603-646-2838

Dartmouth College Web site: http://www.dartmouth.edu/

Quick Facts About the Earth, Ecosystem and Ecological Sciences Program

- Year established: 1993
- Enrollment: 5 doctoral students
- Graduate degrees conferred: doctorate
- Doctoral degree requirements include: dissertation, qualifying exam, oral exam
- Faculty/Advisee ratio: 1:3

Areas of Specialization

Environmental Biogeochemistry (40% of students)
Applied and Quantitative Ecology (20%)
Conservation Biology (20%)
Earth Science (20%)

Special Program Features

The Ph.D. is offered through either the Department of Biological Sciences or the Department of Earth Sciences. Graduate students can cross-register for courses within other departments. Joint degree programs and international program experiences are not offered. The program sponsors regular seminars with visiting lecturers and an annual research retreat.

About the Students

There are 3 male and 2 female graduate students currently enrolled in this program; they range from age 23 to 33, with a median age of 26.

About the Faculty

There are 14 faculty affiliated with this program. The average faculty member teaches 3 courses and advises 1 doctoral student per year. Students choose their faculty advisors. Faculty research is currently being conducted both domestically and internationally. Six faculty specialize in Applied and Quantitative Ecology, 1 in Conservation Biology, 5 in Earth Science, and 2 in Environmental Biogeochemistry.

Tuition and Financial Aid

Tuition in 1996 was $27,740 for the academic year. Teaching fellowships, which include tuition and a stipend, are available to qualified students. Research fellowships are also available.

Facilities

The program sponsors field research sites in Costa Rica, Jamaica, Indonesia, Antarctica, Canada, and the Himalayas.

DUKE UNIVERSITY

With almost 12,000 students (nearly 5,000 of whom are graduate students), Duke University is located on the outskirts of Durham (population 137,000) in the central piedmont "research triangle" region of North Carolina.

☂ Nicholas School of the Environment

PROGRAM/ADMISSIONS CONTACT:

Bertie Belvin, Assistant Dean
Enrollment Services
Nicholas School of the Environment
Box 90330

Duke University
Durham, NC 27708-0330

Phone: 919-613-8070
Fax: 919-684-8741
E-mail: admissions@env.duke.edu

Nicholas School of the Environment Web site: http://www.env.duke.edu

Quick Facts About the Nicholas School of the Environment

- Year established: 1938 as School of Forestry; 1974 as School of Forestry and Environmental studies; 1991 as School of the Environment; 1996 as Nicholas School of the Environment

- Enrollment: Approximately 200 professional students and 20 graduate students

- Graduate degrees conferred: Master of Environmental Management (M.E.M.), Master of Forestry (M.F.), Master of Arts (M.A.), Master of Science (M.S.), doctorate (Ph.D.)

- Professional degree (M.E.M., M.F.) requirements include: 2 years of study or 48 units of credit, master's project

- Graduate master's degree (M.A., M.S.) requirements include: 30 units of credit and minimum of one year in residence, master's thesis

- Doctoral requirements include: Minimum of 60 units of credit, three or more years in residence, dissertation, examination

Areas of Specialization (according to program literature)

Biohazard Science
Coastal Environmental Management
Environmental Toxicology, Chemistry, and Risk Assessment
Forest Resource Management
Resource Ecology
Resource Economics and Policy
Water and Air Resources

Special Program Features

This program is best known for its comprehensive, interdisciplinary, and structured nature, as well as for its relative strength in the subject areas of environmental quality and resource economics and policy. Formal concurrent degree programs are offered with the Fuqua School of Business, School of Law, and Terry Sanford Institute of Public Policy. The Marine Laboratory at Beaufort provides a hands-on opportunity to study coastal and marine processes. Cross-registration is also available through a variety of academic departments within the university, and there are numerous opportunities to take courses at other area universities, including the University of North Carolina at Chapel Hill and North Carolina State University.

Admission to the Program

- Requirements include: previous training in the natural or social sciences; introductory calculus; introductory statistics; working knowledge of computers. Each area of specialization requires additional preparation, as described in the program literature.
- GRE scores and three letters of recommendation are required.
- Transfer students are accepted, and in some cases students may matriculate in the spring term.

About the Faculty

The Nicholas School has over 50 faculty either directly affiliated or associated with its program. Thanks to a major financial gift early in 1996, this number is expected to expand incrementally over the coming years.

Tuition and Financial Aid

Tuition in 1995-96 was $18,403 for the academic year. The program offers financial aid in the form of scholarships, assistantships, and loans. Approximately 45% of professional degree candidates receive some form of financial aid.

Facilities

The Nicholas School of the Environment is housed in the Levine Science Research Center, a three-year-old, state-of-the-art research and teaching facility. There are extensive computer facilities provided, and students have access to a variety of libraries in the Duke system. The Duke Forest encompasses 7,700 acres in five divisions in the Durham area and is used for field research as well as recreational activities. Finally, the Nicholas School adjoins a greenhouse and phytotron with 50 separately controlled growth chambers for research under controlled environmental conditions.

Career Counseling and Job Placement

As a professional degree program, the Nicholas School provides a highly active career counseling and job placement program. Counseling services include one-on-one resumé development, a resumé book, on-campus recruiting, personalized assistance with cover letters and interview techniques, job fairs, and a library of career resource materials and listings of internship and employment opportunities. All students receive assistance in securing summer internships and research funding. Graduates are employed primarily in the areas of environmental consulting, industry, and government, as well as in the nonprofit and academic sectors. Almost all graduates find employment within six months of graduation.

EASTERN KENTUCKY UNIVERSITY

Located in the small, historic town of Richmond, Kentucky, Eastern Kentucky University was established in 1874. It has a total enrollment of 16,870 students.

🎓 Department of Biological Sciences

FACULTY CONTACT:

Barbara Ramey
Professor and Graduate Coordinator
Department of Biological Sciences
235 Moore Building
Eastern Kentucky University
Richmond, KY 40475

ADMISSIONS CONTACT:

The Graduate School
Coates Box 5A
Eastern Kentucky University
521 Lancaster Avenue
Richmond, KY 40475-9981

Phone: 606-622-6258

Eastern Kentucky University Web site: http://www.edu/edu/

Quick Facts About the Department of Biological Sciences

- Enrollment: 49 master's students
- Graduate degree conferred: Master of Science
- Degree requirements for master's students include: required courses, master's thesis
- Faculty/Advisee ratio: 1:4

Areas of Specialization

Applied and Quantitative Ecology (64% of students)
Botany (12%)
Environmental Quality and Public Health (4%)

Special Program Features

This program is best known for its emphasis on wildlife ecology, aquatic ecology, and ornithology. Graduate students can cross-register for courses within other departments. Joint degree programs and international program experiences are not offered.

Admission to the Program

- Admission requirements for master's applicants include: 2 semesters of chemistry, 6 of biology, 1 of calculus; average GRE scores: 450 verbal/500 math
- Master's students accepted each year: 85% of 40 applicants
- Students may matriculate at the start of any term; transfer students are rarely accepted.

About the Students

There are 28 male and 21 female graduate students currently enrolled in this program; 35 are full-time and 14 part-time; none are international; all are Caucasian. Graduate students range from age 22 to 51, with a median age of 27.

About the Faculty

There are 18 faculty affiliated with this program. The average faculty member teaches 4 courses and advises 4 master's students per year. Students choose their faculty advisors. Faculty research is currently being conducted domestically. Eight faculty specialize in Applied and Quantitative Ecology, 4 in Botany, and 1 in Environmental Quality and Public Health.

Tuition and Financial Aid

Tuition in 1996 was $2,070 per year for state residents and $5,740 for non-residents. Some 21–40% of the graduate students in this program receive fi-

nancial aid; 29% of the master's students are awarded teaching or research assistantships.

Facilities

Computer facilities include 8 IBM/clones, 4 Macintoshes, a microcomputer center, and access to the VAX mainframe and to Internet and E-mail. Free or low-cost computer training is available. One building, 10 classrooms, 13 laboratories, 1 library, and various museum collections are available to graduate students. All facilities are handicapped accessible. The school also owns several sites that are available for student research.

Career Counseling and Job Placement

This program offers student internships and cooperative educational opportunities with local industry and state and federal governmental agencies. Career counseling and job placement services include job books and job fairs. Fifty percent of alumni work within the government sector, 25% for private small business, 5% for corporations or industries, and 20% in science or academia; 70% of alumni work in the Southeast. Eighty-five percent of the students find work within six months of graduation.

☛ Other graduate environmental programs at Eastern Kentucky University (no profiles available):

Department of Recreation and Park Administration. *Contact:* Larry Belknap, Chair. *Phone:* 606-622-1833.

THE EVERGREEN STATE COLLEGE

Established in 1972, The Evergreen State College has a total enrollment of 3,350 and is located on a rural campus on the outskirts of Olympia, Washington.

☛ Program in Environmental Studies

PROGRAM CONTACT:
Bonita Evans, Coordinator
Lab 1

ADMISSIONS CONTACT:
Office of Admissions
The Evergreen State College

Graduate Program in   Olympia, WA 98505
    Environmental Studies
The Evergreen State College
Olympia, WA 98505

Phone: 360-866-6000, ext. 6707   *Phone:* 360-866-6000, ext. 6170

Graduate Program in Environmental Studies Web site:
http://192.211.16.13/curricular/MES/home.html

Evergreen State College Web site: http://www.evergreen.edu/

Quick Facts About the Program in Environmental Studies

- Year established: 1984
- Enrollment: 40 master's students per year
- Graduate degrees conferred: Master of Arts, Master of Business Administration, Master of Environmental Science, Master of Public Administration, Master's in Teaching
- Degree requirements for master's students include: required courses, either a 16-credit master's thesis or an 8-credit master's project
- Faculty/Advisee ratio: 1:12

Areas of Specialization

Environmental Quality and Public Health (20% of students)
Environmental Education (15%)
Earth Science (10%)

Special Program Features

Graduate students can cross-register for courses within other departments. International program experiences are not offered.

Admission to the Program

- Admission requirements for master's applicants include: 3 semesters of biology, 1 of calculus, 1 of economics, 1 of social science; GRE scores are required
- Master's students accepted each year: 35% of 160 applicants
- Students may matriculate only in the fall; transfer students are not accepted.

About the Students

There are 50% male and 50% female graduate students currently enrolled in this program; 50% are full-time and 50% part-time; 5% are international and 95% domestic. 90% are Caucasian. Graduate students range from age 23 to 55, with a median age of 34.

About the Faculty

There are 11 faculty affiliated with this program. The average faculty member teaches 3 courses and advises 3–5 master's students per year. Advisors are assigned to students. Five faculty specialize in Applied and Quantitative Ecology, 2 in Botany, 1 in Conservation Biology, 2 in Earth Science, 2 in Environmental Quality and Public Health, 3 in Environmental Studies, 1 in Forestry, and 2 in Resource Policy and Planning.

Tuition and Financial Aid

Tuition in 1996–97 was $3,840 per year for state residents and $11,469 for nonresidents. Under 20% of the graduate students in this program receive financial aid. Under 20% of the master's students are awarded fellowships, under 20% are awarded scholarships, and under 40% are awarded administrative or research assistantships.

Facilities

Computer facilities include access to Internet and E-mail. Free or low-cost computer training is available. There are 2 buildings, many classrooms and laboratories, and 2 libraries available to graduate students. Facilities are handicapped accessible. The school also owns a marine beach and forested area, which is available for natural history research.

Career Counseling and Job Placement

This program offers student internships and individual learning contracts within the local commmunity. Career counseling and job placement services include job books, an alumni database, and job fairs. Seventy-five percent of alumni work within the government sector, 10% for semi-governmental organizations, and 10% for nonprofits; 90% of alumni work in Alaska, California, and the West Coast.

🐦 **Other graduate environmental programs at
The Evergreen State College (no profiles available):**

Graduate Program in Public Administration. *Contact:* Bonita Evans. *Phone:*
360-866-6000, ext. 6707.

FLORIDA INSTITUTE OF TECHNOLOGY

With a total enrollment of 4,000 students, Florida Institute of Technology
(also known as Florida Tech) was established in 1958. Its setting is a residential city on Florida's east coast.

🐦 **Environmental Science Program**

FACULTY CONTACT:

Iver Duedall, Chair
Environmental Science Program
Florida Institute of Technology
150 West University Blvd.
Melbourne, FL 32901-6988

Phone: 407-768-8000
Fax: 407-723-9468

ADMISSIONS CONTACT:

Carolyn Farrior, Associate Dean
Graduate Admissions
Florida Institute of Technology
150 West University Blvd.
Melbourne, FL 32901-6988

Phone: 407-768-8000, ext. 8027
                      or 800-944-4348

University Web site: http://www.fit.edu/

Quick Facts About the Environmental Science Program

- Year established: 1975
- Enrollment: 35 master's students / 5 doctoral students
- Graduate degrees conferred: Master of Science, doctorate
- Master's degree requirements include: master's thesis for some Environ-
  mental Science students, internship experience for all Environmental Re-
  source Management students
- Degree requirements for doctoral students include: dissertation, oral and
  written comprehensive exam
- Faculty/Advisee ratio: 1:5

Areas of Specialization

Environmental Science (75% of students)
Resource Policy and Planning (25%)

Special Program Features

This program is best known for its emphasis on water resources, waste research utilization, and remote sensing. Graduate students can cross-register for courses within other departments. Joint degree programs and international program experiences are not offered.

Admission to the Program

- Admission requirements for master's applicants include: 2 semesters of chemistry, 2 of biology, 2 of calculus, 2 of physical science; average GRE scores: 550 verbal/550 math
- Admission requirements for doctoral applicants include: master's degree (generally); average GRE scores: 550 verbal/550 math
- Master's students accepted each year: 10% of 30 applicants
- Doctoral students accepted each year: 5% of 10 applicants
- Students may matriculate only in the fall and spring; transfer students are not accepted.

About the Students

Of the graduate students currently enrolled in this program, 30 are full-time and 5 part-time; 5 are international and 30 domestic; 70% are Caucasian, 5% Hispanic, 20% Asian, and 5% Native American. Graduate students' median age is 35.

About the Faculty

There are 6 faculty affiliated with this program. The average faculty member teaches 2–3 courses and advises 4 master's and 1–2 doctoral students per year. Faculty research is currently being conducted domestically. One faculty member specializes in Earth Science, 2 in Environmental Quality and Public Health, and 3 in Environmental Science.

Tuition and Financial Aid

Tuition in 1996–97 was $518 per semester credit hour. Some 21–40% of the graduate students in this program receive financial aid; 20% of the master's students are awarded research assistantships; 20% of the doctoral students are awarded research assistantships.

Facilities

Computer facilities include 5 IBM/clones, 3 Macintoshes, a microcenter, and access to Internet and E-mail. Free or low-cost computer training is available. There are 3 buildings, 5 classrooms, 5 laboratories, and 1 library available to graduate students. Facilities are handicapped accessible.

Career Counseling and Job Placement

This program assists students in locating internships for the environmental resource management program. Career counseling and job placement services include job placement counselors, on-campus interviews, and job fairs. Thirty percent of alumni work within the government sector, 10% for nonprofits, 30% for corporations or industries, and 30% in science or academia; 60% of alumni work in Florida, 10% in Washington, D.C., and 25% in international locations. Seventy percent of the students find work within six months of graduation.

☛ Other graduate environmental programs at Florida Institute of Technology (no profiles available):

Program in Environmental Education. *Contact:* Tom Marcinkoski, Coordinator, Department of Science Education. *Phone:* 407-676-1003.

· FROSTBURG STATE UNIVERSITY

Located on a rural 260-acre campus in the mountains of western Maryland, Frostburg State University was founded in 1898 and has a total enrollment of 5,300 students.

☜ Programs in Applied Ecology & Conservation Biology, and Wildlife/Fisheries Biology

FACULTY CONTACT:

Amy Harman,
    Program Coordinator
Department of Biology
Frostburg State University
Frostburg, MD 21532-1099

Phone: 301-687-4175
Fax: 301-687-4737

ADMISSIONS CONTACT:

Office of Graduate Admissions
    and Records
Hitchins Administration Building
Frostburg State University
Frostburg, MD 21532-1099

Phone: 301-687-7053
Fax: 301-687-4597

University Web site: http://www.fsu.umd.edu/

Quick Facts About the Department of Biology

• Year established: 1976
• Enrollment: 69 master's students (in School of Natural and Social Sciences)
• Graduate degree conferred: Master of Science
• Degree requirements for master's students include: required courses, master's thesis

Special Program Features

Graduate students can cross-register for courses within other departments. Joint degree programs are offered with the Political Science and Geography programs. International program experiences include research opportunities in Central America, Africa, and the West Indies.

About the Students

There are 25 men and 44 women enrolled in the School of Natural and Social Sciences; 40 are full-time and 29 part-time; 66 are domestic and 3 international; 65 are Caucasian, 1 Black, 1 Hispanic, and 2 Native American.

About the Faculty

There are 33 faculty affiliated with the School of Natural and Social Sciences.

Tuition and Financial Aid

Tuition in 1996–97 was $156 per credit hour for state residents and $172 for nonresidents. Assitantships and associateships are offered on a competitive basis and include a full tuition waiver.

Career Counseling and Job Placement

This program offers student internships and educational opportunities with the Department of Natural Resources and on Natural Heritage projects. Career counseling and job placement services include active alumni contact. All students find work within six months of graduation.

GEORGE WASHINGTON UNIVERSITY

Located in the heart of Washington, D.C., George Washington University was established in 1821 and has a total enrollment of 16,900 students.

☏ Environmental Law Program

FACULTY CONTACT:

Laurent R. Hourclé
Associate Professor of
   Environmental Law
Environmental Law Program
George Washington University
720 20th Street, NW
Washington, DC 20052

Phone: 202-994-4823

ADMISSIONS CONTACT:

Stephanie Allgaier
Graduate Programs Coordinator
Environmental Law Program
George Washington University
720 20th Street, NW
Washington, DC 20052

Phone: 202-994-4500

Environmental Law Program Web site:
http://www.law.gwu.edu/HTMLnlc/environ.html

University Web site: http://www.gwu.edu/

Law School Web site: http://www.law.gwu.edu/

Quick Facts About the The Environmental Law Program

• Year established: 1970
• Graduate degree conferred: L.LM.

- Degree requirements for master's students include: required courses, master's thesis, 24 credits
- Faculty/Advisee ratio: 1:20

Areas of Specialization

Environmental Law (100% of students)

Special Program Features

This program is best known for its emphasis on pollution control, government contracts, and federal facility compliance. All students specialize in Environmental Law; graduate students can cross-register for courses within other departments. Joint degree programs are offered with the School of Public Health. International program experiences are not offered.

Admission to the Program

- Admission requirements for master's applicants include: LSAT scores; a J.D. law degree
- Master's students accepted each year: 80% of 100 applicants
- Students may matriculate only in the fall; transfer students are not accepted.

About the Students

Graduate students range from age 25 to 50+, with a median age of 35.

About the Faculty

There are 22 faculty, all specializing in Environmental Law, affiliated with this program. The average faculty member teaches 2 courses and advises 2 master's students per year. Students choose their faculty advisors. Faculty research is currently being conducted domestically.

Tuition and Financial Aid

Tuition in 1996 was $20,360 per year. Under 20% of the graduate students in this program receive financial aid; 12% of the master's students are awarded administrative or research assistantships.

Facilities

Computer facilities include 30 IBM/clones, 12 Macintoshes, and access to Internet and E-mail. Free or low-cost computer training is available. There are 4 buildings and 3 libraries available to graduate students. Facilities are handicapped accessible.

Career Counseling and Job Placement

This program offers student internships and educational opportunities with federal agencies such as the Justice Department, Environmental Protection Agency, and Department of Defense. Career counseling and job placement services include job placement counselors, active alumni contact, on-campus interviews, and job books. All students find work within six months of graduation.

☜ Other graduate environmental programs at George Washington University (no profiles available):

Committee on Environmental & Resource Policy. *Contact:* Henry Merchant, 801 22nd Street, Washington, DC 20052. *Phone:* 202-994-7118.

GODDARD COLLEGE

Established in 1938, Goddard College has a total enrollment of only 400 students. It is located on a rural, 250-acre campus in the small village of Plainfield, Vermont.

☜ Goddard/Institute for Social Ecology M.A. Program

FACULTY/STAFF CONTACT:

Daniel Chodorkoff/Claudia Bagiackas
Institute for Social Ecology
Goddard College
Box 89
Plainfield, VT 05667

ADMISSIONS CONTACT:

Graduate Study
Goddard College
Plainfield, VT 05667

Phone: 802-454-8493
Fax: 802-454-1029

Phone: 802-454-8311
     or 800-468-4888

Goddard College Web site: http://goddard.edu/

Quick Facts About the Master's Program in Social Ecology

- Enrollment: 25 master's students
- Graduate degree conferred: Master of Arts
- Degree requirements include: master's thesis, master's project, work experience
- Faculty/Advisee ratio: 1:7

Areas of Specialization

Social Ecology (100% of students)
Environmental Education (50%)
Resource Policy and Planning (15%)
Forestry (10%)

Special Program Features

This program is best known for its emphasis on eco-philosophy, sustainable development, and ecological education. Off-campus study, and the option for students to design their own degree programs, are available, and there is a heavy emphasis on practica, independent research, and seminars. Graduate students can cross-register for courses within other departments, and joint degree programs are offered with the School of Education. International program experiences include research opportunities, internships, and student exchanges in South America. Future program plans include the development of a Ph.D. program.

Admission to the Program

- Admission requirements for master's applicants include: 2 semesters of natural science, 3 of social science; GRE scores not required
- Master's students accepted each year: 50% of 40 applicants
- Students may matriculate at the start of any term; transfer students are accepted.

About the Students

Some 75% of the graduate students are Caucasian, 10% Black, 5% Hispanic, and 5% Asian. Graduate students range from age 23 to 50, with a median age of 30.

About the Faculty

There are 14 faculty affiliated with this program. The average faculty member teaches 3 courses and advises 4 master's students per year. Faculty advisors are chosen by mutual agreement between advisors and students. Faculty research is currently being conducted both domestically and internationally.

Tuition and Financial Aid

Tuition in 1996 was $15,995 for the entire program, plus $4,995 for additional semesters. Over 60% of the graduate students in this program receive financial aid; 25% of the master's students are awarded scholarships; 10% are awarded teaching assistantships.

Facilities

Computer facilities include 5 IBM/clones, 1 terminal for every 5 students, and access to Internet and E-mail. Some facilities are handicapped accessible.

Career Counseling and Job Placement

This program offers student internships and educational opportunities within the local community to meet practicum requirement. Career counseling and job placement services include job placement counselors and active alumni contact. Five percent of alumni work for semi-governmental organizations, 25% for nonprofits, 20% for private small business, and 50% in education. Seventy-five percent of the students find work within six months of graduation.

HARVARD UNIVERSITY

Established in 1636, Harvard University has a total enrollment of over 18,000 students in 12 different schools. It is located in the cosmopolitan city of Cambridge (population 100,000), just across the Charles River from Boston.

☛ Department of Organismic and Evolutionary Biology

CONTACT:

Department of Organismic and Evolutionary Biology

Harvard University
26 Oxford Street
Cambridge, MA 02138

Phone: 617-495-2305
E-mail: yhusain@oeb.harvard.edu

Web site: http://www.oeb.harvard.edu

Quick Facts About the Department of Organismic and Evolutionary Biology

- Graduate degrees offered: doctorate
- Number of graduate students: 60
- Number of faculty members: 35
- Doctoral degree requirements: coursework, reading knowledge of one relevant foreign language, two terms of teaching, oral exam, thesis, thesis seminar, thesis exam

Special Program Features

This program is dedicated to the study of the evolution of the earth's life processes, from the scale of single cells to entire ecosystems. Recognizing the highly interdisciplinary nature of the field, the Department encourages cross-registration with other departments of the University. The Department is known internationally not only for its quality curriculum and research, but also for the work and teaching of its many world-reknowned scientists, including Edward O. Wilson and Stephen J. Gould. Many students travel with their advisors on field trips within the United States and internationally.

Tuition and Financial Aid

Tution at Harvard in 1996–97 was approximately $19,000 per year. Most students who join the program receive a large amount of financial aid, which comes in the form of scholarships, teaching fellowships, research assistantships, and training grant participation.

Facilities

Harvard University provides a range of impressive research facilities, including the oldest and largest library system in the United States. The Department itself makes extensive use of the Museum of Comparative Zoology, the Harvard University Herbaria, the 3,000-acre Harvard Forest, the Concord Field Station, and Arnold Arboretum.

🎓 Other graduate environmental programs at Harvard University (no profiles available):

Department of Earth and Planetary Sciences. *Contact:* Joan Donahue, Harvard University, Department of Earth and Planetary Sciences, 20 Oxford Street, Cambridge, MA 02138. *Web site:* http://www-eps.harvard.edu/

Center for Global Health and the Environment, Harvard Medical School. *Contact:* Eric Chivian, Director, Center for Global Health and the Environment, Oliver Holmes Society, Harvard Medical School, 260 Longwood Ave., Boston, MA 02115. *Phone:* 617-432-0493. *E-mail:* chge@warren.med.harvard.edu

Department of Environment, School of Public Health. *Contact:* Joseph D. Brain, Department of Environmental Health, Harvard School of Public Health, 665 Huntington Ave., Boston, MA 02115. *Phone:* 617-432-1472. *Fax:* 617-277-2382. *Web site:* http://www.hsph.harvard.edu/Academics/eh/index.html

Environment and Natural Resources Program, John F. Kennedy School of Government. *Contact:* Henry Lee, Director, Environment and Natural Resources Program, Kennedy School of Government, 79 Kennedy St., Cambridge, MA 02138. *Phone:* 617-495-1350. *Web site:* http://www.ksg.harvard.edu

Programs in Landscape Architecture and Urban Planning, Graduate School of Design. *Contact:* Office of Student Services, 48 Quincy St., Cambridge, MA 02138. *Phone:* 617-496-1237. *Web site:* http://www.gsd.harvard.edu

A full online list of environmental programs at Harvard can be found at http://environment.harvard.edu. Paper copies of the online guide are available from Geraldine Kaye. *Phone:* 617-495-0368.

HUMBOLDT STATE UNIVERSITY

Located on a 226-acre campus in Arcata, near the redwood forest coast of northern California, Humboldt State University was established in 1913 and has a total enrollment of 7,049 students.

☋ Environmental Systems Graduate Program

FACULTY CONTACT:

Roland Lamberson
Environmental Systems
   Graduate Program
Humboldt State University
Arcata, CA 95521

Phone: 707-826-4926

ADMISSIONS CONTACT:

Office of Admissions, Records
   and School Relations
Humboldt State University
Arcata, CA 95521-8299

Phone: 707-826-4402

University Web site: http://www.humboldt.edu/

Quick Facts About the Environmental Systems Graduate Program

- Year established: 1983
- Enrollment: 24 master's students
- Graduate degree conferred: Master of Science
- Degree requirements for master's students include: required courses, master's thesis, master's project
- Faculty/Advisee ratio: 1:2

Areas of Specialization

Applied and Quantitative Ecology (25% of students)
Earth Science (25%)
Environmental Quality and Public Health (25%)
International Development Technology (25%)

Special Program Features

A program of the Department of Engineering, the Master of Science in Environmental Systems has a heavy natural sciences emphasis and is designed to prepare students for a career in industry, private practice, or government. Graduate students can cross-register for courses within other departments. Joint degree programs are not offered. International program experiences include research opportunities and field stations via the IDT option.

Admission to the Program

- Admission requirements for master's applicants include: average recommended GRE scores: 600 verbal/600 math

- Master's students accepted each year: 33–50% of 50–60 applicants
- Students may matriculate at the start of any term; transfer students are accepted.

About the Students

There are 14 male and 10 female graduate students currently enrolled in this program; all are full-time; 2 are international and 22 domestic. Graduate students range from age 22 to 45, with a median age of 28.

About the Faculty

There are 26 faculty affiliated with this program. The average faculty member teaches 4–6 courses and advises 1–2 master's students per year. Advisors are both assigned to and chosen by students. Faculty research is currently being conducted both domestically and internationally. Twenty-five percent of the faculty specialize in Applied and Quantitative Ecology, 25% in Earth Science, 25% in Environmental Quality and Public Health, and 25% in International Development Technology.

Tuition and Financial Aid

Tuition in 1996 was $0 (plus fees) per year for state residents and $246 per unit for nonresidents. Less than 20% of the graduate students in this program receive financial aid; 50% of the master's students are awarded teaching or research assistantships.

Facilities

Computer facilities include 200 IBM/clones, 200 Macintoshes, 1 terminal per 15 students, a VAX 8700, and access to Internet and E-mail. Free or low-cost computer training is available. There are 4 buildings, 40 classrooms, 10 laboratories, 1 library, and various museum collections available to graduate students. Some facilities are handicapped accessible.

Career Counseling and Job Placement

Career counseling and job placement services include job placement counselors, active alumni contact, on-campus interviews, and job fairs. Forty percent of alumni work within the government sector, 20% for semi-governmental organizations, 10% for private small business, 10% for corporations or industries, and 20% in science or academia. Ninety percent of the students find work within six months of graduation.

☜ Other graduate environmental programs at Humbolt State University (no profiles available):

Environmental Education. *Contact:* Alan Leftridge, Environmental Education Coordinator, Department of Education.

Master of Science in Natural Resources. *Contact:* Program in Natural Resources Planning and Interpretation. *Phone:* 707-826-4147.

Master of Arts in Biology. *Contact:* Department of Biological Sciences. *Phone:* 707-826-3245.

IDAHO STATE UNIVERSITY

Established in 1901, Idaho State University has a total enrollment of 12,000 and is located in the small mountain city of Pocatello, among the Snake River.

☜ Department of Biological Sciences

FACULTY CONTACT:

Jay Anderson
Coordinator of Graduate Programs
Department of Biological Sciences
Campus Box 8007
Idaho State University
Pocatello, ID 83209-8007

Phone: 208-236-3765
Fax: 208-236-4570
E-mail: ANDEJAY@OL.ISU.EDU

ADMISSIONS CONTACT:

Janet Larsen, Admissions
Graduate School
Box 8075
Idaho State University
Pocatello, ID 83209-0009

Phone: 208-236-2270

Department of Biological Sciences Web site:
http://www.isu.edu/departments/bios/

University Web site: http://www.isu.edu/

Quick Facts About the Department of Biological Sciences

- Year established: 1969
- Enrollment: 69 master's students / 25 doctoral students
- Graduate degrees conferred: Master of Science, doctorate, Doctor of Arts
- Degree requirements for master's students include: 30 graduate credits, including two 600-level courses; master's thesis
- Degree requirements for doctoral students include dissertation, qualifying exam, oral exam, comprehensive exam
- Faculty/Advisee ratio: 1:3

Areas of Specialization

Applied and Quantitative Ecology (46% of students)
Environmental Quality and Public Health (15%)
Conservation Biology (8%)
Botany (3%)
Environmental Geography (1%)
Environmental Science (1%)

Special Program Features

This program is best known for its emphasis on stream ecology and community ecology. Graduate students can cross-register for courses within other departments. Joint degree programs are offered with the Engineering and Geology departments.

Admission to the Program

- Admission requirements for master's applicants include: 2 semesters of chemistry, 2 of biology, 1 of calculus, 2 of physical science, 2 of organic chemistry
- GRE scores are required of all graduate applicants
- Master's students accepted each year: 25% of 75 applicants
- Doctoral students accepted each year: 10% of 20 applicants
- Students may matriculate at the start of any term; transfer students are accepted.

About the Students

There are 58 male and 36 female graduate students currently enrolled in this program; 71 are full-time and 23 part-time; 78% are Caucasian, 1% Hispanic, and 4% Asian. Graduate students range from age 22 to 55; their median age is 30.

About the Faculty

There are 31 faculty affiliated with this program. The average faculty member teaches 3.5 courses and advises 3 master's and 1 doctoral students per year. Students choose their faculty advisors. Faculty research is currently being conducted both domestically and internationally. Eight faculty specialize in Applied and Quantitative Ecology, 3 in Botany, and 1 in Conservation Biology.

Tuition and Financial Aid

Tuition in 1996 was $0 (plus fees) per year for state residents and $5,430 for nonresidents. Over 60% of the graduate students in this program receive financial aid; 43% of the master's students are awarded teaching or research assistantships; 50% are hired as part-time help; 32% of the doctoral students are awarded fellowships; and 64% are awarded teaching or research assistantships.

Facilities

Computer facilities include 24 IBM/clones, 12 Macintoshes, and access to Internet and E-mail. Free or low-cost computer training is available. One building, 17 classrooms, 25 laboratories, 1 library, and various museum collections are available to graduate students. Facilities are handicapped accessible. The school also owns riverside property, including riparian and cold-desert steppe habitats, available for student research.

Career Counseling and Job Placement

This program offers cooperative educational opportunities with the Forest Service and Bureau of Land Management. Career counseling and job placement services are not offered. About 80% of the students find work within six months of graduation.

INDIANA UNIVERSITY

With an enrollment of over 35,000 students (7,000 of whom are graduate students), Indiana University is located in the small city of Bloomington, population 60,000.

☚ School of Public and Environmental Affairs

PROGRAM CONTACT:

Allison McMullin
Coordinator of Student Recruitment
School of Public and Environmental Affairs
Office of Academic Programs and Student Services
Indiana University
Bloomington, IN 47405

Phone: 800-765-7755 or 812-855-2840
Fax: 812-855-7802
E-mail: speainfo@indiana.edu or amcmulli@indiana.edu

School of Public and Environmental Affairs Web site:
http://www.indiana.edu/~speaweb/degrees/mses.html

Quick Facts About the School of Public and Environmental Affairs

- Year established: 1972
- Graduate degrees conferred: Master of Science in Environmental Science (M.S.E.S.), Master of Public Affairs (M.P.A.), Ph.D. in Environmental Science
- Degree requirements for M.S.E.S. students include: 2 years of required courses, including (1) environmental science core, (2) environmental management and policy core, (3) concentration area, and (4) internship or research requirement
- Degree requirements for doctoral students include: required courses, dissertation, qualifying exam, oral exam

Areas of Specialization (according to program literature)

Applied Ecology
Environmental Chemistry
Hazardous Materials Management

Water Resources
Specialized

Special Program Features

This program is best known for its applied and interdisciplinary approach to environmental affairs. In addition to the M.S.E.S., students may pursue a three-year joint degree program leading to a Master of Public Affairs (M.P.A.)–M.S.E.S., a joint M.S.E.S.–J.D. (4 years), or a joint M.P.A.–J.D. (4 years). Additional joint degree programs are offered with the Departments of Biology and Geology. This program provides extensive opportunities to study abroad through a variety of international programs.

Admission to the Program

- Minimum requirements for admission to the MSES program include: one course each in calculus, computing, and statistics, and two courses in chemistry.

- Minimum requirements for admission to the MPA program include: one semester of college-level economics, government, and algebra; familiarity with statistics and basic computer applications.

Tuition and Financial Aid

Tuition is approximately $3,000 per year for state residents and $8,500 for nonresidents; 35% of the graduate students in this program receive financial aid.

Career Counseling and Job Placement

This program's career center is fully equipped with the following services: alumni mentor program, alumni receptions, career consultation, career center library, computerized federal job applications, career orientation workshops, job and internship announcements, on- and off-campus recruiting, resumé books, START volunteer service learning program, and workshops on resumé writing, interviewing skills, etc. Recent alumni have found employment in the U.S. Environmental Protection Agency, Department of Energy, World Bank, City of Indianapolis, Radian Corporation, and National Park Service, among others. Ninety-two percent of graduates find work within six months of graduation.

IOWA STATE UNIVERSITY

With a total enrollment of 26,000, Iowa State University was established in 1868. Its setting is a 1,000-acre campus in the small city of Ames, Iowa.

☝ Department of Forestry

FACULTY CONTACT:
David Countryman, Professor
Department of Forestry
Iowa State University
Ames, Iowa 50011

ADMISSIONS CONTACT:
Office of Admissions
Alumni Hall
Iowa State University
Ames, Iowa 50011-2010

Phone: 515-294-1166

Department of Forestry Web site:
http://www.ag.iastate.edu/departments/forestry/Forestry.html

University Web site: http://iastate.edu/

Quick Facts About the Department of Forestry

- Year established: 1904
- Enrollment: 22 master's students / 10 doctoral students
- Graduate degrees conferred: Master of Science, Master of Forestry, doctorate
- Degree requirements for master's students include: required courses, master's thesis, master's project
- Degree requirements for doctoral students include: required courses, dissertation, qualifying exam, oral exam
- Faculty/Advisee ratio: 13/32

Areas of Specialization

Forestry (100% of students)

Special Program Features

This program is best known for its emphasis on forest biology, forest biometry, forest economics, forest administration and management, and wood science. All students specialize in Forestry; graduate students can cross-register for courses within other departments. Joint degree programs are offered with the Business School, interdepartmental offerings within the Colleges of Agriculture, and Liberal Arts and Sciences. International program experiences are not offered.

Admission to the Program

- GRE scores are not required of graduate students
- Advanced degrees are not required of doctoral students
- Master's students accepted each year: 50% of 16 applicants
- Doctoral students accepted each year: 50% of 16 applicants
- Students may matriculate at the start of any term; transfer students are sometimes accepted.

About the Students

There are 20 male and 2 female graduate students currently enrolled in this program; all are full-time; 12 are international and 5 domestic; 47% are Caucasian, 9% Black, and 44% Asian.

About the Faculty

There are 13 faculty affiliated with this program. The average faculty member teaches 3 courses and advises less than 2 master's and less than 1 doctoral students per year. Students choose their faculty advisors. Faculty research is currently being conducted both domestically and internationally. All 13 faculty specialize in Forestry.

Tuition and Financial Aid

Tuition in 1996 was $2,834 per year for state residents and $8,344 for nonresidents. Over 60% of the graduate students in this program receive financial aid; 67% of the master's students are awarded research assistantships; 67% of the doctoral students are awarded research assistantships.

Facilities

Computer facilities include access to Internet and E-mail. Free or low-cost computer training is available. Facilities are handicapped accessible.

Career Counseling and Job Placement

This program does not offer student internships. Career counseling and job placement services include job placement counselors and job announcements.

JACKSON STATE UNIVERSITY

Located on an urban campus in the city of Jackson, Mississippi (population 350,000), Jackson State University has a total enrollment of 6,200 students. This school belongs to the Historically Black Colleges and Universities.

☙ Program in Environmental Science

FACULTY CONTACT:

Dr. Charles Rhyne
Department of Biology
Program in Environmental Science
Jackson State University
Jackson, MS 39217

Phone: 601-968-2586
Fax: 601-973-3664

ADMISSIONS CONTACT:

Graduate Admissions
The Graduate School
Jackson State University
P.O. Box 17095
Jackson, MS 32917-0195

Phone: 601-968-2455

University Web site: http://ccaix.jsums.edu/

Quick Facts About the Program in Environmental Science

• Year established: 1974
• Enrollment: 8 master's students
• Graduate degree conferred: Master of Science
• Degree requirements for master's students include: master's thesis
• Faculty/Advisee ratio: 1:1

Areas of Specialization

Environmental Science (100% of students)

Special Program Features

All students specialize in Environmental Science; graduate students can cross-register for courses within other departments. Joint degree programs and international program experiences are not offered.

Admission to the Program

- Admission requirements for master's applicants include: 2 semesters of chemistry, 4 of biology; average GRE scores: 600 verbal/550 math
- Master's students accepted each year: 70% of 4–6 applicants
- Students may matriculate at the start of any term; transfer students are accepted.

About the Students

There are 2 male and 6 female graduate students currently enrolled in this program; all are full-time; 2 are international and 6 domestic; 50% are Caucasian, 25% Black, and 25% Asian. Graduate students range from age 20 to 55, with a median age of 25.

About the Faculty

There are 7 faculty affiliated with this program. The average faculty member teaches 1–4 courses and advises 2 master's students per year. Students choose their faculty advisors. Faculty research is currently being conducted domestically. One faculty member specializes in Applied and Quantitative Ecology and 6 in Environmental Science.

Tuition and Financial Aid

Tuition in 1996–97 was $2,380 per year for state residents and $4,974 for nonresidents. Under 20% of the graduate students in this program receive financial aid; 10% of the master's students are awarded fellowships; 10% are awarded research assistantships.

Facilities

Computer facilities include 2 IBM/clones, 2 Macintoshes, and access to Internet and E-mail. Free or low-cost computer training is available. There are

2 buildings, 8 classrooms, 5 laboratories, and 1 library available to graduate students. Some facilities are handicapped accessible.

Career Counseling and Job Placement

This program does not offer student internships. Career counseling and job placement services include on-campus interviews and job fairs. Thirty percent of alumni work within the government sector, 10% for semi-governmental organizations, 20% for private small business, 20% for corporations or industries, and 20% in science or academia; 70% of alumni work in the South. All students find work within six months of graduation.

JOHNS HOPKINS UNIVERSITY

Established in 1867, Johns Hopkins University is located on an urban campus one mile from the downtown area of Baltimore, Maryland. Johns Hopkins has a total enrollment of 4,600 students.

☛ Department of Environmental Health Sciences

FACULTY CONTACT:
Robert Fitzgerald, Chair
Department of Environmental
    Health Sciences
Johns Hopkins University
615 North Wolfe Street
Baltimore, MD 21205

ADMISSIONS CONTACT:
Graduate Admissions
140 Garland Hall
3400 N. Charles Street
Baltimore, MD 21218

Phone: 410-955-2212

Phone: 410-516-8174

Department of Environmental Health Sciences Web site:
http://www.sph.jhu.edu/Departments/EHS/

University Web site: http://www.jhu.edu/

Quick Facts About the Environmental Health Sciences Program

• Year established: 1976

• Enrollment: 22 master's students / 79 doctoral students

- Graduate degrees conferred: Master of Science, Master of Health Science, doctorate, Science Doctorate, Doctor of Public Health
- Degree requirements for master's students include: required courses, master's project
- Degree requirements for doctoral students include: required courses, dissertation, oral exam
- Faculty/Advisee ratio: 1:2

Areas of Specialization

Environmental Quality and Public Health (50% of students)
Environmental Science (50%)

Special Program Features

This program is best known for its emphasis on toxicology, molecular dosimetry and epidemiology, and industrial hygiene. Graduate students can cross-register for courses within other departments. Joint degree programs and international program experiences are not offered.

Admission to the Program

- Admission requirements for master's applicants include: 1 semester of chemistry, 1 of biology, 1 of calculus, 1 of physical science
- GRE scores are required for all graduate applicants.

About the Students

There are 79 male and 60 female graduate students currently enrolled in this program; 132 are full-time and 1 part-time; 49 are international and 90 domestic. Graduate students range from age 23 to 47, with a median age of 28.

About the Faculty

There are 77 faculty affiliated with this program. The average faculty member teaches 2 courses and advises 2 doctoral students per year. Advisors are assigned to students. Fifty percent of the faculty specialize in Environmental Quality and Public Health and 50% in Environmental Science.

Tuition and Financial Aid

Tuition in 1996 was $19,750 per academic year. Funds from NIEHS training grants, and departmental funds, are available.

Facilities

Computer facilities include Public Health computer labs.

Career Counseling and Job Placement

This program does not offer student internships, or career counseling and job placement services. All students find work within six months of graduation.

☛ Other graduate environmental programs at Johns Hopkins University (no profiles available):

Program in Environmental Chemistry. *Contact:* Anne Archemeier, Department of Chemistry. *Phone:* 410-516-7429. *Fax:* 410-516-8420.

Department of Geography and Environmental Engineering (including Graduate Program in Ecology). *Contact:* Edward Bouwer, Admissions Coordinator. *Phone:* 410-516-7092. *Fax:* 410-516-8996. *Web site:* http://www.jhu.edu:80/~dogee/

Program in Environmental and Natural Resource. *Contact:* M. Gordon Wolman, Chair, Economics

LEHIGH UNIVERSITY

With a total enrollment of 6,600 students, Lehigh University was established in 1865. It is located on a 1,600-acre campus within the mid-sized city of Bethlehem, Pennsylvania.

☛ Department of Earth and Environmental Sciences

FACULTY CONTACT: ADMISSIONS CONTACT:

Edward Evenson,   Graduate Admission Office
   Graduate Coordinator   Lehigh University

Department of Earth and
  Environmental Sciences
Lehigh University
Bethlehem, PA 18015-3188

Whitaker Laboratory
5 E. Packer Avenue
Bethlehem, PA 18015-3196

Phone: 610-758-3660
Fax: 610-758-3677

Department of Earth and Environmental Sciences Web site:
http://www.lehigh.edu/~inees/inees.html

University Web site: http://www.lehigh.edu/

Graduate School Web site:
http://www.lehigh.edu/~www/academic_research/graduate_school.html

Quick Facts About the Department of Earth and Environmental Sciences

- Year established: 1991
- Enrollment: 4 master's students / 14 doctoral students
- Graduate degrees conferred: Master of Science, doctorate
- Master's degree requirements include: required courses, master's thesis
- Doctoral degree requirements include: dissertation, qualifying exam, oral exam
- Faculty/Advisee ratio: 1:2

Areas of Specialization

Earth Science (60% of students)
Environmental Science (40%)

Special Program Features

This program is best known for its emphasis on aquatic systems, geochronology, glacial geology, and hydrogeology. Graduate students can cross-register for courses within other departments. Joint degree programs and international program experiences are not offered.

Admission to the Program

- Admission requirements for master's applicants include: 2 semesters of chemistry, 1 of biology, 2 of calculus

- GRE scores in the 80th percentile for both verbal and math are required of all graduate applicants.
- Master's students accepted each year: 10% of 10 applicants
- Doctoral students accepted each year: 10% of 20 applicants
- Students may matriculate at the start of any term; transfer students are accepted.

About the Students

There are 15 male and 7 female graduate students currently enrolled in this program; 15 are full-time and 7 part-time; 2 are international and 20 domestic; 90% are Caucasian and 10% Asian. Graduate students range from age 20 to 35, with a median age of 23.

About the Faculty

There are 14 faculty affiliated with this program. The average faculty member teaches 3 courses and advises 2 master's and 1 doctoral student per year. Students choose their faculty advisors. Faculty research is currently being conducted both domestically and internationally. One faculty member specializes in Botany, 8 in Earth Science, 1 in Environmental Geography, and 4 in Environmental Science.

Tuition and Financial Aid

Tuition in 1996 was $740 per credit. Over 60% of the graduate students in this program receive financial aid. Ten percent of the master's students are awarded fellowships; 90% are awarded teaching or research assistantships. Twenty percent of the doctoral students are awarded fellowships; 80% are awarded teaching or research assistantships.

Facilities

Computer facilities include 5 IBM/clones, 30 Macintoshes, a central computer lab, and access to Internet and E-mail. Free or low-cost computer training is available. One building, 8 classrooms, 14 laboratories, and 2 libraries are available to graduate students. Facilities are handicapped accessible.

Career Counseling and Job Placement

This program does not offer student internships or career counseling and job placement services. Fifty percent of alumni work for private small business, and 50% in science or academia; 90% of alumni work in the northeastern United States. Most students find work within six months of graduation.

LEHMAN COLLEGE AT THE CITY UNIVERSITY OF NEW YORK

Located in the Bronx, New York, Lehman College has a total enrollment of 10,100 students. This school belongs to the Hispanic Association of Colleges and Universities.

☚ Recreation Program

FACULTY CONTACT:

Robin Kunstler, Associate Professor
Program in Recreation
Department of Exercise, Sport
  and Leisure Sciences
Lehman College at the
  City University of New York
Bronx, NY 10468

ADMISSIONS CONTACT:

Admissions Office
Lehman College at the
  City University of New York
Bronx, NY 10468

Phone: 718-960-8067

Phone: 718-960-8731

Lehman College Web site: http://www.lehman.cuny.edu/

Quick Facts About the Recreation Program

- Year established: 1970
- Enrollment: 70 master's students
- Graduate degree conferred: Master of Science
- Master's degree requirements include: required courses; either master's thesis, or comprehensive exam plus 6 credits
- Faculty/Advisee ratio: 1:20

Special Program Features

This program is best known for its emphasis on therapeutic recreation and recreation administration. All students specialize in Recreation Management and Leisure Studies; graduate students can cross-register for courses within other departments. Joint degree programs and international program experiences are not offered.

Admission to the Program

- GRE scores are not required.
- Master's students accepted each year: 100% of 25 applicants (50% conditionally)
- Students may matriculate at the start of any term; transfer students are accepted.

About the Students

There are 25 male and 45 female graduate students currently enrolled in this program; 5 are full-time and 65 part-time; 5 are international and 65 domestic; 33% are Caucasian, 33% Black, 33% Hispanic, and 1% Asian. Graduate students range from age 22 to 55, with a median age of 30.

About the Faculty

There are 3 faculty affiliated with this program. The average faculty member teaches 2 courses and advises 2 master's students per year. Faculty research is currently being conducted domestically. All 3 faculty specialize in Recreation Management and Leisure Studies.

Tuition and Financial Aid

Tuition in 1996 was $4,350 per year for state residents and $7,600 for nonresidents. Under 20% of the graduate students in this program receive financial aid.

Facilities

Computer facilities include one terminal per 3 students, a computer center, and access to Internet and E-mail. Free or low-cost computer training is available. One building, 4 classrooms, 4 laboratories, 25 libraries, and the nearby New York Botanical Garden are available to graduate students. Facilities are handicapped accessible.

Career Counseling and Job Placement

This program offers a 3 credit internship course (90 hours of field experience plus assignments). Career counseling and job placement services include active alumni contact and job books. Twenty percent of alumni work within the government sector, 5% for semi-governmental organizations, 20% for nonprofits, and 5% for private small business. All alumni work in the Northeast. All students find work within six months of graduation.

☜ Other graduate environmental programs at Lehman College of the City University of New York (no profiles available):

Program in Plant Science. *Contact:* Dwight Kincaid, Ph.D. *Phone:* 718-960-8651.

MANKATO STATE UNIVERSITY

Established in 1894, Mankato State University has a total enrollment of 15,220 students. Its setting is a suburban campus on the Minnesota River, 80 miles from Minneapolis–St. Paul, Minnesota.

☜ Environmental Sciences Program

FACULTY CONTACT:
Dr. Beth Proctor, Director
Environmental Sciences Program
Mankato State University
P.O. Box 8400, MSU Box 34
Mankato, MN 56001-8400

Phone: 507-389-5697
Fax: 507-389-5974

ADMISSIONS CONTACT:
College of Graduate Studies
125 Administration Building
Mankato State University
Mankato, MN 56001-8400

Phone: 507-389-2321

Environmental Sciences Program gopher server:
gopher://Gopher.Mankato.MSUS.EDU:70/0F-1%3A8361%3AEnviron-
mental%20Sciences

Mankato State University Web site: http://www.mankato.msus.edu/

Graduate School Web site:
http://www.mankato.msus.edu/dept/gradstud/GRAD/grad.html

Quick Facts About the Environmental Sciences Program

- Year established: 1987
- Enrollment: 23 master's students
- Graduate degree conferred: Master of Science
- Master's degree requirements include: required courses, master's thesis, qualifying exam, oral defense of thesis
- Faculty/Advisee ratio: 1:4

Areas of Specialization

Environmental Science (45% of students)
Earth Science (25%)
Applied and Quantitative Ecology (15%)
Environmental Education (5%)
Environmental Quality and Public Health (5%)

Special Program Features

Graduate students can cross-register for courses within other departments.
Joint degree programs are not offered. International program experiences include research opportunities, and internships in Japan. Future program
plans include changes in several "core" courses.

Admission to the Program

- Admission requirements for master's applicants include: 3 quarters of chemistry, 5 quarters of biology; GPA above 2.75; GRE scores are not re- quired
- Master's students accepted each year: 70% of 28 applicants

- Students may matriculate at the start of any term; transfer students are sometimes accepted.

About the Students

Graduate students range from age 22 to 37, with a median age of 26.

About the Faculty

There are 100 faculty affiliated with this program. The average faculty member teaches 9 courses (quarters) and advises 3 master's students per year. Each student has a primary advisor plus a thesis advisory committee. Faculty research is currently being conducted domestically. Twenty faculty specialize in Applied and Quantitative Ecology, 10 in Botany, 10 in Environmental Education, 10 in Environmental Quality and Public Health, and 50 in Environmental Science.

Tuition and Financial Aid

Tuition in 1994 was $80 per credit for state residents and $110 per credit for nonresidents. Over 60% of the graduate students in this program receive financial aid; 10% of the master's students are awarded scholarships; 90% are awarded teaching, administrative, or research assistantships.

Facilities

Computer facilities include 475 microcomputers and access to Internet and E-mail. Free or low-cost computer training is available. There are 2 buildings, 31 laboratories, and 1 library available to graduate students. Facilities are handicapped accessible.

Career Counseling and Job Placement

This program offers student internships or educational opportunities with the local, state, and federal government; industry (i.e., 3M); and consulting firms. Career counseling and job placement services include job placement counselors, active alumni contact, on-campus interviews, job books, and job fairs. Thirty percent of alumni work within the government sector, 30% for private small business, and 40% for corporations or industries; 75% of alumni work in the Great Lakes States and 5% in Washington, D.C. Eighty-three percent of the students find work within six months of graduation.

McNEESE STATE UNIVERSITY

With a total enrollment of 7,420, McNeese State University was established in 1939. Its setting is a 90-acre campus in the mid-sized, industrial city of Lake Charles, Lousiana.

☎ Department of Biological and Environmental Sciences

FACULTY CONTACT:

Robert Maples, Head
Department of Biological and
  Environmental Sciences
McNeese State University
P.O. Box 92000
Lake Charles, LA 70609-2000

Phone: 318-475-5674

ADMISSIONS CONTACT:

Enrollment Information Center
McNeese State University
Box 92895
Lake Charles, LA 70609-2895

Phone: 318-475-5146
    or 800-622-3352

McNeese State University Web site: http://www.mcneese.edu/

Quick Facts About the Department of Biological and Environmental Sciences

- Year established: 1968
- Enrollment: 35 master's students
- Graduate degree conferred: Master of Science
- Master's degree requirements include: required courses; master's thesis, or 15 hours additional coursework
- Faculty/Advisee ratio: 1:4

Areas of Specialization

Environmental Science (90% of students)
Environmental Quality and Public Health (10%)

Special Program Features

This program is best known for its emphasis on air pollution, environmental compliance, aquatic toxicology, and wastewater. Graduate students can cross-register for courses within other departments. Joint degree programs and international program experiences are not offered.

Admission to the Program

- Admission requirements for master's applicants include: 4 semesters of chemistry, 2 of biology, 1 of natural science, 2 of physical science, 1 of social science; average GRE scores: 1,100 total
- Master's students accepted each year: 50% of 10 applicants
- Students may matriculate at the start of any term; transfer students are accepted.

About the Students

There are 28 male and 7 female graduate students currently enrolled in this program; 15 are full-time and 20 part-time; 1 international and 34 domestic; 60% are Caucasian, 30% Black, and 10% Asian. Graduate students range from age 24 to 35, with a median age of 29.

About the Faculty

There are 10 faculty affiliated with this program. The average faculty member teaches 4–5 courses and advises 1 master's student per year. Students choose their faculty advisors. Faculty research is currently being conducted domestically. Two faculty specialize in Environmental Quality and Public Health, 8 in Environmental Science, and 1 in Air Pollution.

Tuition and Financial Aid

Tuition in 1996 was $1,650 per year for state residents and $4,850 for nonresidents. Some 21–40% of the graduate students in this program receive financial aid; 20% of the master's students are awarded teaching assistantships.

Facilities

Computer facilities include 25 IBM/clones, 5 Macintoshes, and access to Internet and E-mail. Free or low-cost computer training is available. There

are 2 buildings, 10 classrooms, 15 laboratories, 1 library, and various museum collections available to graduate students. All facilities are handicapped accessible. McNeese Farm, Sam Hunter State Park, and Cameron
Prairie Freshwater Wetland are also available for student research.

Career Counseling and Job Placement

This program offers cooperative educational opportunities with the local
petro-chemical industry. Career counseling and job placement services include job placement counselors, on-campus interviews, and an alumni database. Ten percent of alumni work within the government sector, 80% for
corporations or industries, and 10% in science or academia; 90% of alumni
work in Louisiana and 10% in the Southwest. Ninety-five percent of the students find work within six months of graduation.

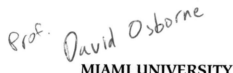

MIAMI UNIVERSITY

Situated on a 500-acre campus in the small town of Oxford, Ohio, Miami
University has a total enrollment of 16,000 students and was established in
1809.

☂ Institute of Environmental Sciences

FACULTY CONTACT: ADMISSIONS CONTACT:
Gene Willeke, Director   The Graduate School
Institute of Environmental Sciences 102 Roudebush Hall
Miami University   Miami University
102 Boyd Hall   Oxford, OH 45056
Oxford, OH 45056

Phone: 513-529-5811   Phone: 513-529-4125

Miami University Web site: http://www.muohio.edu/

Graduate School Web site: http://www.muohio.edu/graduateschool/

Quick Facts About the Institute of Environmental Sciences

• Year established: 1969

• Enrollment: 72 master's students

- Graduate degree conferred: Master of Environmental Science
- Master's degree requirements include: required courses; students choose either a master's thesis, practicum, or internship
- Faculty/Advisee ratio: 1:4

Areas of Specialization

Applied and Quantitative Ecology (29% of students)
Resource Policy and Planning (17%)
Earth Science (15%)
Environmental Education (12%)
Resource Analysis (11%)
Environmental Quality and Public Health (6%)
Parks and Recreation Management (6%)
Conservation Biology (4%)

Special Program Features

Graduate students can cross-register for courses within other departments. Joint degree programs are not offered. International program experiences include student exchanges, and field stations in Central America. Future program plans include expansion of environmental science offerings to undergraduates.

Admission to the Program

- GRE scores are not required.
- Master's students accepted each year: 20% of 125 applicants
- Students may matriculate at the start of any term; transfer students are sometimes accepted.

About the Students

There are 38 male and 34 female graduate students currently enrolled in this program; 67 are full-time and 5 part-time; 6 are international and 66 domestic; 94% are Caucasian, 3% Black, .6% Hispanic, 1.6% Asian, and 0.1% Native American. Graduate students range from age 22 to 48, with a median age of 27.

About the Faculty

There are 65 faculty affiliated with this program. The average faculty member teaches 6 courses and advises 3 master's students per year. Advisors are initially assigned to and then chosen by students. Faculty research is currently being conducted both domestically and internationally. 9 faculty specialize in Applied and Quantitative Ecology, 5 in Botany, 1 in Conservation Biology, 3 in Corporate Environmental Management, 6 in Earth Science, 3 in Environmental Education, 6 in Environmental Geography, 1 in Environmental Law, 2 in Environmental Quality and Public Health, 4 in Environmental Science, 7 in Environmental Studies, 1 in Parks and Recreation Management, 9 in Resource Policy and Planning, and 2 in Social Ecology.

Tuition and Financial Aid

Tuition in 1996 was $5,110 per year for state residents and $5,430 for nonresidents. Over 60% of the graduate students in this program receive financial aid. Four percent of the master's students are awarded fellowships, 4% are awarded scholarships, and 73% are awarded teaching, administrative, or research assistantships.

Facilities

Computer facilities include 19 IBM/clones, one terminal per 4 students, 8 open computer labs across campus, and access to Internet and E-mail. Free or low-cost computer training is available. There are 32 laboratories, 6 libraries, and various museum collections available to graduate students. All facilities are handicapped accessible. The Bachelor Wildlife & Game Reserve, Ecology Research Center, Hueston Woods State Park, Peffer Park, and Silvoor Nature Preserve are also available for student research.

Career Counseling and Job Placement

This program offers student internships or educational opportunities within the local commmunity. Career counseling and job placement services include active alumni contact, job books, an alumni database, and job fairs. Sixteen percent of alumni work within the government sector, 13% for semigovernmental organizations, 12% for nonprofits, 34% for private small business, 12% for corporations or industries, and 3% in science or academia; 58% of alumni work in the Midwest and 4% in international locations. Eighty-four percent of the students find work within six months of graduation.

MICHIGAN TECHNOLOGICAL UNIVERSITY

Established in 1885, Michigan Technological University (also known as Michigan Tech) has a total enrollment of 6,500 students. Its campus stretches for a mile along Portage Lake in Houghton, Michigan.

🎓 School of Forestry and Wood Products

FACULTY CONTACT:

Warren E. Frayer, Dean
School of Forestry and
   Wood Products
Michigan Technological University
1400 Townshend Drive
Houghton, MI 49931-1295

Phone: 906-487-2454`
Fax: 906-487-2915

ADMISSIONS CONTACT:

Graduate School Office
Michigan Technological University
1400 Townshend Drive
Houghton, MI 49931-1295

Phone: 906-487-2327

Michigan Technological University Web site: http://www.mtu.edu/

Quick Facts About the School of Forestry and Wood Products

- Year established: 1936
- Enrollment: 25 master's students / 25 doctoral students
- Graduate degrees conferred: Master of Science, doctorate
- Master's degree requirements include: required courses, master's thesis or master's project
- Doctoral degree requirements include: required courses, dissertation, qualifying exam, oral exam
- Faculty/Advisee ratio: 1:2.5

Areas of Specialization

Applied and Quantitative Ecology (50% of students)
Environmental Science (20%)
Environmental Studies (20%)
Botany (10%)
Forestry (10%)

Special Program Features

This program is best known for its emphasis on landscape ecology and biotechnology. Graduate students can cross-register for courses within other departments. Joint degree programs are not offered. International program experiences include student exchanges in China.

Admission to the Program

- Admission requirements for master's applicants include: B.S. degree; average GRE scores: 550 verbal/550 math
- Admission requirements for doctoral applicants include: master's degree; average GRE scores: 550 verbal/550 math
- Master's students accepted each year: 30% of 35 applicants
- Doctoral students accepted each year: 40% of 20 applicants
- Students may matriculate at the start of any term; transfer students are accepted.

About the Students

There are 30 male and 20 female graduate students currently enrolled in this program; all 50 are full-time; 25 are international and 25 domestic; 60% are Caucasian, 5% Black, 5% Hispanic, and 30% Asian. Graduate students range from age 21 to 44; the median age is 27.

About the Faculty

There are 20 faculty affiliated with this program. The average faculty member teaches 3 courses and advises 1 master's and 1 doctoral student per year. Students choose their faculty advisors. Faculty research is currently being conducted both domestically and internationally. Ten faculty specialize in Applied and Quantitative Ecology, 2 in Botany, 1 in Environmental Geography, 2 in Environmental Science, and 2 in Resource Policy and Planning.

Tuition and Financial Aid

Tuition in 1996 was $3,717 per year for state residents and $8,607 for nonresidents. Over 60% of the graduate students in this program receive financial aid. Ninety percent of the master's students are awarded research assistantships. Fifty percent of the doctoral students are awarded fellowships; 50% are awarded research assistantships.

Facilities

Computer facilities include 21 IBM/clones, one terminal per 3 students, and access to Internet and E-mail. Free or low-cost computer training is available. There are 4 buildings, 6 classrooms, 14 laboratories, and 1 library available to graduate students. Some facilities are handicapped accessible. The school also owns the Ford Forestry Research Center (35 buildings and a 4,500-acre forest), which is available for student research.

Career Counseling and Job Placement

This program does not offer student internships, career counseling, or job placement services. Thirty percent of alumni work within the government sector, 10% for private small business, 50% for corporations or industries, and 10% in science or academia; 40% of alumni work in the Great Lakes States and 40% in international locations. Ninety percent of the students find work within six months of graduation.

MISSISSIPPI STATE UNIVERSITY

Established in 1878, Mississippi State University is located in a small town and has a total enrollment of 13,000 students.

🎓 Department of Wildlife and Fisheries

FACULTY CONTACT:

Dr. H. Randall Robinette, Head
Department of Wildlife
  and Fisheries
Mississippi State University
Box 9690
Mississippi State, MS 39762-9690

Phone: 601-325-3133
Fax: 601-325-8726

ADMISSIONS CONTACT:

Graduate School
Mississippi State University
P.O. Box G
157 Allen Hall
Mississippi State, MS 39762

Phone: 601-325-7400

Mississippi State University Web site: http://www.msstate.edu/

Department of Wildlife and Fisheries Web site:
http://www.cfr.msstate.edu/wildlife/main.htm

Quick Facts About the Department of Wildlife and Fisheries

- Year established: 1968
- Enrollment: 25 master's students / 15 doctoral students
- Graduate degrees conferred: Master of Science, doctorate
- Master's degree requirements include: master's thesis, oral examination
- Doctoral degree requirements include: dissertation, oral examination
- Faculty/Advisee ratio: 1:5

Areas of Specialization

Applied and Quantitative Ecology (100% of students)

Special Program Features

All students specialize in Applied and Quantitative Ecology; graduate students can cross-register for courses within other departments. Joint degree programs and international program experiences are not offered. Future program plans include offering aquaculture courses.

Admission to the Program

- Admission requirements for master's applicants include: B.S. degree, with GPA above 3.0; average GRE scores: 500 verbal/500 math
- Admission requirements for doctoral applicants include: master's degree; average GRE scores: 500 verbal/500 math
- Master's students accepted each year: 25% of 40 applicants
- Doctoral students accepted each year: 25% of 10 applicants
- Students may matriculate at the start of any term; transfer students are accepted.

About the Students

There are 37 male and 3 female graduate students currently enrolled in this program; all 40 are part-time; 6 are international and 34 domestic; 80% are Caucasian, 5% Black, and 15% Asian. Graduate students range from age 22 to 25, with a median age of 24.

About the Faculty

There are 14 faculty affiliated with this program. The average faculty member teaches 1.5 courses and advises 5 master's and 2 doctoral students per year. Faculty advisors choose their students. Faculty research is currently being conducted domestically. All 14 faculty specialize in Applied and Quantitative Ecology.

Tuition and Financial Aid

Tuition in 1996 was $4,320 per year for state residents and $9,030 for non-residents. Over 60% of the graduate students in this program receive financial aid. Ninety percent of the master's students are awarded research assistantships, and 90% of the doctoral students are awarded administrative assistantships.

Facilities

Computer facilities include a mainframe and access to Internet and E-mail. Free or low-cost computer training is available. One building, 8 laboratories, and 2 libraries are available to graduate students. Facilities are handicapped accessible. The school also owns 10,000 acres of pine forest and bottomland hardwood forest that are available for student research.

Career Counseling and Job Placement

This program does not offer student internships. Career counseling and job placement services include on-campus interviews and job books. Forty-five percent of alumni work within the government sector, 8% for nonprofits, 13% for private small business, 3% for corporations or industries, and 17% in science or academia; 65% of alumni work in the Southeast, 3% in Washington, D.C., and 8% in international locations. Ninety-nine percent of the students find work within six months of graduation.

🐾 Department of Forestry

CONTACT:

Dr. Douglas Richards, Head
Department of Forestry
Mississippi State University

Phone: 601-325-2949

College of Forestry Web site: http://www.cfr.msstate.edu/

Department of Forestry Web site:
http://www.cfr.msstate.edu/forestry/main.htm

Quick Facts About the Department of Forestry

- Year established: 1938
- Enrollment: 29 master's students / 10 doctoral students
- Graduate degrees conferred: Master of Science, doctorate
- Master's degree requirements include: required courses, master's thesis, master's project, oral exam which includes thesis defense
- Doctoral degree requirements include: required courses, dissertation, qualifying exam, oral exam
- Faculty/Advisee ratio: 1:2

Special Program Features

This program is best known for its emphasis on bottomland hardwood management, timber harvesting, and forest biometrics. Graduate students can cross-register for courses within other departments. Joint degree programs are offered with the Business School. International program experiences are not offered.

Admission to the Program

- GRE scores are required for all graduate applicants; doctoral applicants must have a master's degree.
- Master's students accepted each year: 65% of 15 applicants
- Doctoral students accepted each year: 50% of 8 applicants
- Students may matriculate at the start of any term; transfer students are sometimes accepted.

Tuition and Financial Aid

Tuition in 1994 was $2,000 for state residents and $4,500 for nonresidents. Over 60% of the graduate students in this program receive financial aid. Sixty percent of the master's and 60% of the doctoral students are awarded research assistantships.

Career Counseling and Job Placement

Career counseling and job placement services include job placement counselors, on-campus interviews, and job books. Twenty percent of alumni work within the government sector, 60% for private small business, and 20% in science or academia; 60% of alumni work in the South. Ninety percent of the students find work within six months of graduation.

MONTANA STATE UNIVERSITY

With a total enrollment of 10,540 students, Montana State University was established in 1893 and is located in the small city of Bozeman, Montana.

⚲ Land Rehabilitation Program

FACULTY CONTACT:

Frank Munshower, Director
Land Rehabilitation Program
Reclamation Research Unit
106 Linfield Hall
Montana State University
Bozeman, MT 59717-0290

Phone: 406-994-3721

ADMISSIONS CONTACT:

College of Graduate Studies
Montana State University
Bozeman, MT 59717

Phone: 406-994-4145

Montana State University Web site: http://www.montana.edu/

Quick Facts About the Land Rehabilitation Program

- Year established: 1981
- Enrollment: 13 master's students
- Graduate degree conferred: Master of Science
- Master's degree requirements include a 4-course core in land rehabilitation
- Faculty/Advisee ratio: 1:6

Special Program Features

This program is best known for its emphasis on the rehabilitation of violently disturbed land. All students specialize in Applied and Quantitative

Ecology; graduate students can cross-register for courses within other departments. Joint degree programs and international program experiences are not offered.

Admission to the Program

- Admission requirements for master's applicants include: 2 semesters of chemistry, 2 of biology, 1 of calculus; average GRE scores: 550 verbal/550 math
- Master's students accepted each year: 25% of 8 applicants
- Students may matriculate at the start of any term; transfer students are sometimes accepted.

About the Students

There are 7 male and 6 female graduate students currently enrolled in this program; 12 are full-time and 1 part-time; 1 is international and 12 domestic; 90% are Caucasian and 8% Asian. Graduate students range from age 23 to 45, with a median age of over 30.

About the Faculty

There are 3 faculty affiliated with this program. The average faculty member teaches 1.5 courses and advises 3 master's students per year. Students choose their faculty advisors. Faculty research is currently being conducted domestically. Two faculty specialize in Applied and Quantitative Ecology and one in Analytical Chemistry.

Tuition and Financial Aid

Tuition in 1996 was $1,759 per year for state residents and $3,715 for non-residents. Under 20% of the graduate students in this program receive financial aid. Ten percent of the master's students are awarded research assistantships; 20% receive employment.

Facilities

Computer facilities include 4 IBM/clones, one terminal per 3 students, student computer facilities in most buildings, and access to Internet and E-mail. Free or low-cost computer training is available. One building, 2 laboratories, and 1 library are available to graduate students. Some facilities are handicapped accessible. The school also owns a ranch that has numerous old mining disturbances that are available for student research.

Career Counseling and Job Placement

This program offers a student internship in cooperation with the Montana Department of State Lands. Career counseling and job placement services include an alumni database. Forty-three percent of alumni work within the government sector, 50% for private small business, 2.5% for corporations or industries, and 5% in science or academia; 75% of alumni work in the Rocky Mountain region and 2.5% in international locations. Ninety percent of the students find work within six months of graduation.

☙ Fish and Wildlife Management Program

CONTACT:

Lynn Irby, Director
Fish and Wildlife Management Program
Montana State University
Bozeman, MT 59717

Phone: 406-994-4549

Quick Facts About the Fish and Wildlife Management Program

- Year established: 1937
- Enrollment: 35 master's students / 5 doctoral students
- Graduate degrees conferred: Master of Science, doctorate in Biology
- Master's degree requirements include: required courses, master's thesis, qualifying oral exam
- Doctoral degree requirements include: required courses, dissertation, qualifying exam, oral exam
- Faculty/Advisee ratio: 7:40

Areas of Specialization

Applied and Quantitative Ecology (100% of students)

Special Program Features

This program is best known for its emphasis on applied wildlife and fisheries management. Graduate students cannot cross-register for courses within other departments. Joint degree programs and international program experiences are not offered.

Admission to the Program

- Admission requirements for master's applicants include: 2 semesters of chemistry, 8 of biology, 1 of calculus, 1 of economics, 1 of physical science
- Average GRE scores required of all graduate students: 550 verbal/550 math
- Master's degree not required for doctoral applicants
- Master's students accepted each year: 15% of 150 applicants
- Doctoral students accepted each year: 5–10% of 50 applicants
- Students may matriculate at the start of any term; transfer students are sometimes accepted.

Tuition and Financial Aid

Five percent of the master's students and 5% of the doctoral students are awarded fellowships; 95% of the master's students and 95% of the doctoral students are awarded teaching or research assistantships.

Career Counseling and Job Placement

This program does not offer student internships. Career counseling and job placement services are available. Eighty percent of alumni work within the government sector, 5% for nonprofits, 5% for private small business, and 10% in science or academia; 80% of alumni work in the West. Ninety-five percent of the students find work within six months of graduation.

☚ Other graduate environmental programs at Montana State University (no profiles available):

Biology Department. *Contact:* Robert Moore. *Phone:* 406-994-4548.
Department of Animal and Range Sciences. *Contact:* Frank Munshower. *Phone:* 406-994-3721

Dr. John Smallwood Birdguy

MONTCLAIR STATE UNIVERSITY

With a total enrollment of 13,700 students, Montclair State University has a main campus in the suburban town of Branchville, New Jersey, as well as a rural 240-acre field campus in Stokes Forest. This school belongs to the Hispanic Association of Colleges and Universities.

☞ New Jersey School of Conservation

FACULTY/ADMISSIONS CONTACT:

John Kirk, Director
New Jersey School of Conservation
Montclair State University
RD #2, Box 272
Branchville, NJ 07826

Phone: 201-948-4646

Montclair State University Web site: http://www.montclair.edu/

Quick Facts About the New Jersey School of Conservation

• Year established: 1949
• Enrollment: 20 master's students
• Graduate degree conferred: Master of Arts
• Master's degree requirements include: required courses
• Faculty/Advisee ratio: 1:20

Special Program Features

This program is best known for its emphasis on curriculum development in environmental education. All students specialize in Environmental Education; graduate students can cross-register for courses within other departments. Joint degree programs are not offered. The school offers nondegree internships to students from 27 countries. Future program plans include new courses in environmental ethics and biodiversity, and continuing to train classroom teachers in environmental education.

Admission to the Program

• Admission requirements for master's applicants include: B.S. or B.A. in education or related field; average GRE scores: 500 verbal/500 math

- Master's students accepted each year: 80% of 13 applicants
- Students may matriculate at the start of any term; transfer students are sometimes accepted.

About the Students

There are 6 male and 14 female graduate students currently enrolled in this program; 6 are full-time and 14 part-time; none are international; 90% are Caucasian, 1% Black, 8% Hispanic, and 1% Asian. Graduate students range from age 24 to 60; the median age is 32.

About the Faculty

There are 5 faculty affiliated with this program. Faculty advisors are assigned to students. All faculty specialize in Environmental Education.

Tuition and Financial Aid

Tuition in 1996 was $158 per credit for state residents and $200 for non-residents. Under 20% of the graduate students in this program receive financial aid. Twenty percent of the master's students are awarded fellowships.

Facilities

Computer facilities include 6 Macintoshes and access to Internet and E-mail. Free or low-cost computer training is not available. There are 60 buildings, 6 classrooms, 1 laboratory, and 1 library available to graduate students. Facilities are handicapped accessible. The school is located amidst 29,000 acres of state park and forest land. It is the environmental field campus for Montclair State College, 57 miles away.

Career Counseling and Job Placement

This program offers 4 full teaching fellowships per year. No career counseling and job placement services are offered. Two percent of alumni work for nonprofits, 2% for private small business; 96% are already classroom teachers; 98% of alumni work in New Jersey.

MOSS LANDING MARINE LABS

☜ Marine Labs School/Program

CONTACT:

Gail Johnston, Assistant Director
Marine Labs School/Program
Moss Landing Marine Labs
P.O. Box 450
Moss Landing, CA 95039

Phone: 408-633-3304
Moss Landing Marine Labs Web site: http://arnica.csustan.edu/mlml.html

Quick Facts About the Marine Labs School/Program

- Year established: 1964
- Total enrollment: 110 (90% master's students)
- Tuition in 1994: varies by campus
- Setting: rural, oceanside campus; other classes in small agricultural city of Salinas, California
- Graduate degree conferred: Master of Science, in conjunction with 6 consortium campuses
- Master's degree requirements include: required courses, master's thesis
- Faculty/Advisee ratio: 1:12

Areas of Specialization

Oceanography (35% of students)
Fisheries Science (30%)

Special Program Features

A research and educational institution of the California State University system, this program is best known for its emphasis on marine science. Graduate students can cross-register for courses within other departments. Joint degree programs and international program experiences are not offered.

Admission to the Program

- Admission requirements for master's applicants include: 2 semesters of chemistry, 2 of biology, 2 of calculus; GRE scores are strongly recommended
- Master's students accepted each year (on average): 45% of 120 applicants
- Students may matriculate at the start of any term; transfer students are not accepted.

About the Students

There are 40% male and 60% female graduate students currently enrolled in this program; 25% are full-time and 75% part-time; 1% are international and 99% domestic; 90% are Caucasian, 1% Black, 2% Hispanic, and 7% Asian. Graduate students range from age 22 to 40, with a median age of 25.

About the Faculty

There are 7 faculty affiliated with this program. The average faculty member teaches 4 courses and advises 12–20 master's students per year. Advisors are temporarily assigned to and then chosen by students. Faculty research is currently being conducted both domestically and internationally. Four faculty specialize in Applied and Quantitative Ecology and 3 in Oceanography.

Tuition and Financial Aid

Some 41–60% of the graduate students in this program receive financial aid; 60% of the master's students are awarded teaching or research assistantships.

Facilities

Computer facilities include 10 IBM/clones, 10 Macintoshes, 5 GIS computers, and access to Internet and E-mail. Free or low-cost computer training is available. Moss Landing is currently in temporary facilities, due to the 1989 earthquake. These facilities are handicapped accessible.

Career Counseling and Job Placement

This program does not offer student internships or career counseling services. Sixty percent of alumni work within the government sector, 20% for private small business, and 20% in science or academia; 60% of alumni work in the West Coast region. Sixty-five percent of the students find work within six months of graduation.

NEW JERSEY INSTITUTE OF TECHNOLOGY

Established in 1881, New Jersey Institute of Technology has a total enrollment of 7,700. It is located on a 40-acre campus in Newark—New Jersey's largest city.

♔ Environmental Policy Studies Program

FACULTY CONTACT:

John Opie, Professor
Department of Humanities
  and Social Science
New Jersey Institute of Technology
University Heights
Newark, NJ 07102

ADMISSIONS CONTACT

Office of University Admissions
New Jersey Institute of Technology
University Heights
Newark, NJ 07102

Phone: 201-596-3269

Phone: 201-596-3460

Department of Humanities and Social Science Web site:
http://www.njit.edu/njIT/instruct/degree/envipol.html

New Jersey Institute of Technology Web site: http://www.njit.edu/

Quick Facts About the Environmental Policy Studies Program

- Year established: 1993
- Enrollment: 8 master's students
- Graduate degree conferred: Master of Science
- Master's degree requirements include: required courses, master's thesis, master's project, work experience
- Faculty/Advisee ratio: 1:1

Areas of Specialization (no statistics available)

Applied and Quantitative Ecology
Environmental Quality and Public Health

Environmental Studies
Resource Policy and Planning

Special Program Features

This program is best known for its emphasis on environmental history and philosophy. Graduate students can cross-register for courses within other departments. Joint degree programs and international program experiences are not offered. Possible future program plans include additional faculty and the development of joint degree programs.

Admission to the Program

- Admission requirements for master's applicants include: GPA above 3.0; faculty recommendation letters; average GRE scores: 500 verbal/600 quantitative/550 analytical (1650 minimum)
- Master's students accepted each year: 50% of 10 applicants
- Students may matriculate at the start of any term; transfer students are accepted.

About the Students

There are 4 male and 4 female graduate students currently enrolled in this program; 6 are full-time and 2 part-time; all are Caucasian. Graduate students range from age 25 to 33, with a median age of 27.

About the Faculty

There are 18 faculty affiliated with this program. The average faculty member teaches 4 courses and advises 1 master's student per year. Advisors are assigned to students. Faculty research is currently being conducted both domestically and internationally. One faculty member specializes in Applied and Quantitative Ecology, 1 in Corporate Environmental Management, 1 in Environmental Geography, 1 in Environmental Law, 3 in Environmental Quality and Public Health, 6 in Environmental Studies, 9 in Resource Policy and Planning, and 1 in Architecture.

Tuition and Financial Aid

Tuition in 1996 was $6,776 per year for state residents and $9,372 for non-residents. Over 60% of the graduate students in this program receive financial aid. Eighty percent of the master's students are awarded research assistantships; 20% receive hourly employment.

Facilities

Computer facilities include IBM/clones, Macintoshes, various computer labs, and access to Internet and E-mail. Free or low-cost computer training is available. There are 22 buildings and 4 libraries available to graduate students. All facilities are handicapped accessible.

Career Counseling and Job Placement

This program offers various student internships or educational opportunities within the local commmunity. Career counseling and job placement services include job placement counselors, active alumni contact, on-campus interviews, job books, an alumni database, and job fairs. Twenty-five percent of alumni work within the government sector, 25% for nonprofits, 25% for private small business, and 25% for corporations or industries. Eighty percent of the students find work within six months of graduation.

NEW YORK UNIVERSITY

With a total enrollment of 40,000 students, New York University was established in 1831 and is located on an urban campus in New York City's Greenwich Village.

☗ Department of Applied Science, Energy Science Program

FACULTY CONTACT:

Gabriel Miller
Director of Graduate Studies
Department of Applied Science,
   Energy Science Program
New York University
Washington Square
New York, NY 10003

Phone: 212-998-8995

ADMISSIONS CONTACT:

The Graduate School of
   Arts & Science
New York University
6 Washington Square North
P.O. Box 907, Cooper Station
New York, NY 10003

Phone: 212-998-8050

Department of Applied Science Web site:
http://www.nyu.edu/gsas/program/applied/

New York University Web site: http://www.nyu.edu/

Quick Facts About the Department of Applied Science

- Year established: 1974
- Enrollment: 30 master's students / 15 doctoral students
- Graduate degrees conferred: Master of Science, doctorate
- Master's degree requirements include: required courses, master's project
- Doctoral degree requirements include: required courses, dissertation, qualifying exam, oral exam, and one language
- Faculty/Advisee ratio: 1:4

Special Program Features

This program is best known for its emphasis on climate modeling and energy utilization. All students specialize in Earth Science; graduate students can cross-register for courses within other departments. Joint degree programs and international program experiences are not offered. Future program plans include more course offerings in environmental science.

Admission to the Program

- GRE scores are not required for graduate applicants
- Admission requirements for master's applicants include: 2 semesters of chemistry, 3 of calculus, 2 of physical science
- Master's degrees are required for doctoral applicants
- Master's students accepted each year: 80% of 30 applicants
- Doctoral students accepted each year: 30% of 10 applicants
- Students may matriculate at the start of any term; transfer students are accepted.

About the Students

There are 25 male and 3 female graduate students currently enrolled in this program; 15 are full-time and 6 part-time; 15 are international and 10 domestic; 50% are Caucasian, 20% Black, and 30% Asian. Graduate students range from age 22 to 45, with a median age of 28.

About the Faculty

There are 9 faculty affiliated with this program. The average faculty member teaches 3 courses and advises 2 master's and 2 doctoral students per year. Students choose their advisors. Faculty research is currently being conducted both domestically and internationally. All faculty specialize in Earth Science.

Tuition and Financial Aid

Tuition in 1996 was $600 per credit. Some 21–40% of the graduate students in this program receive financial aid. Twenty percent of the master's students are awarded scholarships. Thirty percent of the doctoral students are awarded scholarships, and 30% are awarded research assistantships.

Facilities

Computer facilities include 3 IBM/clones, 5 Macintoshes, 8 terminals, and access to Internet and E-mail. Free or low-cost computer training is available. One building, 2 classrooms, 3 laboratories, and 3 libraries are available to graduate students. Some facilities are handicapped accessible.

Career Counseling and Job Placement

This program offers student internships at a number of research institutions. Career counseling and job placement services include job placement counselors and active alumni contact. Twenty percent of alumni work within the government sector, 30% for private small business, 30% for corporations or industries, and 20% in science or academia; 40% of alumni work in the Mid-Atlantic region, 10% in Washington, D.C., and 30% in international locations. Eighty-five percent of the students find work within six months of graduation.

☜ Other graduate environmental programs at New York University (no profiles available):

Department of Biology. *Contact:* Gloria Cosuzzi, Director of Graduate Studies. *Phone:* 212-998-8200.

Environmental Conservation Education Graduate Program. *Contact:* Thomas Colwell, Coordinator. *Phone:* 212-998-5637.

Nelson Institute of Environmental Medicine. *Contact:* Katie Shadow. *Phone:* 212-263-7300, ext. 885-5281.

Science & Environmental Reporting Program. *Contact:* William Burrows, Director, Department of Journalism & Mass Communication. *Phone:* 212-998-7970.

NORTH CAROLINA STATE UNIVERSITY

Established in 1887, North Carolina State University has a total enrollment of 27,000 students. It is located in the state capital of Raleigh and enjoys collaborative relationships with the numerous educational institutions in the Raleigh–Durham–Chapel Hill "research triangle" region.

☜ Program in Parks, Recreation and Tourism Management

FACULTY CONTACT:

Larry Gustke
Graduate Administrator
Program in Parks, Recreation
    and Tourism Management
North Carolina State University
Raleigh, NC 27695

Phone: 919-515-3276

ADMISSIONS CONTACT:

The Graduate School
North Carolina State University
Box 7102
Raleigh, NC 27695-7102

Phone: 919-515-2872

Parks, Recreation and Tourism Management Web site:
http://www2.acs.ncsu.edu/grad/catalog/prg-prt.htm

North Carolina State University Web site: http://www.ncsu.edu/

Graduate School Web site: http://www2.acs.ncsu.edu/grad/   .

*Quick Facts About the Program in Parks, Recreation
and Tourism Management*

- Year established: 1947
- Enrollment: 60 master's students
- Graduate degrees conferred: Master of Science; Master of Parks, Recreation and Tourism Management
- Master's degree requirements include: required courses (11 hours core), master's thesis, master's project
- Faculty/Advisee ratio: 1:8

Areas of Specialization

Parks and Recreation Management (80% of students)
Resource Policy and Planning (15%)
Forestry (5%)

Special Program Features

This program is best known for its emphasis on geographical information systems and travel and tourism management. Graduate students can cross-register for courses within other departments. A co-major in Public Administration is offered. International program experiences are not offered.

Admission to the Program

- Admission requirements for master's applicants include: average GRE scores: 463 verbal/452 math
- Master's students accepted each year: 75% of 43 applicants
- Students may matriculate at the start of any term; transfer students are accepted.

About the Students

There are 49 male and 21 female graduate students currently enrolled in this program; 45 are full-time and 15 part-time; 2 are international and 58 domestic; 90% are Caucasian, 5% Black, and 5% Asian. Graduate students range from age 22 to 48, with a median age of 24.

About the Faculty

There are 9 faculty affiliated with this program. The average faculty member teaches 4 courses and advises 8 master's students per year. Advisors are assigned to students. Faculty research is currently being conducted both domestically and internationally. One faculty member specializes in Environmental Education, 2 in Environmental Geography, 3 in Forestry, 9 in Parks and Recreation Management, and 4 in Resource Policy and Planning.

Tuition and Financial Aid

Tuition in 1996 was $1,692 per year for state residents and $9,854 for non-residents. Some 21–40% of the graduate students in this program receive fi-

nancial aid; 30% of the master's students are awarded teaching or research assistantships.

Facilities

Computer facilities include 15 computers for GIS and access to Internet and E-mail. Free or low-cost computer training is available. One building, 3 classrooms, 2 laboratories, and 2 libraries are available to graduate students. Facilities are handicapped accessible. The school also owns a mixed hardwood/softwood forest with lake access; two on-campus field facilities with laboratory space, streams, ponds, and terrestrial habitats; and three aquaculture facilities: one near the coast, one in the mountains, and one on campus. Various agricultural research stations throughout the state are also available for student research.

Career Counseling and Job Placement

This program offers student internships with parks and recreation departments, state parks, and state government agencies. No career counseling and job placement services are offered. Seventy-five percent of the students find work within six months of graduation.

☜ Program in Fisheries and Wildlife Sciences

CONTACT:

Richard L. Noble, Coordinator
Program in Fisheries and Wildlife Sciences
North Carolina State University
Raleigh, NC 27695

Phone: 919-515-7586

Quick Facts About the Program in Fisheries and Wildlife Sciences

- Year established: 1977
- Graduate degrees conferred: Master of Science, Master of Wildlife Biology (non-thesis), doctorate
- Master's degree requirements include: required courses, master's thesis for M.S.; master's project and work experience for M.W.B.

- Doctoral degree requirements include: dissertation, qualifying exam, oral exam
- Faculty/Advisee ratio: 1:3

Areas of Specialization

Applied and Quantitative Ecology (90% of students)
Aquaculture (10%)

Special Program Features

This program is best known for its emphasis on fish recruitment, habitat ecology, and wildlife statistics. Graduate students can cross-register for courses within other departments. Joint degree programs and international program experiences are not offered.

(*Note:* As a program, rather than a department, faculty and their resources are admistered through their primary departments. Students, under the mentorship of 25 faculty, may pursue 12 graduate degree titles through 6 departments.)

Admission to the Program

- GRE scores are required for all graduate applicants.
- Students may matriculate at the start of any term; transfer students are sometimes accepted.

Tuition and Financial Aid

Tuition in 1994 was $1,070. Over 60% of the graduate students in this program receive financial aid. All graduate sttudents are awarded teaching or research assistantships.

Career Counseling and Job Placement

This program does not offer student internships. Career counseling and job placement services include job placement counselors, on-campus interviews, job books, an alumni database, and job fairs. All students find work within six months of graduation.

☜ Program in Marine, Earth and Atmospheric Sciences

CONTACT:

Gerald Janowitz
Graduate Administrator
Program in Marine, Earth and Atmospheric Sciences
North Carolina State University
Raleigh, NC 27695

Phone: 919-515-3837

Quick Facts About the Program in Marine, Earth and Atmospheric Sciences

- Year established: M.S. in Geology, 1939 / Ph.D. in Marine Science, 1969
- Enrollment: 58 master's students / 47 doctoral students
- Graduate degrees conferred: Master of Science, doctorate
- Master's degree requirements include: master's thesis, oral exam
- Doctoral degree requirements include: dissertation, qualifying exam, oral exam
- Faculty/Advisee ratio: 1:3

Areas of Specialization

Earth Science (100% of students)

Special Program Features

Graduate students can cross-register for courses within other departments. Joint degree programs and international program experiences are not offered.

Admission to the Program

- Admission requirements for master's applicants include: 2 semesters of chemistry, 3 of calculus, 3 of physical science; average GRE scores: 550 verbal/600 math
- Admission requirements for doctoral applicants include: master's degree; average GRE scores: 550 verbal/600 math
- Master's students accepted each year: 75% of 100 applicants

- Doctoral students accepted each year: 50% of 30 applicants
- Students may matriculate at the start of any term; transfer students are sometimes accepted.

About the Students

There are 74 male and 31 female graduate students currently enrolled in this program; 28 are international and 77 domestic; 65% are Caucasian and 35% Asian.

Tuition and Financial Aid

Tuition in 1994 was $1,500 per year for state residents and $8,540 for non-residents. Over 60% of the graduate students in this program receive financial aid. Eighty percent of the master's students are awarded teaching or research assistantships, and 90% of the doctoral students are awarded research assistantships.

Career Counseling and Job Placement

This program does not offer student internships. Career counseling and job placement services include on-campus interviews and job books. All students find work within six months of graduation.

✿ Department of Zoology

CONTACT:

James Gilliam
Director of Graduate Programs
Department of Zoology
North Carolina State University
Raleigh, NC 27695

Phone: 919-515-3273

Department of Zoology Web site:
http://www2.acs.ncsu.edu/grad/catalog/prg-zo.htm

Quick Facts About the Department of Zoology

- Enrollment: 60 master's students / 38 doctoral students
- Graduate degrees conferred: Master of Science, Master of Life Science (non-thesis), doctorate

- Master's degree requirements include: required courses, master's thesis
- Doctoral degree requirements include: required courses, dissertation, qualifying exam, oral exam
- Faculty/Advisee ratio: 1:3

Areas of Specialization

Applied and Quantitative Ecology (60% of students)
Conservation Biology (30%)

Special Program Features

This program is best known for its emphasis on aquatic ecology. Graduate students can cross-register for courses within other departments. Joint degree programs are not offered. International program experiences include research opportunities and field stations in many countries.

Admission to the Program

- Admission requirements for master's applicants include: 4 semesters of chemistry, 6 of biology, 1 of calculus, and 2 of physical science
- GRE scores are required of all graduate applicants.
- No master's degree is required for doctoral applicants.
- Master's students accepted each year: 20% of 60 applicants
- Doctoral students accepted each year: 20% of 30 applicants
- Students may matriculate at the start of any term; transfer students are accepted.

About the Students

There are 32 male and 66 female graduate students in this program; 70% are Caucasian, 5% Black, 10% Hispanic, and 5% Asian.

About the Faculty

Forty-three faculty are affiliated with this program.

Tuition and Financial Aid

Over 60% of the graduate students receive financial aid. Six percent of the master's students are awarded fellowships; 75% receive teaching or research assistantships. Ten percent of the doctoral students are awarded fellowships; 90% receive teaching or research assistantships.

Career Counseling and Job Placement

This program offers student internships with state and federal agencies and occasionally with industry. Career counseling and job placement services include job placement counselors, on-campus interviews, job books, and job fairs. Roughly 30% of alumni work within the government sector, 10% for nonprofits, 10% for private small business, 10% for corporations or industries, and 40% in science or academia. All students find work within six months of graduation.

☀ Other graduate environmental programs at North Carolina State University (no profiles available):

Conservation Biology. *Contact:* Martha Groom, Assistant Professor. *Phone:* 919-515-4588.

NORTHWESTERN SCHOOL OF LAW, LEWIS AND CLARK COLLEGE

Located on an urban campus in the city of Portland, Oregon, Lewis and Clark College has a total enrollment of 3,440 students.

☀ Natural Resources Law Institute

FACULTY CONTACT:

Janice Weis
Natural Resources Law Institute
Northwestern School of Law
Lewis & Clark College
10015 SW Terwillinger Blvd.
Portland, OR 97219-7799

Phone: 503-768-6649
Fax: 503-768-6671

Northwestern School of Law Web site:
http://www.lclark.edu/LAW/index.html

ADMISSIONS CONTACT:

Director of Admissions
Northwestern School of Law
of Lewis & Clark College
10015 SW Terwillinger Blvd.
Portland, OR 97219-7799

Phone: 503-768-6613

Quick Facts About the Natural Resources Law Institute

- Year established: Juris Doctorate (J.D.) program, 1970 / Master of Laws (L.LM.), 1988
- Enrollment: 756 law students
- Graduate degrees conferred: Juris Doctorate, Master of Laws (an advanced legal degree in Environmental and Natural Resources Law)
- J.D. requirements include: required courses, 2 papers
- L.LM. requirements include: required courses, dissertation, graduate seminar, graduate thesis

Special Program Features

This program is best known for its emphasis on environmental and natural resources law. All L.LM. and 30% of J.D. students specialize in Environmental Law; graduate students can cross-register for courses within other departments. Joint degree programs are offered with the School of Public Policy. International program experiences are not offered.

Admission to the Program

- Admission requirements for L.LM. applicants include: J.D. degree; LSAT scores
- J.D. students accepted each year: 30% of 2,500 applicants
- L.LM. students accepted each year: 33% of 45 applicants
- J.D. students may matriculate only in the fall; L.LM. students may matriculate at the start of any term; transfer students are sometimes accepted.

About the Faculty

The average faculty member teaches 4 courses and advises 2 L.LM. students per year. Faculty research is currently being conducted both domestically and internationally. Faculty specialize in Environmental Law.

Tuition and Financial Aid

Tuition in 1996 was $362 per semester hour. Over 60% of the graduate students in this program receive financial aid. Ten percent of the J.D. students are awarded scholarships; 10% are awarded research assistantships. Forty percent of the L.LM. students are awarded research assistantships.

Facilities

Computer facilities include 100 IBM/clones and access to Internet and E-mail. Free or low-cost computer training is available. There are 4 buildings, 10 classrooms, 2 laboratories, and 2 libraries available to graduate students. Facilities are handicapped accessible.

Career Counseling and Job Placement

This program offers student internships or educational opportunities within the local commmunity. Career counseling and job placement services include job placement counselors, active alumni contact, on-campus interviews, job books, and an alumni database. Eighty-two percent of the students find work within six months of graduation.

NOVA SOUTHEASTERN UNIVERSITY

With a total enrollment of 11,100, Nova Southeastern University was established in 1964. It is located in the subtropical, coastal town of Dania, Florida.

☞ Institute of Marine and Coastal Studies

FACULTY / ADMISSIONS CONTACT:

Richard Dodge
Administrator: Master's Degree Programs
Oceanographic Center
Institute of Marine and Coastal Studies
Nova Southeastern University
Oceanographic Center
8000 North Ocean Drive
Dania, FL 33004

Phone: 305-920-1909
Fax: 305-947-8559
E-mail: dodge@ocean.nova.edu

Nova Southeastern University Web site: http://www.nova.edu/

Quick Facts About the Institute of Marine and Coastal Studies

- Year established: 1970

- Enrollment: 50 master's students / 6 doctoral students
- Graduate degrees conferred: Master of Science, doctorate
- Master's degree requirements include: master's thesis, or non-thesis option
- Doctoral degree requirements include: dissertation, qualifying exam, oral exam
- Faculty/Advisee ratio: 1:6

Special Program Features

This program is best known for its emphasis on marine biology and coastal zone management. All students specialize in Marine and Coastal Studies; graduate students cannot cross-register for courses within other departments. Joint degree programs are offered with the undergraduate college. International program experiences are not offered.

Admission to the Program

- GRE scores of over 1000 are preferred for all graduate applicants
- Admission requirements for master's applicants include an undergraduate degree; marine biology applicants require a major in biology, oceanography, or science education
- Master's degrees are required for doctoral applicants
- Master's students accepted each year: 75% of 125 applicants
- Doctoral students accepted each year: 10% of 10 applicants
- Students may matriculate at the start of any term; transfer students are not accepted.

About the Students

There are 31 male and 19 female graduate students currently enrolled in this program; 50 are full-time and 6 part-time; 7 are international and 43 domestic; 98% are Caucasian and 1% Asian. Graduate students range from age 22 to 45, with a median age of 25.

About the Faculty

There are 9 faculty affiliated with this program. The average faculty member teaches 3 courses and advises 30 master's and 6 doctoral students per

year. Advisors are assigned to students. Faculty research is currently being conducted both domestically and internationally. All faculty specialize in Marine and Coastal Studies.

Tuition and Financial Aid

Tuition in 1996 was $212 per credit hour. Some 21–40% of the graduate students in this program receive financial aid.

Facilities

Computer facilities include IBM/clones, one terminal per 5 students, and access to Internet and E-mail. Free or low-cost computer training is available. There are 2 buildings, 2 classrooms, 4 laboratories, and 2 libraries available to graduate students. Some facilities are handicapped accessible.

Career Counseling and Job Placement

This program does not offer student internships or career counseling and job placement services. Twenty-five percent of alumni work within the government sector, 25% for private small business, and 25% in science or academia; 75% of alumni work in Florida. Ninety-nine percent of the students find work within six months of graduation.

THE OHIO STATE UNIVERSITY

Located on an urban campus in the capital city of Columbus, Ohio State University was established in 1968 and has a total enrollment of 58,600 students.

☛ Environmental Science Graduate Program

FACULTY CONTACT:
Samual Traina, Program Director
Environmental Science
   Graduate Program

ADMISSIONS CONTACT:
Admissions Office
The Ohio State University
Third Floor Lincoln Tower

The Ohio State University   1800 Cannon Drive
412B Kottman Hall   Columbus, OH 43210-1200
2021 Coffey Road
Columbus, OH 43210-1086

Phone: 614-292-9762   *Phone:* 614-292-3980
Fax: 614-292-7432
E-mail: enviro@osu.edu

Environmental Science Graduate Program Web site:
http://www-esgp.ag.ohio-state.edu/homebase.html

Ohio State University Web site: http://www.osu.edu/

Quick Facts About the Environmental Science Graduate Program

- Year established: 1989
- Enrollment: 36 master's students / 46 doctoral students
- Graduate degrees conferred: Master of Science, doctorate
- Master's degree requirements include: master's thesis, comprehensive written exam prepared by student's advisory committee
- Doctoral degree requirements include: dissertation, qualifying exam, oral exam
- Faculty/Advisee ratio: 1:4

Areas of Specialization

Applied and Quantitative Ecology (40% of students)
Environmental Science (23%)
Environmental Quality and Public Health (10%)
Earth Science (9%)
Botany (4%)
Conservation Biology (2%)
Environmental Geography (1%)
Environmental Law (1%)

Special Program Features

This campus-wide program is administered through the Graduate School and includes the colleges of Food, Agriculture, and Environmental Science; Biological Sciences; Engineering; Pharmacy; Medicine; Veterinary Medicine; Mathematical and Physical Sciences; and Social and Behavioral Sciences. Graduate students can cross-register for courses within other departments. Joint degree programs are not offered. International program experiences include research opportunities, student exchanges, and field stations in South America, Europe, India, and China.

Admission to the Program

- Admission requirements for master's applicants include: 2 semesters of chemistry, 2 of biology, 1 of calculus, 1 of physical science; average GRE scores: 600 verbal/600 math

- Admission requirements for doctoral applicants include: master's degree; average GRE scores: 650 verbal/650 math

- Graduate students accepted last year: 22 out of 150 applicants

- Students may matriculate only in the fall; transfer students are sometimes accepted.

About the Students

There are 47 male and 35 female graduate students currently enrolled in this program; 70 are full-time and 12 part-time; 36 are international and 46 domestic; 57% are Caucasian, 2% Black, 8% Hispanic, and 22% Asian. Graduate students range from age 24 to 36, with a median age of 26.

About the Faculty

There are 64 faculty respresenting 22 departments and schools affiliated with this program. The average faculty member advises 1 master's and 1.3 doctoral students per year. Students choose their faculty advisors. Faculty research is currently being conducted both domestically and internationally. 20 faculty specialize in Applied and Quantitative Ecology, 4 in Botany, 10 in Earth Science, 3 in Environmental Geography, 3 in Environmental Law, 10 in Environmental Quality and Public Health, and 10 in Environmental Science.

Tuition and Financial Aid

Tuition in 1996 was $4,473 per year for state residents and $11,988 for non-residents. Over 60% of the graduate students in this program receive financial aid. Five percent of the master's students are awarded fellowships; 34% are awarded teaching or research assistantships. Six percent of the doctoral students are awarded fellowships; 55% are awarded teaching or research assistantships.

Facilities

Computer facilities include access to Internet and E-mail. Free or low-cost computer training is available. There are various buildings, classrooms, laboratories, and museum collections, and 16 libraries available to graduate students. All facilities are handicapped accessible. The school also owns the Ohio Agriculture Research & Development Center—a research farm located in Wooster, Ohio (70 miles away), equipped with labs, greenhouses, growth chambers, and field plot areas, including 8 branch stations, available for student research.

Career Counseling and Job Placement

This program does not offer student internships. Career counseling and job placement services are provided by supporting colleges.

☂ School of Natural Resources

CONTACT:

Dr. Robert E. Roth, Associate Director
School of Natural Resources
The Ohio State University
2021 Coffey Road
Columbus, OH 43210-1085

Phone: 614-292-2265
Fax: 614-292-7432

School of Natural Resources Web site:
http://www.ag.ohio-state.edu/~natres/

Quick Facts About the School of Natural Resources

- Year established: 1972
- Enrollment: 80 master's students
- Graduate degree conferred: Master of Science

- Master's degree requirements include: master's thesis, or 2 papers
- Faculty/Advisee ratio: 1:5

Special Program Features

Graduate students can cross-register for courses within other departments. Joint degree programs are offered with the Law School and the School of Public Policy. International program experiences include research opportunities, field stations, and technical assistance in many countries. A Ph.D. degree program is in the process of being approved.

Admission to the Program

- Admission requirements for master's applicants include: 10 hours of chemistry, 10 of biology, 10 of calculus, 15 of social science, and 15 of humanities; average GRE scores: 513 verbal/624 math
- Master's students accepted each year: 75% of 45 applicants
- Students may matriculate only in the fall; transfer students are sometimes accepted.

About the Faculty

There are 42 faculty affiliated with this program.

Tuition and Financial Aid

Over 60% of the graduate students in this program receive financial aid. All are awarded teaching or research assistantships.

Career Counseling and Job Placement

This program offers voluntary student internships or educational opportunities within the local commmunity. Career counseling and job placement services include job books and job fairs. Forty percent of alumni work within the government sector, 10% for semi-governmental organizations, 10% for nonprofits, 30% for private small business, and 10% in science or academia; 60% of alumni work in Ohio, 5% in Washington, D.C., and 5% in international locations. Seventy percent of the students find work within six months of graduation.

OHIO UNIVERSITY

Established in 1804, Ohio University has a total enrollment of 27,250 students and is located in the rural small town of Athens, Ohio.

☜ Environmental Studies Graduate Program

FACULTY CONTACT:

Dr. Gene Mapes, Director
Environmental Studies
  Graduate Program
Ohio University
Athens, OH 45701-2979

Phone: 614-593-4686

ADMISSIONS CONTACT:

Office of Graduate
  Student Services
Ohio University
Athens, OH 45701-2979

Phone: 614-593-2800

Quick Facts About the Environmental Studies Graduate Program

- Year established: 1971
- Enrollment: 50 master's students
- Graduate degree conferred: Master of Science
- Master's degree requirements include: required courses, master's thesis, master's project
- Faculty/Advisee ratio: 1:1

Areas of Specialization

Environmental Geography (30% of students)
Applied and Quantitative Ecology (15%)
Botany (10%)
Earth Science (10%)
Environmental Law (10%)
Environmental Science (10%)
Resource Policy and Planning (10%)
Environmental Quality and Public Health (5%)

Special Program Features

This program is best known for its emphasis on hydrogeology, GIS, and ecology. Graduate students can cross-register for courses within other departments. Joint degree programs and international program experiences are not offered.

Admission to the Program

- Average GRE scores (recommended): 550 verbal/550 math
- Master's students accepted each year: 50% of 80 applicants
- Students may matriculate at the start of any term; transfer students are accepted.

About the Students

There are 32 male and 18 female graduate students currently enrolled in this program; 48 are full-time and 2 part-time; 7 are international and 43 domestic; 90% are Caucasian and 10% Asian. Graduate students range from age 22 to 45, with a median age of 25.

About the Faculty

There are 50 faculty affiliated with this program. The average faculty member teaches 6 courses (quarter system) and advises 1 master's student per year. Students choose their faculty advisors. Faculty research is currently being conducted both domestically and internationally. Ten faculty specialize in Applied and Quantitative Ecology, 5 in Botany, 5 in Conservation Biology, 8 in Earth Science, 2 in Environmental Geography, 2 in Environmental Law, 3 in Environmental Quality and Public Health, 2 in Environmental Science, 2 in Forestry, and 2 in Resource Policy and Planning.

Tuition and Financial Aid

Tuition in 1996 was $4,431 per year for state residents and $8,670 for nonresidents. Some 21–40% of the graduate students in this program receive financial aid. Thirty percent of the master's students are awarded scholarships; 10% are awarded teaching assistantships.

Facilities

There is a library, with a computer center, available to graduate students. All facilities are handicapped accessible.

Career Counseling and Job Placement

This program does not offer student internships or career counseling and job placement services. Fifty percent of alumni work within the government sector, 20% for nonprofits, 20% for private small business, and 10% for corporations or industries; 80% of alumni work in the mid-Atlantic region, 5% in Washington, D.C., and 5% in international locations. Ninety percent of the students find work within six months of graduation.

OKLAHOMA STATE UNIVERSITY

With a total enrollment of 18,500 on its Stillwater campus, this land-grant institution was established in 1890 and is located on a 900-acre campus in the small town of Stillwater, near the geographic center of the United States. Stillwater is recognized nationally as one of the safest cities in the country.

☂ Zoology Program

FACULTY CONTACT:

Jerry Wilhm, Head
Department of Zoology
430 Life Sciences West
Oklahoma State University
Stillwater, OK 74078-0459

Phone: 405-744-5555
Fax: 405-744-7074

ADMISSIONS CONTACT:

The Graduate College
Oklahoma State University
Stillwater, OK 74078-0050

Phone: 405-744-6368

Department of Zoology Web site:
http://www.osu-ours.okstate.edu/gradcoll/dept/zoo.htm

Oklahoma State University Web site:
http://bubba.ucc.okstate.edu/indexold.html

Quick Facts About the Zoology Program

- Year established: 1945
- Enrollment: 38 master's students / 20 doctoral students
- Graduate degrees conferred: Master of Science, doctorate

- Master's degree requirements include: required courses, master's thesis, master's project, oral exam, special skills

- Doctoral degree requirements include: required courses, dissertation, qualifying exam, oral exam, special skills, public seminar, and final defense

- Faculty/Advisee ratio: 1:4

Areas of Specialization

Applied and Quantitative Ecology (60% of students)
Environmental Quality and Public Health (30%)
Conservation Biology (5%)
Environmental Science (5%)

Special Program Features

This program is best known for its emphasis on environmental toxicology and wildlife and fisheries ecology. Graduate students can cross-register for courses within other departments. Joint degree programs are offered with the Environmental Science program. International program experiences are not offered.

Admission to the Program

- Admission requirements for master's applicants include: 40 hours of biology; average GRE scores: 481 verbal/559 math

- Admission requirements for doctoral applicants include: master's degree; average GRE scores: 500 verbal/600 math

- Master's students accepted each year: 50% of 40 applicants

- Doctoral students accepted each year: 50% of 15 applicants

- Students may matriculate at the start of any term; transfer students are accepted.

About the Students

There are 40 male and 18 female graduate students currently enrolled in this program; 54 are full-time and 4 part-time; 4 are international and 54 domestic; 92% are Caucasian, 2% Hispanic, 2% Asian, and 4% Native American. Graduate students range from age 22 to 41, with a median age of 27.

About the Faculty

There are 15 faculty affiliated with this program. The average faculty member teaches 3 courses and advises 3 master's and 1 doctoral student per year. Students choose an advisory committee. Faculty research is currently being conducted both domestically and internationally. Seven faculty specialize in Applied and Quantitative Ecology, 3 in Conservation Biology, and 7 in Environmental Quality and Public Health.

Tuition and Financial Aid

Tuition in 1996 was $1,932 per year for state residents and $4,919 for non-residents. Over 60% of the graduate students in this program receive financial aid. All students are awarded teaching or research assistantships.

Facilities

Computer facilities include 8 IBM/clones, 1 Macintosh, one terminal per 6 students, a university computer center, student work stations, and access to Internet and E-mail. Free or low-cost computer training is available. One building, 3 classrooms, 36 laboratories, 1 library, and various museum collections are available to graduate students. Some facilities are handicapped accessible. The school also owns a lake, agricultural properties, agricultural research stations, and a cross timbers research area, which are available for student research.

Career Counseling and Job Placement

This program offers student internships or educational opportunities with the U.S. Fish and Wildlife Service Cooperation Research Unit and the Oklahoma Department of Wildlife Conservation. Career counseling and job placement services are not available. Sixty percent of alumni work within the government sector, 15% for private small business, and 25% in science or academia. Ninety-five percent of the students find work within six months of graduation.

☜ Other graduate environmental programs at Oklahoma State University (no profiles available):

Environmental Sciences Graduate Program. *Contact:* Gary Ostrander, Director, Oklahoma State University, Environmental Sciences Graduate Program, 002 Life Science East, Stillwater, OK 74078. *Phone:* 405-744-

9229 or 1-800-227-GRAD. *Fax:* 405-744-7673. *E-mail:* osuei@seic.lse. okstate.edu. *Web site:* http://www.osu-ours.okstate.edu/gradcoll/dept/ envsci.htm

Department of Forestry. *Contact:* Stephen Hallgren, Chairman, Graduate Committee. *Phone:* 405-744-6805. *Fax:* 405-744-9693.

OREGON GRADUATE INSTITUTE OF SCIENCE & TECHNOLOGY

Located 10 miles from downtown Portland, Oregon Graduate Institute of Science & Technology was established in 1965 and has a total enrollment of 400 graduate students.

☞ Environmental Science & Engineering Program

FACULTY CONTACT:

Dr. William Fish,
   Associate Professor
   Department of Environmental
   Science & Engineering
Oregon Graduate Institute of
   Science & Technology
19600 NW von Neumann Drive
Beaverton, OR 97006-1999

Phone: 503-690-1099
Fax: 503-690-1273

ADMISSIONS CONTACT:

Margaret Day
Director of Admissions and Records
Oregon Graduate Institute of
   Science & Technology
19600 NW von Neumann Drive
Beaverton, OR 97006-1999

Phone: 503-690-1028
Fax: 503-690-1029

Department of Environmental Science and Engineering Web site: http://www.ese.ogi.edu/

Oregon Graduate Institute of Science and Technology Web site: http://www.ogi.edu/welcome.html

Quick Facts About the Environmental Science & Engineering Program

- Year established: 1985
- Enrollment: 30 master's students / 30 doctoral students
- Graduate degrees conferred: Master of Science, doctorate

- Master's degree requirements include: required courses (45 credit hours), master's thesis for thesis program; 12-month non-thesis program is also available
- Doctoral degree requirements include: required courses, dissertation, work experience, qualifying exam, oral exam
- Faculty/Advisee ratio: 1:4

Areas of Specialization (no statistics available)

Applied and Quantitative Ecology
Earth Science
Environmental Science

Special Program Features

This program is best known for its emphasis on contaminant hydrology, environmental chemistry, and the global climate. Students may pursue M.S. and Ph.D. programs in (1) Environmental Science and Engineering and (2) Atmospheric Physics. Graduate students can cross-register for courses within other departments. Joint degree programs are offered with the Electrical Engineering & Applied Physics and Chemistry, and the Biology & Molecular Biology departments. International program experiences are available. Future program plans include more courses in air pollution and air quality.

Admission to the Program

- Admission requirements for master's applicants include: 2 semesters of chemistry, 1 of biology, 2+ of calculus, 2 of natural science, 2 of physical science; average GRE scores: 615 verbal/615 math
- Admission requirements for doctoral applicants include: average GRE scores: 640 verbal/645 math
- Master's students accepted each year: 56% of 65 applicants
- Doctoral students accepted each year: 2% of 75 applicants
- Students may matriculate only in the fall; transfer students are sometimes accepted.

About the Students

There are 35 male and 25 female graduate students currently enrolled in this program; 56 are full-time and 4 part-time; 14 are international and 46

domestic; 80% are Caucasian, 10% Asian, and 10% Native American. Graduate students range from age 26 to 35, with a median age of 28.

About the Faculty

There are 11 faculty affiliated with this program. The average faculty member teaches 3 courses and advises 1–2 master's and 3–4 doctoral students per year. Teams of advisors are assigned to students. Faculty research is currently being conducted both domestically and internationally. Three faculty specialize in Applied and Quantitative Ecology, 5 in Earth Science, 1 in Environmental Quality and Public Health, and 11 in Environmental Science.

Tuition and Financial Aid

Tuition in 1996 was $14,000 for the academic year. Some 41–60% of the graduate students in this program receive financial aid. All doctoral students are awarded teaching or research assistantships.

Facilities

Computer facilities include 6 IBM/clones, 5 Macintoshes, one terminal per 3 students, 10 Unix stations, 5 CPUs, and access to Internet and E-mail. Free or low-cost computer training is available. There are 7 buildings, 8 classrooms, 9 laboratories, and 2 libraries available to graduate students. Facilities are handicapped accessible. The school also owns property adjacent to campus, available for student research.

Career Counseling and Job Placement

Career counseling and job placement services include active alumni contact. Thirty percent of alumni work within the government sector, 30% for private small business, 15% for corporations or industries, and 15% in science or academia; 4% of alumni work in international locations. All students find work within six months of graduation.

OREGON STATE UNIVERSITY

Established in 1858, Oregon State University has a total enrollment of 14,340 students. Its setting is a 400-acre campus in the small city of Corvallis, in a region known for its mild climate.

☜ College of Forestry

CONTACT:

George Brown, Dean
College of Forestry
Oregon State University
Corvallis, OR 97331-5710

Phone: 503-737-2005
Fax: 503-737-2668

College of Forestry Web site: http://www.cof.orst.edu/

Oregon State University Web site: http://www.orst.edu/

Quick Facts About the College of Forestry

- Enrollment: 24 master's students / 14 doctoral students
- Graduate degrees conferred: Master of Science, Master of Forestry, doctorate
- Master's degree requirements include: required courses, master's thesis, master's project, oral exam
- Doctoral degree requirements include: required courses, dissertation, qualifying exam, oral exam
- Faculty/Advisee ratio: 2:3

Areas of Specialization

Resource Policy and Planning (24% of students)
Parks and Recreation Management (9%)
Environmental Geography (4%)
Forestry (4%)
Environmental Education (3%)
Applied and Quantitative Ecology (2%)

Special Program Features

This program is best known for its emphasis on forest policy and planning, and modeling. Graduate students can cross-register for courses within other departments. Joint degree programs are offered with the Forest Engineering and Forest Science Departments. International program experiences are not offered.

Admission to the Program

- Admission requirements for master's applicants include: average GRE scores: 530 verbal/610 math
- Admission requirements for doctoral applicants include: average GRE scores: 590 verbal/640 math
- Master's students accepted each year: 50% of 24 applicants
- Doctoral students accepted each year: 40% of 12 applicants
- Students may matriculate at the start of any term; transfer students are sometimes accepted.

About the Students

There are 25 male and 13 female graduate students currently enrolled in this program; 9 are international and 29 domestic; 98% are Caucasian and 2% Hispanic. Graduate students range from age 23 to 40, with a median age of 32.

About the Faculty

There are 22 faculty affiliated with this program. The average faculty member teaches 2 courses and advises 2 master's and 1.5 doctoral students per year. Advisors are assigned to students. Faculty research is currently being conducted both domestically and internationally. Two faculty specialize in Applied and Quantitative Ecology, 1 in Environmental Education, 3 in Environmental Geography, 2 in Forestry, 5 in Parks and Recreation Management, and 9 in Resource Policy and Planning.

Tuition and Financial Aid

Tuition in 1996 was $4,584 per year for state residents and $8,016 for nonresidents. Over 60% of the graduate students in this program receive financial aid. Twenty percent of the graduate students are awarded fellowships; all are awarded teaching or research assistantships.

Facilities

Computer facilities include 20 IBM/clones, one terminal per student, a 30-station teaching lab for GIS, extensive university-wide computer labs, four mainframe academic systems, four general-access computer facilities, and access to Internet and E-mail. Free or low-cost computer training is available. There are 3 buildings, 11 classrooms, 34 laboratories, 2 libraries, and various museum collections available to graduate students. Major facilities are handicapped accessible. The school also owns research forests, a coastal marine lab, a geology field camp, and a variety of rangelands and forests in several different ecoclimatic zones all over the state. A national estuarine sanctuary (at Coos Bay) is also available for student research.

Career Counseling and Job Placement

This program does not offer student internships. Career counseling and job placement services include job placement counselors, active alumni contact, on-campus interviews, job books, an alumni database, and job fairs. Twenty percent of alumni work within the government sector, 30% for private small business, 20% for corporations or industries, and 30% in science or academia; 50% of alumni work in the Pacific Northwest. All students find work within six months of graduation.

☜ Marine Resource Management Program

CONTACT:

Irma Delson
COAS Head Advisor and Coordinator
Marine Resource Management Program
College of Oceanic and Atmospheric Sciences (COAS)
Oregon State University
Corvallis, OR 97331-5503

Phone: 503-737-3504

College of Oceanic and Atmospheric Sciences Web site:
http://www.orst.edu/mc/coldep/oceatm/oceatm.htm

Quick Facts About the Marine Resource Management Program

- Year established: 1974
- Enrollment: 25 master's students
- Graduate degree conferred: Master of Science
- Master's degree requirements include: required courses; either master's thesis, master's project, or internship report; final seminar; and oral exam
- Faculty/Advisee ratio: 1:2

Special Program Features

Graduate students can cross-register for courses within other departments. Joint degree programs are offered in business and other areas. International program experiences include internships in Micronesia and other South and mid-Pacific nations. Future program plans include continual revision and improvement.

Admission to the Program

- Admission requirements for master's applicants include: 2 semesters of chemistry, 2 of calculus, 2 of physical science; average GRE scores above 80th percentile
- Master's students accepted each year: 35% of 45 applicants
- Students may matriculate at the start of any term; transfer students are rarely accepted.

About the Faculty

There are 15 faculty affiliated with this program. Advisors are assigned to or chosen by students.

Tuition and Financial Aid

Over 60% of the graduate students in this program receive financial aid. Master's students are rarely awarded fellowships or scholarships, but commonly receive research assistantships.

Career Counseling and Job Placement

This program offers student internships nationwide. Career counseling and job placement services are available at the university level and include job placement counselors and on-campus interviews. Alumni work in all sectors. All students find work within four months of graduation.

☂ Fisheries and Wildlife Program

CONTACT:
Charlotte Vickers
Administrative Specialist

Department of Fisheries and Wildlife
Oregon State University
Nash Hall 104
Corvalis, OR 97331-3803

Phone: 503-737-1941

Department of Fisheries and Wildlife Web site:
http://www.orst.edu/dept/fish_wild/

Quick Facts About the Fisheries and Wildlife Program

- Year established: 1934
- Enrollment: 56 master's students / 34 doctoral students
- Graduate degrees conferred: Master of Science, Master of Interdiscipli-
  nary Studies (MAIS–in Resource Management), Master of Agriculture
  (MAgr–in Aquaculture), doctorate
- Master's degree requirements include: required courses, master's thesis,
  master's project for MAIS and MAgr
- Doctoral degree requirements include: required courses, dissertation,
  qualifying exam, oral exam
- Faculty/Advisee ratio: 1:7

Areas of Specialization

Applied and Quantitative Ecology (95% of students)
Conservation Biology (5%)

Special Program Features

Graduate students can cross-register for courses within other departments.
Joint degree programs and international program experiences are not offered.

Admission to the Program

- Admission requirements for master's applicants include: 2 semesters of
  chemistry, 2 of biology, 1 of calculus, 2 of natural science, 2 of physical
  science; GRE scores
- Admission requirements for doctoral applicants include: master's degree;
  GRE scores

- Master's students accepted each year (on average): 12% of 90 applicants
- Doctoral students accepted each year (on average): 10% of 25 applicants
- Students may matriculate at the start of any term; transfer students are accepted.

About the Faculty

There are 19 faculty affiliated with this program.

Tuition and Financial Aid

Over 60% of the graduate students in this program receive financial aid. Five percent of the master's students are awarded scholarships, 95% are awarded teaching or research assistantships. All doctoral students are awarded teaching or research assistantships.

Career Counseling and Job Placement

This program does not offer student internships. Career counseling and job placement services include job placement counselors, active alumni contact, on-campus interviews, and job books. Eighty percent of alumni work within the government sector, 5% for private small business, and 5% in science or academia. Ninety percent of the students find work within six months of graduation.

☚ Geosciences Program

CONTACT:

Cyrus Field, Chair
Department of Geosciences, Geology and Geography Programs
Oregon State University
Wilkinson Hall 104
Corvallis, OR 97331-5506

Phone: 503-737-1219

Department of Geosciences, Geology and Geography Programs Web site:
http://www.orst.edu/dept/geosciences/

Quick Facts About the Geosciences Program

- Year established: 1934, Geology/1949, Geography/1989, Geosciences

- Enrollment: 50 master's students / 25 doctoral students
- Graduate degrees conferred: Master of Science, Master of Arts, doctorate
- Master's degree requirements include: required courses, master's thesis or master's project
- Doctoral degree requirements include: required courses, dissertation, qualifying exam, oral exam, an international language
- Faculty/Advisee ratio: 1:4

Special Program Features

This program is best known for its emphasis on resource geography, physical geography, and landscape ecology. Graduate students can cross-register for courses within other departments. Joint degree programs are offered, with Engineering, Forestry, and Agriculture as minors. International program experiences are not offered. Future program plans include additional hydrogeology courses.

Admission to the Program

- GRE scores are required of all graduate applicants; doctoral applicants require a master's degree
- Master's students accepted each year: 40% of 150 applicants
- Doctoral students accepted each year: 30% of 50 applicants
- Students may matriculate at the start of any term; transfer students are accepted.

About the Faculty

There are 25 faculty affiliated with this program.

Tuition and Financial Aid

Over 60% of the graduate students in this program receive financial aid. Twenty percent of the master's students are awarded scholarships; 80% are awarded teaching or research assistantships. Twenty percent of the doctoral students are awarded scholarships; 90% are awarded teaching or research assistantships.

Career Counseling and Job Placement

This program offers student internships. Career counseling and job placement services include active alumni contact, on-campus interviews, job books, and advisor assistance. Forty percent of alumni work within the government sector, 5% for semi-governmental organizations, 5% for nonprofits, 10% for private small business, 30% for corporations or industries, and 10% in science or academia; 50% of alumni work in the Pacific Northwest and 20% in international locations. Ninety-five percent of the students find work within six months of graduation.

☜ Rangeland Resources Program

CONTACT:

William Krueger, Head
Department of Rangeland Resources
Oregon State University
Strand Agricultural Hall 202
Corvallis, OR 97331-2218

Phone: 503-737-1615

Department of Rangeland Resources Web site:
http://ranger.range.orst.edu/

Quick Facts About the Rangeland Resources Program

- Year established: 1949
- Enrollment: 16 master's students / 8 doctoral students
- Graduate degrees conferred: Master of Science, Master of Agriculture, doctorate
- Master's degree requirements include: master's thesis, 8 hour written exam
- Doctoral degree requirements include: dissertation, oral exam, 40-hour written exam
- Faculty/Advisee ratio: 1:3

Areas of Specialization

Range Management (95%)

Special Program Features

Graduate students can cross-register for courses within other departments. Joint degree programs are not offered. International program experiences include student exchanges in Australia/New Zealand.

Admission to the Program

- GRE scores are not required
- Admission requirements for master's applicants include: a 3.0 GPA on the last 90 hours of undergraduate work
- Master's students accepted each year: 50% of 10 applicants
- Doctoral students accepted each year: 50% of 10 applicants
- Students may matriculate at the start of any term; transfer students are not accepted.

About the Faculty

There are 11 faculty affiliated with this program.

Tuition and Financial Aid

Over 60% of the graduate students in this program receive financial aid; 80% of the graduate students are awarded research assistantships.

Career Counseling and Job Placement

This program does not offer student internships or career counseling and job placement services. Thirty percent of alumni work within the government sector, 20% for private small business, and 50% in science or academia; 90% of alumni work in the Western region. Ninety percent of the students find work within six months of graduation.

PACE UNIVERSITY SCHOOL OF LAW

With a total enrollment of 836 students, Pace University Law School was established in 1976 and is located on a suburban campus in White Plains, New York.

☜ Environmental Law Program

FACULTY CONTACT:

William Slye
Director of Environmental
    Legal Studies
Environmental Law Program
Pace University School of Law
78 North Broadway
White Plains, NY 10603

Phone: 914-422-4201

ADMISSIONS CONTACT:

The Office of Admissions
Pace University School of Law
78 North Broadway
White Plains, NY 10603

Phone: 914-422-4210

Pace University Law School Web site: http://willy.law.pace.edu/

Quick Facts About the Environmental Law Program

- Year established: 1985
- Enrollment: 24 Master of Laws (L.LM.) students
- Graduate degree conferred: L.LM
- Master's degree requirements include: Master's thesis (optional); 24 credits, including 3 law review quality papers, and a B average
- Program director is the de facto advisor

Special Program Features

All students specialize in Environmental Law; graduate students can not cross-register for courses within other departments. Joint degree programs and international program experiences are not offered. Future program plans include offering a Doctor of Juridical Science (SJD) in environmental law, pending approval.

Admission to the Program

- Admission requirements for master's applicants include a Juris Doctorate degree; GRE scores are not required
- Master's students accepted each year: 90% of 70 applicants
- Students may matriculate only in the fall; transfer students are not accepted.

About the Faculty

There are 9 faculty affiliated with this program. Faculty research is currently being conducted internationally. All faculty specialize in Environmental Law.

Tuition and Financial Aid

Tuition in 1996 was $18,220 per year. Under 20% of the graduate students in this program receive financial aid. Two percent of the master's students are awarded fellowships; 5% are awarded research assistantships.

Facilities

IBM/clones and free or low-cost computer training are available. The West-chester library system is available to graduate students. Some facilities are handicapped accessible.

Career Counseling and Job Placement

This program does not offer student internships. Career counseling and job placement services include job placement counselors and on-campus interviews.

PORTLAND STATE UNIVERSITY

With a total enrollment of 11,500 students (over 3,000 of whom are graduate students), Portland State University is located in the environmentally progressive city of Portland, Oregon, known for its pleasant quality of life and innovative land-use strategies.

☚ Environmental Sciences and Resources Doctoral Program

FACULTY CONTACT:

Larry Crawshaw, Director
Environmental Sciences
   and Resources
College of Liberal Arts and Sciences
Portland State University

ADMISSIONS CONTACT:

Portland State University
Office of Admissions
P.O. Box 751
Portland, OR 97207-0751

P.O. Box 751
Portland, OR 97207-0751

Phone: 503-725-4980   *Phone:* 503-725-3511 or
                                                  800-547-8887, ext. 3511
Environmental Sciences and Resources Web site:
http://www.esr.pdx.edu/environ/esr.html#program

Quick Facts About the Environmental Sciences and Resources Doctoral Program

- Year established: 1969

- Graduate degree conferred: doctorate in environmental sciences and resources

- Doctoral degree requirements include: course work, dissertation, oral examination

Areas of Specialization

Biology
Chemistry
Civil Engineering
Geology
Physics

Special Program Features

All students enrolled in this program take a seminar and one-year course in environmental sciences and resources, followed by in-depth course work within the specific department in which they choose to specialize (see above list of Areas of Specialization). However, each dissertation committee is composed of faculty members from a range of departments.

About the Faculty

There are 50–60 faculty members associated with this program.

Facilities

Students enrolled in this program have access to approximately 6,000 square meters of research laboratories, as well as greenhouses, a herbarium, extensive research equipment, and computer facilities.

Tuition and Financial Aid

Tuition in 1996 was $4,584 per year. Most entering graduate students are supported by teaching assistantships, which usually require 15 hours per week of activity. Advanced graduate students generally receive research assistantships. Both types of assistantship result in a full tuition waiver.

PRESCOTT COLLEGE

Established in 1966, Prescott College has a total enrollment of 690 and is located near the center of the small town of Prescott, Arizona. Prescott provides a variety of off-campus field research areas.

☂ Master of Arts Program

CONTACT:

Joan Clingan
Master of Arts Program
Prescott College
220 Grove Avenue
Prescott, AZ 86301

Phone: 520-445-8048
Fax: 520-776-5137

Quick Facts About the Master of Arts Program

- Year established: 1991
- Enrollment: 86 master's students
- Graduate degree conferred: Master of Arts
- Master's degree requirements include: required courses, master's thesis, internship experience
- Faculty/Advisee ratio: 1:1

Areas of Specialization

Environmental Education (30% of students)
Environmental Studies (30%)
Applied and Quantitative Ecology (10%)

Botany (10%)
Resource Policy and Planning (10%)

Special Program Features

Graduate students can not cross-register for courses within other departments. Joint degree programs and international program experiences are not offered. Future program plans may include students self-designing their curriculum.

Admission to the Program

- Admission requirements for master's applicants include: course work in biology, natural science, and physical science equivalent to an undergraduate degree in the sciences; 2 years of work experience; GRE scores not required

- Master's students accepted each year (on average): 50% of 100 applicants

- Students may matriculate at the start of any term; transfer students are accepted.

About the Students

There are 38 male and 62 female graduate students currently enrolled in this program; 84 are full-time and 2 part-time; 2 are international and 84 domestic; 82% are Caucasian, 4% Black, 5% Hispanic, 8% Native American, and 1% Asian. Graduate students range from age 22 to 67, with a median age of 42.

About the Faculty

There are 61 adjunct professors affiliated with this program. The average professor advises 1 master's student per year. Academic research is currently being conducted both domestically and internationally. One professor specializes in Applied and Quantitative Ecology, 1 in Botany, 2 in Environmental Education, and 4 in Environmental Studies.

Tuition and Financial Aid

Tuition in 1996 was $7,360 per year. Over 60% of the graduate students in this program receive financial aid. Two percent of the master's students are awarded teaching assistantships.

Facilities

Computer facilities include access to Internet and E-mail. Free or low-cost computer training is available. There are 4 buildings, 9 classrooms, and various libraries available to graduate students. Facilities are handicapped accessible. The school also owns a 90-acre wilderness area, with petroglyphs, available for student research.

Career Counseling and Job Placement

This program does not offer career counseling and job placement services, but does assist with networking to facilitate student internships or educational opportunities within the local commmunity. Seventy-five percent of alumni work in Arizona; 100% work in the Southwest. All students find work within six months of graduation.

PRINCETON UNIVERSITY

Located in an attractive town of 30,000 in central New Jersey, Princeton University was established in 1746 and has a total enrollment of 6,400 students.

☛ Ecology and Evolutionary Biology Program

PROGRAM CONTACT:

Evelyn Wolfe,
    Administrative Assistant
Department of Ecology and
    Evolutionary Biology
Room 102, Guyot Hall
Princeton University
Princeton, NJ 08544-1003

Phone: 609-258-3977
Fax: 609-258-1712

ADMISSIONS CONTACT:

Office of Graduate Admission
Graduate School
Princeton University
P.O. Box 270
Princeton, NJ 08540

Phone: 609-258-3034

Department of Ecology and Evolutionary Biology Web site:
http://www.eeb.princeton.edu/index.html

Princeton University Web site: http://www.princeton.edu/

Quick Facts About the Ecology and Evolutionary Biology Program

- Enrollment: 30 doctoral students
- Graduate degrees conferred: Master of Arts, doctorate
- Master's degree requirements include: master's thesis; general exam makes student eligible for M.A.
- Doctoral degree requirements include: dissertation, oral exam
- Faculty/Advisee ratio: 1:1

Special Program Features

This program is best known for its strength in the areas of evolutionary ecology, behvioral ecology, theoretical ecology, population and community ecology, physiology, ecological and evolutionary genetics, molecular evolution, epidemiology of infectious diseases, and conservation biology. Graduate students can cross-register for courses within other departments. Joint degree programs are an option if students present an acceptable program of study. Future program plans include more courses in physiology.

Admission to the Program

- Admission requirements for master's applicants include: 2 semesters of chemistry, 2 of biology, 2 of calculus, 2 of natural science, 2 of physical science; GRE scores required
- Admission requirements for doctoral applicants include: average GRE scores: 600 verbal/600 math
- Doctoral students accepted each year (on average): 5% of 96 applicants
- Students may matriculate only in the fall; transfer students are not accepted.

About the Students

There are 19 male and 11 female graduate students currently enrolled in this program; all are full-time; 13 are international and 17 domestic.

About the Faculty

There are 17 faculty affiliated with this program. The average faculty member teaches 2 courses and advises 2 master's and 3 doctoral students per

year. Advisors are both assigned to and chosen by students. Faculty research is currently being conducted both domestically and internationally. Two faculty specialize in Applied and Quantitative Ecology, 1 in Botany, 2 in Conservation Biology, 1 in Earth Science, 1 in Environmental Studies, 1 in Forestry, and 4 in Social Ecology; 5 are Behaviorists.

Tuition and Financial Aid

Tuition in 1996 was $21,640 for the academic year. Over 60% of the graduate students in this program receive financial aid. Ninety percent of the doctoral students are awarded fellowships, 80% are awarded research assistantships, and 10% receive outside awards.

Facilities

Computer facilities include access to Internet and E-mail. Free or low-cost computer training is available. There are 2 buildings, 4 classrooms, 3 laboratories, and 2 libraries available to graduate students. Facilities are handicapped accessible. The school also owns a 99-acre natural state fallow farm that is available for student research.

Career Counseling and Job Placement

This program does not offer student internships or career counseling and job placement services, although some on-campus interviews are provided by others. Twenty-five percent of alumni work within the government sector and 75% in science or academia. Eighty percent of the students find work within six months of graduation.

☛ Other graduate environmental programs at Princeton University (no profiles available):

Program in Science, Technology & Public Policy, Environmental Policy Concentration. *Contact:* Henry Bienen, Dean, Princeton, NJ 08544-1013. *Web site:* http://www.wws.princeton.edu/programs/stpp.html

PURDUE UNIVERSITY

Located on a 650-acre campus in the small city of West Lafayette, Indiana, Purdue University was established in 1869 and has a total enrollment of 40,940 students.

☜ Forestry and Natural Resources Program

FACULTY CONTACT:

Carl Eckelman
Chair, Graduate Committee
Department of Forestry and
 Natural Resources
Purdue University
1159 Forestry Building
West Lafayette, IN 47907-1159

ADMISSIONS CONTACT:

Director of Graduate Admissions
Department of Forestry and
 Natural Resources
Purdue University
West Lafayette, IN 47907-1159

Phone: 317-494-3640

Phone: 317-494-3640

Department of Forestry and Natural Resources Web site:
http://omni.cc.purdue.edu/~fnr/

Purdue University Web site: http://www.purdue.edu/

Quick Facts About the Forestry and Natural Resources Program

- Year established: 1914
- Enrollment: 39 master's students / 32 doctoral students
- Graduate degrees conferred: Master of Science, Master of Science in Forestry, doctorate
- Master's degree requirements include: required courses, master's thesis, final exam
- Doctoral degree requirements include: required courses, dissertation, qualifying exam (prelim), oral exam (final)

Areas of Specialization

Applied and Quantitative Ecology (36 students)
Parks and Recreation Management (12)
Wood Science (11)
Environmental Geography (5)
Resource Policy and Planning (3)
Forestry (1)
Forest Biometrics (1)

Special Program Features

Graduate students can cross-register for courses within other departments.

Admission to the Program

- Admission requirements for master's applicants include: 2 semesters of chemistry, 2 of biology, 2 of calculus (all depending upon subject area); average GRE scores: 500 verbal/500 math
- Admission requirements for doctoral applicants include: master's degree; average GRE scores: 500 verbal/500 math
- Students may matriculate at the start of any term; transfer students are accepted.

About the Students

There are 47 male and 24 female graduate students currently enrolled in this program; 67 are full-time and 4 part-time; 26 are international and 45 domestic.

About the Faculty

There are 22 faculty affiliated with this program. Advisors are both assigned to and chosen by students. Twelve faculty specialize in Applied and Quantitative Ecology, 2 in Environmental Geography, 2 in Parks and Recreation Management, 2 in Resource Policy and Planning, and 4 in Wood Science.

Tuition and Financial Aid

Tuition in 1996 was $3,056 per year for state residents and $10,128 for non-residents. Teaching and research assistantships are available on a competitive basis.

Facilities

This program has computer facilities and property available for student research.

☛ Other graduate environmental programs at Purdue University (no profiles available):

Department of Earth and Atmospheric Science. *Contact:* E. Agee, Head.
GIS and Remote Sensing Program. *Contact:* C. Johannsen.
Program in Environmental and Population Biology. *Contact:* L. Sherman.
Water Resources Program. *Contact:* J. Wright.

RENSSELAER POLYTECHNIC INSTITUTE

Established in 1824, Rensselaer Polytechnic Institute (also known as RPI) has a total enrollment of 6,300 students. Its setting is a 260-acre hillside campus in the mid-sized city of Troy, New York.

☎ Environmental Management & Policy Program

FACULTY CONTACT:

Bruce Piasecki, Director
Environmental Management
    & Policy
Russell Sage Laboratory
Rensselaer Polytechnic Institute
Sage Hall, 2502-A
Troy, NY 12180-3950

Phone: 518-276-6565

ADMISSIONS CONTACT:

Director of Graduate Admissions
Graduate Center
Rensselaer Polytechnic Institute
Troy, NY 12180-3590

Phone: 518-276-6789

Rensselaer Polytechnic Institute Web site: http://www.rpi.edu/

Quick Facts About the Environmental Management & Policy Program

- Year established: 1990
- Enrollment: 25 master's students
- Graduate degrees conferred: Master of Science, doctorate
- Master's degree requirements include: internship experience, 4 core classes plus distribution requirements
- Doctoral degree requirements include: dissertation, qualifying exam
- Faculty/Advisee ratio: 1:12

Areas of Specialization

Corporate Environmental Management (70% of students)
Environmental Quality and Public Health (20%)

Special Program Features

This program is best known for its emphasis on the integration of managerial and technical competencies. Graduate students can cross-register for courses within other departments. Joint degree programs are offered with the Business School. International program experiences are not offered. Future program plans include increased availability in course work developed specifically for the program, plus increased research funding in intellectual products.

Admission to the Program

- GRE scores are required for all graduate students
- Admission requirements for master's applicants include: 2 semesters of chemistry, 1 of biology, 2 of calculus, 2 of economics, 2 of physical science, 4 of social science
- Master's students accepted each year (on average): 25% of 90 applicants
- Doctoral students accepted each year (on average): 20% of 10 applicants
- Students may matriculate at the start of any term; transfer students are accepted.

About the Students

There are 18 male and 7 female graduate students currently enrolled in this program; 15 are full-time and 10 part-time; 3 are international and 22 domestic; 98% are Caucasian and 2% Asian. Graduate students range from age 22 to 56, with a median age of 27.

About the Faculty

There are 30 faculty affiliated with this program. The average faculty member teaches 3 courses and advises 12 master's and 4 doctoral students per year. Students receive course and professional advice from the director and assistant director. Faculty research is currently being conducted domestically. Two faculty specialize in Applied and Quantitative Ecology, 2 in Botany, 2 in Conservation Biology, 6 in Corporate Environmental Management, 4 in Earth Science, 1 in Environmental Education, 1 in Environmental Law, 6 in Environmental Quality and Public Health, 2 in Environmental Science, 3 in Environmental Studies, and 3 in Resource Policy and Planning.

Tuition and Financial Aid

Tuition in 1996 was $540 per credit hour. Some 21–40% of the graduate students in this program receive financial aid. Some master's students are awarded tuition waivers. Seventy-five percent of the doctoral students are awarded research assistantships.

Facilities

Computer facilities include 150 IBM/clones, 45 Macintoshes, one terminal per 20 students, and access to Internet and E-mail. The university has 2 mainframe systems with about 60 terminals, plus a networked system of mincomputers with about 200 terminals. Free or low-cost computer training is available. There are 17 buildings, 400 classrooms, 60 laboratories, and 15 libraries available to graduate students. All facilities are handicapped accessible. The school also owns a 100-acre managed woodlot that is available for student research.

Career Counseling and Job Placement

This program requires a 6-credit, 1 term, 250-hour minimum applied internship experience in a managerial, industrial, nonprofit, or agency setting. Career counseling and job placement services include job placement counselors, active alumni contact, job books, and an alumni database. Seventy percent of alumni work within the government sector, 10% for semi-governmental organizations, 10% for nonprofits, 30% for private small business, and 20% for corporations or industries; 70% of alumni work in the mid-Atlantic region and 10% in Washington, D.C. Ninety percent of the students find work within six months of graduation.

☏ Environmental Engineering Program

CONTACT:

Dr. Simeon Kumisar
Assistant Professor
Department of Civil and Environmental Engineering
Rensselaer Polytechnic Institute
Troy, NY 12180

Phone: 518-276-4893

This program is part of the broader Environmental Studies Program, which includes three separate majors. Please refer to the Environmental Studies Program Web site: http://www.rpi.edu/dept/environ/www/index.html

Quick Facts About the Environmental Engineering Program

- Year established: 1958
- Enrollment: 50 master's students / 5 doctoral students

- Graduate degrees conferred: Master of Science, Master of Engineering (M.Eng.), doctorate
- Master's degree requirements include: required courses, master's thesis for M.S., master's project for M.Eng.
- Doctoral degree requirements include: required courses, dissertation, qualifying exam, oral exam
- Faculty/Advisee ratio: 1:5

Special Program Features

This program is best known for its emphasis on bioremediation, aquatic plant management, and water treatment. Graduate students can cross-register for courses within other departments. Joint degree programs and international program experiences are not offered. Future program plans include a joint thrust with environmental management and environmental science.

Admission to the Program

- Admission requirements for master's applicants include: 4 semesters of chemistry, 1 of biology, 4 of calculus, 2 of natural science, 4 of physical science; average GRE scores: 560 verbal/650 math
- Admission requirements for doctoral applicants include: master's degree; average GRE scores: 600 verbal/750 math
- Master's students accepted each year (on average): 25% of 80 applicants
- Doctoral students accepted each year (on average): 2–5% of 50 applicants
- Students may matriculate at the start of any term; transfer students are sometimes accepted.

About the Students

There are 30 male and 25 female graduate students currently enrolled in this program; 15 are full-time and 40 part-time; 7 are international and 43 domestic; 73% are Caucasian, 2% Black, and 25% Asian. Graduate students range from age 23 to 45, with a median age of 30.

About the Faculty

There are 4 faculty affiliated with this program. The average faculty member teaches 3 courses and advises 5 master's and 1 doctoral students per year. Faculty research is currently being conducted both domestically and internationally.

Tuition and Financial Aid

Tuition in 1994 was $1,500. Some 41–60% of the graduate students in this program receive financial aid. Ten percent of the master's students are awarded fellowships, and 40% are awarded teaching or research assistantships. Fifty percent of the doctoral students are awarded teaching assistantships, and 50% research assistantships.

Career Counseling and Job Placement

This program's internships are student-driven. Career counseling and job placement services include job placement counselors, active alumni contact, on-campus interviews, job books, an alumni database, job fairs, and contact with professional societies. Thirty percent of alumni work within the government sector, 40% for private small business, 25% for corporations or industries, and 5% in science or academia. All students find work within six months of graduation.

☛ Other graduate environmental programs at Rensselaer Polytechnic Institute (no profiles available):

Department of Earth and Environmental Sciences. *Contact:* E. Bruce Watson, Chair. *Phone:* 518-276-6474.

RICE UNIVERSITY

Located on an urban campus in the city of Houston, Texas, Rice University was established in 1891 and has a total enrollment of 3,700 students.

☛ Environmental Science & Engineering Program

PROGRAM CONTACT: ADMISSIONS CONTACT:
Vicky Wynne, Department Secretary   Rice University

Department of Environmental
    Science & Engineering
Rice University
P.O. Box 1891
Houston, TX 77251-1891

Department of Environmental
    Science & Engineering
Graduate Admissions
P.O. Box 1892
Houston, TX 77251-1892

Phone: 713-527-4951
Fax: 713-285-5203
E-mail: ENVI@rice.edu

Department of Environmental Science and Engineering Web site:
http://www.ruf.rice.edu/~envi/

Rice University Web site: http://www.rice.edu/

Quick Facts About the Environmental Science & Engineering Program

- Year established: 1967
- Enrollment: 18 master's students / 15 doctoral students
- Graduate degrees conferred: Master of Science, Master of Electrical Engineering (M.EE), Master of Environmental Science (M.ES), doctorate
- Master's degree requirements include: required courses, master's thesis (not required for M.ES and M.EE degrees)
- Doctoral degree requirements include: required courses, dissertation, qualifying exam, oral exam
- Faculty/Advisee ratio: 1:6

Areas of Specialization

Environmental Engineering (60% of students)
Environmental Science (40%)

Special Program Features

This program is best known for its emphasis on membrane technologies, groundwater modeling, and bioremediation. Graduate students can cross-register for courses within other departments. Joint degree programs are offered with the Business School. International program experiences include research opportunities and student exchanges in Western Europe. Future program plans include the addition of another faculty member or two within the next several years to broaden the scope of the program.

Admission to the Program

- Admission requirements for master's applicants include: 2 semesters of chemistry, 4 of calculus, 2 of physical science; course work in fluid mechanics and computer science is very helpful; average GRE scores: 580 verbal/730 math/650 analytical

- Admission requirements for doctoral applicants include: master's degree; average GRE scores: 620 verbal/750 math/670 analytical

- Master's students accepted each year (on average): 11% of 180 applicants

- Doctoral students accepted each year (on average): 11% of 60 applicants

- Students may matriculate usually only in the fall; transfer students are not accepted.

About the Students

There are 16 male and 17 female graduate students currently enrolled in this program; all are full-time; 7 are international and 26 domestic; 59% are Caucasian, 6% Black, 6% Hispanic, and 13% Asian. Graduate students range from age 22 to 43, with a median age of 28.

About the Faculty

There are 7 faculty affiliated with this program. The average faculty member teaches 3 courses and advises 3 master's and 3 doctoral students per year. Faculty advisors choose their students. Faculty research is currently being conducted both domestically and internationally. One faculty member specializes in Earth Science, 1 in Environmental Law, 2 in Environmental Science, 1 in Groundwater Hydrology, 1 in Physical/Chemical Processes, and 1 in Biological Process Engineering.

Tuition and Financial Aid

Tuition in 1996 was $12,300 per year. Over 60% of the graduate students in this program receive financial aid (with the exception of M.ES and M.EE candidates). Ninety-five percent of the master's students are awarded research assistantships. Sixteen percent of the doctoral students are awarded scholarships, and 100% are awarded research assistantships.

Facilities

Computer facilities include 6 IBM/clones, 15 Macintoshes, 2 terminals per 3 students, a computer center, 3 Sun/SPARC workstations, and access to

Internet and E-mail. Free or low-cost computer training is available. There are 2 buildings, 2 classrooms, 5 laboratories, and libraries available to graduate students. Facilities are handicapped accessible.

Career Counseling and Job Placement

This program does not offer student internships. Career counseling and job placement services include job placement counselors, active alumni contact, on-campus interviews, job books, an alumni database, and job fairs. Seven and one-half percent of alumni work within the government sector, 7.5% for semi-governmental organizations, 2.5% for nonprofits, 32.5% for private small business, 32.5% for corporations or industries, and 17.5% in science or academia; 57% of alumni work in Texas, 20% in the New England area, and 7.5% in international locations. Ninety-five percent of the students find work within six months of graduation.

ROWAN COLLEGE OF NEW JERSEY

Established in 1923, Rowan College of New Jersey (formerly Glassboro State College) has a total enrollment of 9,855 students. Its setting is a 200-acre campus in the small town of Glassboro.

🎓 Graduate Program in Environmental Education & Conservation

FACULTY CONTACT:

Frank Gary Patterson, Program Advisor
Graduate Program in Environmental
  Education & Conservation
Rowan College of New Jersey
Glassboro, NJ 08028

ADMISSIONS CONTACT:

Office of Graduate Studies
Rowan College of New Jersey
201 Mullica Hill Road
Glassboro, NJ 08028-1701

Phone: 609-256-4500, ext. 3587

Rowan College of New Jersey Web site: http://www.rowan.edu/

Quick Facts About the Graduate Program in Environmental Education & Conservation

• Year established: 1966

- Enrollment: 68 master's students
- Graduate degree conferred: Master of Arts
- Master's degree requirements include: required courses, master's thesis
- Faculty/Advisee ratio: 1:50

Areas of Specialization

Environmental Studies (100% of students)
Environmental Education (50%)
Applied and Quantitative Ecology (25%)
Resource Policy and Planning (15%)
Environmental Law (5%)
Environmental Quality and Public Health (5%)

Special Program Features

This program is best known for its emphasis on environmental education and program development. Graduate students can cross-register for courses within other departments. Joint degree programs are offered with the School of Education. International program experiences are not offered. Future program plans include new courses in environmental science and a Ph.D. in Environmental Studies.

Admission to the Program

- Admission requirements for master's applicants include: a bachelor's degree; average GRE scores: 460 verbal/510 math
- Master's students accepted each year (on average): 95% of 15–20 applicants
- Students may matriculate at the start of any term; transfer students are accepted.

About the Students

There are 32 male and 36 female graduate students currently enrolled in this program; 6 are full-time and 62 part-time; none are international; 90% are Caucasian, 5% Hispanic, and 5% Asian. Graduate students range from age 22 to 62, with a median age of 34.

About the Faculty

This is an interdisciplinary program, with numerous classes offered by many faculty in different college departments. The average faculty member teaches 8 courses and advises 10–15 master's students per year. Faculty research is currently being conducted domestically.

Tuition and Financial Aid

Tuition in 1996 was $3,935 per year for state residents and $6,240 for non-residents. Under 20% of the graduate students in this program receive financial aid; 5% of the master's students are awarded fellowships.

Facilities

Computer facilities include computer rooms in each classroom building and dormitory, with 25 computers per room. Free or low-cost computer training is available. There are 2 libraries available to graduate students. Facilities are handicapped accessible. The school also sponsors the Pinelands Institute for Natural and Environmental Studies (PINES), a field center for environmental education in Lebanon State Forest.

Career Counseling and Job Placement

This program offers student internships within the local commmunity. Career counseling and job placement services include active alumni contact. Twenty percent of alumni work within the government sector, 10% for nonprofits, 5% for private small business, 5% for corporations or industries, and 60% in science or academia; 80% of alumni work in New Jersey and 5% in international locations. Most students are already employed prior to graduation.

RUTGERS, THE STATE UNIVERSITY OF NEW JERSEY

Established in 1766, Rutgers University has a total enrollment of 47,000 students on three campuses. Its main campus is located in the city of New Brunswick, New Jersey.

☜ Geography Graduate Program

FACULTY CONTACT:

Dr. David A. Robinson, Director
Geography Graduate Program
Rutgers University
P.O. Box 5053
New Brunswick, NJ 08903-5053

Phone: 908-932-4741

ADMISSIONS CONTACT:

Office of Graduate
  and Professional Admissions
Rutgers University
Van Nest Hall
New Brunswick, NJ 08903

Phone: 908-932-7711

Geography Graduate Program Web site:
http://climate.rutgers.edu/geography/

Rutgers University Web site:
http://www.rutgers.edu/

Quick Facts About the Geography Graduate Program

- Year established: 1955
- Enrollment: 20 master's students / 30 doctoral students
- Graduate degrees conferred: Master of Science, Master of Arts, doctorate
- Master's degree requirements include: one required course; master's thesis and non-thesis options available
- Doctoral degree requirements include: required courses, dissertation, qualifying exam, oral exam
- Faculty/Advisee ratio: 1:3

Areas of Specialization

Resource Policy and Planning (20% of students)
Environmental Geography (16%)
Earth Science (14%)
Applied and Quantitative Ecology (10%)
Environmental Education (10%)
Environmental Quality and Public Health (8%)

Special Program Features

This program is best known for its emphasis on remote sensing, GIS, hazards, and urban environments. Graduate students can cross-register for courses within other departments. Joint degree programs and international program experiences are not offered. Future program plans include more emphasis on society/environment issues.

Admission to the Program

- GRE scores are required of all graduate applicants
- Students may matriculate only in the fall; transfer students are accepted.

About the Students

There are 24 male and 26 female graduate students currently enrolled in this program; 27 are full-time and 23 part-time; 12 are international and 38 domestic; 80% are Caucasian, 4% Black, 6% Hispanic, and 10% Asian. Graduate students range from age 23 to 47, with a median age of 30.

About the Faculty

There are 23 faculty affiliated with this program. The average faculty member teaches 0.5 courses and advises 1 master's and 1.5 doctoral students per year. Faculty research is currently being conducted both domestically and internationally. Two faculty specialize in Marine Ecology, 7 in Earth Science, 1 in Environmental Education, 3 in Environmental Geography, 3 in Risk Assessment, and 7 in Urban and Regional Planning.

Tuition and Financial Aid

Tuition in 1996 was $5,389 per year for state residents and $7,899 for nonresidents. Some 41–60% of the graduate students in this program receive financial aid. Twenty percent of the master's students are awarded teaching or research assistantships. Twenty-five percent of the doctoral students are awarded fellowships, 10% are awarded scholarships, and 40% are awarded teaching or research assistantships.

Facilities

Computer facilities include access to Internet and E-mail. Free or low-cost computer training is available. One main building, numerous classrooms, 4 laboratories, and 4 libraries are available to graduate students. All facilities are handicapped accessible. The school also owns numerous sites statewide that are available for student research.

Career Counseling and Job Placement

This program does not offer student internships or career counseling and job placement services. Forty percent of alumni work within the government sector, 5% for semi-governmental organizations, 5% for nonprofits, 15% for private small business, 10% for corporations or industries, and 25% in science or academia; 60% of alumni work in the mid-Atlantic region, 5% in Washington, D.C., and 10% in international locations. Ninety-five percent of the students find work within six months of graduation.

☜ Environmental Sciences Program

CONTACT:

Alan Appleby, Program Director
Graduate Program in Environmental Sciences
Department of Environmental Sciences
Rutgers University
New Brunswick, NJ 08903-0231

Phone: 908-932-9185

Department of Environmental Sciences Web site:
http://snowfall.rutgers.edu

Quick Facts About the Environmental Sciences Program

- Year established: 1920
- Enrollment: 103 master's students / 99 doctoral students
- Graduate degrees conferred: Master of Science, doctorate
- Master's degree requirements include: required courses, master's project
- Doctoral degree requirements include: required courses, dissertation, qualifying exam, oral exam, research thesis
- Faculty/Advisee ratio: 1:3

Areas of Specialization

Environmental Quality and Public Health (35% of students)
Earth Science (32%)
Environmental Law (3%)
Environmental Chemistry (15%)
Radiation Science (15%)

Special Program Features

Graduate students can cross-register for courses within other departments. Joint degree programs are offered with the Medical School. International program experiences are not offered. Future program plans include a 30–50% increase in faculty over the next 3 years.

Admission to the Program

- Average GRE scores of 650 verbal/650 math required of all graduate applicants
- Admission requirements for master's applicants include: 2 semesters of chemistry, 2 of biology, 2 of calculus
- Master's students accepted each year (on average): 25% of 80 applicants
- Doctoral students accepted each year (on average): 25% of 40 applicants
- Students may matriculate at the start of any term; transfer students are accepted.

About the Students

There are 101 male and 101 female graduate students currently enrolled in this program; 85 are full-time and 127 part-time.

About the Faculty

There are 43 faculty affiliated with this program. The average faculty member teaches 3 courses and advises 3 master's and 2 doctoral students per year. Advisors are both assigned to and chosen by students.

Tuition and Financial Aid

Under 20% of the graduate students in this program receive financial aid. Two percent of the master's students are awarded teaching assistantships, and 25% of the doctoral students are awarded research assistantships.

Career Counseling and Job Placement

Student internships in some option areas are required; these may be satisfied at local hospitals, industries, or national labs. Career counseling and job placement services are not offered. Thirty percent of alumni work within the government sector, 10% for private small business, 40% for corporations or industries, and 20% in science or academia. All students find work within six months of graduation.

☜ Ecology and Evolution Program

CONTACT:

Thomas Meagher, Director
Graduate Program in Ecology and Evolution
Nelson Biological Laboratories
Rutgers University
P.O. Box 1059
Piscataway, NJ 08855-1059

Phone: 908-445-2077

Quick Facts About the Ecology and Evolution Program

- Year established: 1985
- Graduate degrees conferred: Master of Science, Master of Arts, doctorate
- Master's degree requirements include: required courses, master's thesis
- Doctoral degree requirements include: required courses, dissertation, qualifying exam, oral exam
- Faculty/Advisee ratio: 1:1

Areas of Specialization

Applied and Quantitative Ecology (40% of students)
Molecular Evolution, Population Genetics, and Evolution (40%)
Conservation Biology (20%)

Special Program Features

This program is best known for its emphasis on plant ecology, population genetics, ornithology, and marine sciences. Graduate students can cross-register for courses within other departments. Joint degree programs are not offered.

Admission to the Program

GRE scores are required of all graduate applicants.

About the Faculty

There are 62 faculty affiliated with this program. The average faculty member teaches 2 courses and advises 2 master's and 1 doctoral students per year. Advisors are both assigned to and chosen by students.

Career Counseling and Job Placement

This program does not offer student internships or career counseling and job placement services. Ten percent of alumni work within the government sector, 5% for nonprofits, 10% for corporations or industries, and 75% in science or academia. Ninety percent of the students find work within six months of graduation.

SONOMA STATE UNIVERSITY

Located in the wine country north of San Francisco, Sonoma State University has a total enrollment of 6,611 students.

☞ Biology Program

FACULTY CONTACT:

John Hopkirk, Graduate Coordinator
Department of Biology
Sonoma State University
1801 E. Cotati Avenue
Rohnert Park, CA 94928-3609

Phone: 707-664-2189

ADMISSIONS CONTACT:

Office of Admissions and Records
Sonoma State University
1801 E. Cotati Avenue
Rohnert Park, CA 94928-3609

Phone: 707-664-2SSU

Department of Biology Web site: http://www.sonoma.edu/biology/

Sonoma State University Web site: http://www.sonoma.edu/

Quick Facts About the Biology Program

- Year established: 1962
- Enrollment: 40 master's students
- Graduate degree conferred: Master of Arts
- Master's degree requirements include: required courses, master's thesis, oral exam, thesis defense
- Faculty/Advisee ratio: 1:4

Areas of Specialization

Applied and Quantitative Ecology (30% of students)
Botany (20%)
Conservation Biology (10%)
Environmental Quality and Public Health (10%)
Environmental Science (10%)
Environmental Studies (10%)

Special Program Features

This program is best known for its emphasis on marine biology. Graduate students can cross-register for courses within other departments. Joint degree programs and international program experiences are not offered. Faculty retirements are expected within the next few years.

Admission to the Program

- Admission requirements for master's applicants include: 3 semesters of chemistry, 8 of biology, 1 of physical science, GRE scores required
- Master's students accepted each year (on average): 50% of 20 applicants
- Students may matriculate at the start of any term; transfer students are not accepted.

About the Students

There are 15 male and 25 female graduate students currently enrolled in this program; 20 are full-time and 20 part-time; 80% are Caucasian, 10% Hispanic, and 10% Native American. Graduate students range from age 22 to 53, with a median age of 27.

About the Faculty

There are 13 faculty affiliated with this program. The average faculty member advises 2 master's students per year. Students choose their faculty advisors. Faculty research is currently being conducted domestically. Eight faculty specialize in Applied and Quantitative Ecology, 2 in Botany, and 1 in Environmental Science.

Tuition and Financial Aid

Tuition in 1996 was $0 (plus fees) per year for state residents and $246 per credit for nonresidents. Some 21–40% of the graduate students in this program receive financial aid. Forty percent of the master's students are awarded teaching assistantships.

Facilities

Computer facilities include 48 Macintoshes, one GIS computer, and access to Internet and E-mail. Free or low-cost computer training is available. One building, 10 classrooms, 8 laboratories, and 1 library areavailable to graduate students. Facilities are handicapped accessible. The school also owns a biological preserve that is available for student research.

Career Counseling and Job Placement

This program does not offer student internships or career counseling and job placement services. Forty percent of alumni work within the government sector, 20% for nonprofits, 20% for private small business, and 20% in science or academia. All students find work within six months of graduation.

SOUTHERN ILLINOIS UNIVERSITY AT CARBONDALE

With a total enrollment of 24,000 students, Southern Illinois University was established in 1869. It is located on a 4,000-acre campus within the small city of Carbondale.

☚ Department of Forestry

FACULTY CONTACT:

Dwight McCurdy, Chair
Department of Forestry
Southern Illinois University
   at Carbondale
Carbondale, IL 62901-4411

Phone: 618-453-3341
Fax: 618-453-4562

ADMISSIONS CONTACT:

Graduate School
Southern Illinois University
   at Carbondale
Carbondale, IL 62901-4716

Phone: 618-536-7791

Southern Illinois University Web site: http://www.siu.edu/

Quick Facts About the Department of Forestry
• Year established: 1957

- Enrollment: 30 master's students
- Graduate degrees conferred: Master of Science
- Master's degree requirements include: required courses (statistics, research methods), master's thesis
- Faculty/Advisee ratio: 1:3

Areas of Specialization (no statistics available)

Applied and Quantitative Ecology
Environmental Geography
Environmental Studies
Forestry
Resource Policy and Planning;

Special Program Features

Graduate students can cross-register for courses within other departments. Joint degree programs and international program experiences are not offered.

Admission to the Program

- Master's students accepted each year (on average): 50% of 60 applicants
- Students may matriculate at the start of any term; transfer students are accepted.

About the Students

There are 17 male and 13 female graduate students currently enrolled in this program; all are full-time; 5 are international and 25 domestic.

About the Faculty

There are 11 faculty affiliated with this program. The average faculty member teaches 4 courses and advises 3 master's students per year. Students choose their faculty advisors. Faculty research is currently being conducted both domestically and internationally. Eleven faculty specialize in Applied and Quantitative Ecology, 2 in Botany, 1 in Earth Science, 1 in Environmental Education, 2 in Environmental Geography, 11 in Environmental Studies, 11 in Forestry, 9 in Parks and Recreation Management, and 3 in Resource Policy and Planning.

Tuition and Financial Aid

Tuition in 1996 was $1,920 per year for state residents and $5,760 for non-residents. Over 60% of the graduate students in this program receive financial aid. All master's students are awarded teaching or research assistantships.

Career Counseling and Job Placement

Career counseling and job placement services include job placement counselors, active alumni contact, on-campus interviews, job books, and job fairs. Sixty percent of alumni work within the government sector and 40% in science or academia. All students find work within six months of graduation.

☛ Other graduate environmental programs at Southern Illinois University at Carbondale (no profiles available):

Department of Curriculum and Instruction/Environmental Education. *Contact:* Trudi Volk. *Phone:* 618-453-4214.

SOUTHERN OREGON STATE COLLEGE

Located in the small, agricultural community of Ashland, Southern Oregon State College has a total enrollment of 4,480 students.

☛ Program in Environmental Education

FACULTY CONTACT:

Stewart Janes, Associate
  Biology Professor
Environmental Education Program
Southern Oregon State College
1250 Siskiyou Boulevard
Ashland, OR 97520

Phone: 503-552-6797

ADMISSIONS CONTACT:

Office of Admissions
Southern Oregon State College
1250 Siskiyou Boulevard
Ashland, OR 97520-5032

Phone: 503-552-6411

Program in Environmental Education Web site:
http://www.sosc.osshe.edu/biology/enveduc.htm

Southern Oregon State College Web site: http://www.sosc.osshe.edu/

Quick Facts About the Program in Environmental Education

- Year established: 1990
- Enrollment: 20 master's students
- Graduate degree conferred: Master of Science
- Master's degree requirements include: required courses
- Faculty/Advisee ratio: 1:10

Areas of Specialization

Applied and Quantitative Ecology (70% of students)
Teaching and other areas (30%)

Special Program Features

This program is best known for its emphasis on field courses. Graduate students can cross-register for courses within other departments. Joint degree programs and international program experiences are not offered. Future program plans include a self-sustaining summer program.

Admission to the Program

- Admission requirements for master's applicants include: 18 quarter hours of natural science, GRE scores
- Master's students accepted each year (on average): 100% of 20 applicants
- Students may matriculate at the start of any term; transfer students are not accepted.

About the Students

There are 10 male and 10 female graduate students currently enrolled in this program; 10 are full-time and 10 part-time; none are international; 90% are Caucasian, 2% Black, 2% Hispanic, 2% Native American, and 2% Asian. Graduate students range from age 25 to 45, with a median age of 35.

About the Faculty

There are 2 faculty affiliated with this program. The average faculty member teaches 6–9 courses and advises 2 master's students per year. Advisors are assigned to students. Faculty research is currently being conducted domestically. One faculty member specializes in Applied and Quantitative Ecology, and 1 in Science Education.

Tuition and Financial Aid

Tuition in 1996 was $4,611 per year for state residents and $7,851 for non-residents. Some 41–60% of the graduate students in this program receive financial aid.

Facilities

Computer facilities include a computer lab with 135 IBM/clones and 40 Macintoshes, computers in other departments, and access to Internet and E-mail. There are 2 libraries available to graduate students. Facilities are handicapped accessible.

Career Counseling and Job Placement

This program offers student internships or educational opportunities with the Bureau of Land Management, Forest Service, National Park Service, and Estuarine Reserve. Career counseling and job placement services include job placement counselors, on-campus interviews, job books, job fairs, and bulletin boards. Thirty percent of alumni work within the government sector, 30% for nonprofits, and 30% in science or academia. Eighty percent of the students find work within six months of graduation.

SOUTHERN UNIVERSITY

Established in 1880, Southern University has a total enrollment of 9,900 students and is located in the city of Baton Rouge, Louisiana.

☜ Environmental Science Program

CONTACT:

Robert H. Miller, Jr., Chair
Department of Chemistry
Environmental Science Program
Southern University

P.O. Box 9440
Baton Rouge, LA 70813

Phone: 504-771-3990

Quick Facts About the Environmental Science Program

- Year established: 1985
- Enrollment: 18 master's students
- Graduate degree conferred: Master of Science
- Master's degree requirements include: required courses, master's thesis, master's project,
- Faculty/Advisee ratio: 1:2

Areas of Specialization

Environmental Science (60%)
Environmental Quality and Public Health (40%)

Special Program Features

Graduate students can cross-register for courses within other departments. Joint degree programs are offered with the School of Public Policy. International program experiences are not offered.

Admission to the Program

- Admission requirements for master's applicants include: 6 semesters of chemistry; GRE scores are not required
- Master's students accepted each year (on average): 4% of 10 applicants
- Students may matriculate at the start of any term; transfer students are not accepted.

About the Students

There are 8 male and 10 female graduate students currently enrolled in this program; 7 are full-time and 11 part-time; 5 are international and 13 domestic; 3% are Caucasian, 85% Black, 2% Hispanic, and 4% Asian. Graduate students range from age 22 to 40, with a median age of 31.

About the Faculty

There are 7 faculty affiliated with this program. The average faculty member teaches 2 courses and advises 1 master's student per year. Advisors are chosen by students. Faculty research is currently being conducted domestically. Two faculty specialize in Environmental Quality and Public Health and 5 in Environmental Science.

Tuition and Financial Aid

Tuition in 1996 was $2,046 per year for state residents and $3,822 for nonresidents. Some 41–60% of the graduate students in this program receive financial aid. Fifty-two percent of the master's students are awarded teaching, administrative, or research assistantships.

Facilities

Computer facilities include 20 IBM/clones, 8 Macintoshes, one terminal per student, 28 GIS computers, and access to Internet and E-mail. Free or low-cost computer training is available. There are 2 buildings, 6 classrooms, 8 laboratories, and 2 libraries available to graduate students. All facilities are handicapped accessible. The school's Agriculture Department owns an experimental farm and a number of greenhouses that are available for student research.

Career Counseling and Job Placement

This program offers student internships with the state's Department of Environmental Quality; students also do research in collaboration with several local industries. Career counseling and job placement services include on-campus interviews. Twenty percent of alumni work within the government sector, 70% for corporations or industries, and 10% in science or academia; 60% of alumni work in Louisiana and 40% in the Southwest. Ninety percent of the students find work within six months of graduation.

STANFORD UNIVERSITY

Located on an 8,000-acre campus in the San Francisco Bay Area of California, Stanford University was established in 1885 and has a total enrollment of 13,900 students.

☏ Earth Systems Program

FACULTY CONTACT:

Jonathan Roughgarden, Director
Earth Systems Program
Stanford University
Building 360-Room 360A
Stanford, CA 94305

Phone: 415-725-3183

ADMISSIONS CONTACT:

Graduate Admissions
Office of the Registrar
Stanford University
Stanford, CA 94305-3005

Phone: 415-723-4291

Earth Systems Program Web site: http://pangea.stanford.edu/ESYS.html

Stanford University Web site: http://www.stanford.edu/

Quick Facts About the Earth Systems Program

- Year established: 1993
- Enrollment: 10 master's students / 10 doctoral students
- Graduate degree conferred: coterminal Master of Science (available only to current Stanford undergraduates)
- Master's degree requirements include: required courses
- Faculty/Advisee ratio: 1:2

Areas of Specialization

Conservation Biology (25% of students)
Environmental Science (25%)
Environmental Studies (20%)
Corporate Environmental Management (10%)
Environmental Geography (10%)

Special Program Features

This program is best known for its emphasis on in-depth interdisciplinary environmental science and for its coterminal bachelor's/master's degree. Graduate students can cross-register for courses within other departments. Joint degree programs and international program experiences are not offered. Future program plans include further review; as a very new program, requirements are still being established.

Admission to the Program

- Admission requirements for master's applicants include: 2 quarters of chemistry, 1 of biology, 3 of calculus, 3 of economics, 2 of natural science, 2 of physical science; 1/4 year internship experience; GRE scores not required

- Master's students accepted each year (on average): 100% of 10 applicants

- Students may matriculate at the start of any term; transfer students are sometimes accepted.

About the Students

There are 8 male and 2 female graduate students currently enrolled in this program; all are full-time; 1 is international and 9 domestic; 60% are Caucasian, 10% Black, and 20% Asian. Graduate students' median age is 21.5.

About the Faculty

There are 20 faculty affiliated with this program. The average faculty member advises less than 1 master's student per year. Students choose their faculty advisors.

Tuition and Financial Aid

Tuition in 1996 was $19,695 per year. Under 20% of the graduate students in this program receive financial aid; 50% of the master's students are awarded teaching assistantships.

Facilities

Computer facilities include 3 Macintoshes, 1 terminal per 3 students, university-wide computer clusters, and access to Internet and E-mail. Free or low-cost computer training is available. One building and 22 libraries are available to graduate students. Some facilities are handicapped accessible.

Career Counseling and Job Placement

This program does not offer student internships. Career counseling and job placement services include job placement counselors, active alumni contact, on-campus interviews, job books, an alumni database, and job fairs.

Thirty-three percent of alumni work for private small business and 67% in science or academia. All alumni work in the San Francisco Bay Area. All students find work within six months of graduation.

☜ Department of Biological Sciences

DEPARTMENT CONTACT:

Lorie Langdon
Student Services Office
Department of Biological Sciences
Stanford University
Stanford, CA 94305

ADMISSIONS CONTACT:

Office of Graduate Admissions
Stanford University
Stanford, CA 94305-4291

Phone: 415-723-5413
Fax: 415-723-6132
E-mail: Lorie.Langdon@Forsythe.Stanford.EDU

Phone: 415-723-4291

Department of Biological Sciences Web site:
http://www-leland.stanford.edu/group/biosci/

Quick Facts About the Department of Biological Sciences

• Enrollment: 110 graduate students / 90 postdoctoral fellows
• Graduate degrees conferred: Master of Science, doctorate
• Doctoral degree requirements include: course work, dissertation, plus teaching experience in at least three courses
• Faculty/Advisee ratio: 1:3

Areas of Specialization

Molecular Biology, Cell Biology, Development Biology, Genetics (40–50 students)
Plant Biology (35 students)
Population and Evolutionary Biology, Ecology (20 students)
Marine Biology (15 students)

Special Program Features

This program specializes in scholarly research and in the preparation of students for professional careers focused on biological research. Informal laboratory instruction and participation in seminars constitute a large part of the educational process. The Department's faculty roster includes several internationally known environmental scientists, including Paul Ehrlich, Stephen Schneider, and Peter Vitousek, among others.

About the Faculty

There are 35 professorial faculty members, 9 associated faculty, and 90 postdoctoral fellows affiliated with this program.

Facilities

The Department of Biology makes extensive use of the Herrin/Gilber laboratories, situated on the Stanford campus; the 1,300-acre Jasper Ridge Biological Preserve, just five miles from campus; and the Hopkins Marine Station, located in Pacific Grove on the Monterey Peninsula.

Tuition and Financial Aid

Doctoral candidates generally receive enough financial support to cover tuition and the cost of living.

☂ Other graduate environmental programs at Stanford University (no profiles available):

Program in Ecology & Evolutionary Biology. *Contact:* Lorie Landon, Student Services Officer, Department of Biological Sciences. *Phone:* 415-723-5413.

Department of Geological and Environmental Sciences. *Contact:* Jonathan Stebbins. *Phone:* 415-723-1140.

STATE UNIVERSITY OF NEW YORK COLLEGE OF ENVIRONMENTAL SCIENCE AND FORESTRY

Established in 1911, the State University of New York (also know as SUNY) College of Environmental Science and Forestry at Syracuse has a total enrollment of 1,840 students. It is located in on a 12-acre campus in a large city in upstate New York, adjacent to Syracuse University.

☜ Environmental Science and Forestry Program

FACULTY AND ADMISSIONS CONTACT:

Robert Frey
Dean of Instruction & Graduate Studies
College of Environmental Science and Forestry
SUNY-Syracuse
227 Bray Hall
Syracuse, NY 13210-2781

Phone: 315-470-6599
Fax: 315-470-6779
E-mail: RHFREY@SUADMIN

College of Environmental Science and Forestry Web site: http://www.esf.edu/

Quick Facts About the Environmental Science and Forestry Program

- Year established: 1911
- Enrollment: 350 master's students / 200 doctoral students
- Graduate degrees conferred: Master of Science, Master of Landscape Architecture, doctorate
- Master's degree requirements include: required courses, master's thesis, master's project, internship experience
- Doctoral degree requirements include: dissertation, qualifying exam, oral exam
- Faculty/Advisee ratio: 1:5

Special Program Features

Students enrolled in this program may pursue graduate degree programs in six major areas: (1) Environmental and Forest Biology, (2) Forest Chemistry, (3) Forest Resource Management, (4) Environmental and Resource Engineering, (5) Landscape Architecture, and (6) Environmental Science. Graduate students can cross-register for courses within other departments. Joint degree programs are offered with the Law School, School of Public Policy, Business School, and School of Education at Syracuse University. International program experiences are not offered. Future program plans include offering an Master of Professional Studies (M.P.S.) degree in 1996, in 6 of the 8 specialization areas.

Admission to the Program

- Average GRE scores of 550 verbal/600 math required for all graduate applicants
- Master's degree not required for doctoral applicants
- Master's students accepted each year (on average): 50% of 400 applicants
- Doctoral students accepted each year (on average): 40% of 200 applicants
- Students may matriculate at the start of any term; transfer students are accepted.

About the Students

There are 400 male and 150 female graduate students currently enrolled in this program; 400 are full-time and 150 part-time; 60 are international and 490 domestic; 85% are Caucasian, 5% Black, 5% Hispanic, and 5% Native American. Graduate students range from age 22 to 55, with a median age of 30.

About the Faculty

There are 140 faculty affiliated with this program. The average faculty member teaches 3 courses and advises 4 master's and 3 doctoral students per year. Advisors are assigned to students. Faculty research is currently being conducted domestically.

Tuition and Financial Aid

Tuition in 1996 was $5,100 per year for state residents and $8,416 for nonresidents. Some 21–40% of the graduate students in this program receive financial aid. Forty-five percent of the master's students are awarded teaching or research assistantships, and 55% of the doctoral students are awarded teaching or research assistantships.

Facilities

Computer facilities include 120 IBM/clones, 75 Macintoshes, 40 GIS computers, all resources of Syracuse University, and access to Internet and E-mail. Free or low-cost computer training is available. There are 15 buildings, 25 classrooms, 30 laboratories, and various libraries available to graduate students. Facilities are handicapped accessible. The school also owns 30,000 acres of property that is available for student research.

Career Counseling and Job Placement

This program offers student internships. Career counseling and job placement services include job placement counselors and an alumni database. Fifty percent of alumni work within the government sector, 5% for nonprofits, 20% for private small business, and 25% for corporations or industries. Most students find work within six months of graduation.

TENNESSEE TECHNOLOGICAL UNIVERSITY

Located in the small town of Cookeville, Tennessee Technological University was established in 1915 and has a total enrollment of 8,240 students.

☞ Program in Environmental Biology

FACULTY CONTACT:
Michael Harvey, Chair
Department of Biology
Program in Environmental Biology
Tennessee Technological University
Cookeville, TN 38505

Phone: 615-372-3140

ADMISSIONS CONTACT:
Graduate School
Tennessee Technological University
Cookeville, TN 38505

Phone: 615-372-3233

Tennessee Technological University Web site: http://www.tntech.edu/

Quick Facts About the Environmental Biology Program
- Year established: long ago
- Enrollment: 60 master's students
- Graduate degree conferred: Master of Science
- Master's degree requirements include: required courses, master's thesis
- Faculty/Advisee ratio: varies

Special Program Features

This program is best known for its emphasis on fisheries and wildlife. Graduate students can cross-register for courses within other departments. Joint degree programs are not offered.

Admission to the Program

- GRE scores are required for master's applicants
- Master's students accepted each year (on average): 75% of 30 applicants
- Students may matriculate at the start of any term; transfer students are accepted.

About the Students

There are 60 full-time graduate students currently enrolled in this program.

About the Faculty

There are 18 faculty affiliated with this program. The average faculty member teaches 4 courses and advises 3 master's students per year. Students choose their faculty advisors. Faculty research is currently being conducted domestically.

Tuition and Financial Aid

Tuition in 1996 was $2,366 per year for state residents and $5,312 for nonresidents. Over 60% of the graduate students in this program receive financial aid. Eighty percent of the master's students are awarded teaching or research assistantships.

Facilities

One building, 10 classrooms, 1 library and various computer facilities are available to graduate students. Facilities are handicapped accessible.

Career Counseling and Job Placement

This program does not offer student internships or career counseling and job placement services. Most students find work within six months of graduation.

TEXAS CHRISTIAN UNIVERSITY

Established in 1873, Texas Christian University has a total enrollment of 6,730 students. Its setting is an urban campus within the mid-sized city of Fort Worth.

🎓 Environmental Sciences Program

FACULTY CONTACT:
Leo Newland, Director
Environmental Sciences Program
Texas Christian University
Box 30798
Fort Worth, TX 76129

ADMISSIONS CONTACT:
Dean of Graduate Studies
  and Research
Texas Christian University
Box 32871
Fort Worth, TX 76129

Phone: 817-921-7271

Environmental Sciences Program Web site:
http://geowww.geo.tcu.edu/ensc/ensc.html

Texas Christian University Web site: http://www.tcu.edu/

Quick Facts About the Environmental Sciences Program
- Year established: 1967
- Enrollment: 35 master's students
- Graduate degree conferred: Master of Science
- Master's degree requirements include: master's thesis
- Faculty/Advisee ratio: 1:5

Areas of Specialization
Environmental Geography (40% of students)
Applied and Quantitative Ecology (25%)
Environmental Science (20%)
Earth Science (10%)
Environmental Quality and Public Health (5%)

Special Program Features
This program is best known for its emphasis on remote sensing/GIS, aquatic ecology, and environmental chemistry. Graduate students can cross-register

for courses within other departments. Joint degree programs and international program experiences are not offered.

Admission to the Program

- Admission requirements for master's applicants include: 2 semesters of chemistry, 2 of biology, 1 of calculus, 1 of geology; average GRE scores: 500 verbal/500 math
- Master's students accepted each year (on average): 60% of 20 applicants
- Students may matriculate at the start of any term; transfer students are accepted.

About the Students

There are 16 male and 19 female graduate students currently enrolled in this program; 2 are international and 33 domestic; 90% are Caucasian. Graduate students range from age 21 to 51, with a median age of 30.

About the Faculty

There are 16 faculty affiliated with this program. The average faculty member teaches 2–3 courses and advises 2–3 master's students per year. Students choose their faculty advisors. Faculty research is currently being conducted both domestically and internationally. Four faculty specialize in Applied and Quantitative Ecology, 5 in Earth Science, 2 in Environmental Geography, 1 in Environmental Law, 1 in Environmental Quality and Public Health, 2 in Environmental Science, and 1 in Forestry.

Tuition and Financial Aid

Tuition in 1996 was $7,200 per year. 21-40% of the graduate students in this program receive financial aid. Thirty percent of the master's students are awarded teaching or research assistantships.

Facilities

Computer facilities include 6 IBM/clones, 17 Macintoshes, one Unix terminal per 20 students, 5 GIS computers, and access to Internet and E-mail. Free or low-cost computer training is available. One building, 10–12 classrooms, and 10–12 laboratories are available to graduate students. Facilities are handicapped accessible. The school also owns a fish hatchery that is available for student research.

Career Counseling and Job Placement

This program offers student internships or educational opportunities within the local commmunity. Career counseling and job placement services include job placement counselors, active alumni contact, on-campus interviews, job books, and an alumni database. Forty percent of alumni work within the government sector, 10% for semi-governmental organizations, 30% for private small business, and 10% for corporations or industries; 60% of alumni work in Texas, 5% in Washington, D.C., and 10% in international locations. Eighty-five percent of the students find work within six months of graduation.

TEXAS TECH UNIVERSITY

With a total enrollment of 24,215 students, Texas Tech University was established in 1922 and is located on a 1,839-acre campus in the mid-sized city of Lubbock.

☞ Range and Wildlife Management Program

FACULTY CONTACT:

Carlton Britton, Professor
Department of Range and
  Wildlife Management
Texas Technological University
Lubbock, TX 79409-2125

Phone: 806-742-2841
Fax: 806-742-2280

ADMISSIONS CONTACT:

Graduate Admissions
Texas Technological University
Box 41030
Lubbock, TX 79409

Phone: 806-742-2787

Department of Range and Wildlife Management Web site:
http://www.ttu.edu/~rwfmhp/

Texas Tech University Web site: http://www.ttu.edu/home.htm

Quick Facts About the Range and Wildlife Management Program

• Year established: 1965

- Enrollment: 27 master's students / 12 doctoral students
- Graduate degrees conferred: Master of Science, doctorate
- Master's degree requirements include: master's thesis, master's project
- Doctoral degree requirements include: dissertation qualifying exam, oral exam
- Faculty/Advisee ratio: 1:3

Areas of Specialization

Wildlife Management (21 students)
Range Management (15 students)
Fisheries Science (4 students)

Special Program Features

This program is best known for its emphasis on fire ecology, wildlife habitat, and playa ecosystems. Graduate students can cross-register for courses within other departments. Joint degree programs are not offered. International program experiences include research opportunities in South America.

Admission to the Program

- Admission requirements for master's applicants include: 3 semesters of chemistry, 5 of biology, 2 of calculus, 2 of economics, 8 of natural science; average GRE scores: 450 verbal/600 math
- Admission requirements for doctoral applicants include: master's degree; average GRE scores: 500 verbal/650 math
- Master's students accepted each year (on average): 7% of 200 applicants
- Doctoral students accepted each year (on average): 5% of 60 applicants
- Students may matriculate at the start of any term; transfer students are somctimes accepted.

About the Students

There are 34 male and 5 female graduate students currently enrolled in this program; all are full-time; 10 are international and 29 domestic; 73% are

Caucasian, 15% Hispanic, and 12% Asian. Graduate students range from age 23 to 35, with a median age of 27.

About the Faculty

There are 15 faculty affiliated with this program. The average faculty member teaches 2 courses and advises 3 master's and 1 doctoral students per year. Faculty advisors select students. Faculty research is currently being conducted both domestically and internationally. Fourteen faculty specialize in Applied and Quantitative Ecology and one in Environmental Geography.

Tuition and Financial Aid

Tuition in 1996 was $30 per credit hour for state residents and $176 for nonresidents. All graduate students in this program receive financial aid. Five percent of the master's students are awarded fellowships, 95% are awarded teaching or research assistantships. Ten percent of the doctoral students are awarded fellowships, 90% are awarded teaching or research assistantships.

Facilities

Computer facilities include 20 IBM/clones, 15 Macintoshes, one terminal per 9 students, a university mainframe, VAX, 2 GIS computers, and access to Internet and E-mail. Free or low-cost computer training is available. One building, 4 classrooms, 2 laboratories, various museum collections, and 2 libraries are available to graduate students. Facilities are handicapped accessible. The school also owns Texas Tech Experimental Ranch, which is available for student research.

Career Counseling and Job Placement

This program does not offer student internships. Career counseling and job placement services include job placement counselors, active alumni contact, on-campus interviews, and job books. Fifty percent of alumni work within the government sector, 10% for semi-governmental organizations, 10% for nonprofits, 10% for private small business, and 20% in science or academia; 30% of alumni work in the Southwest, 10% in Washington, D.C., and 10% in international locations. Seventy percent of the students find work within six months of graduation.

TUFTS UNIVERSITY

Located on a suburban campus about seven miles from downtown Boston,
Tufts University was established in 1852 and has a total enrollment of 7,500
students.

☂ International Environmental and Resource Policy Program

FACULTY CONTACT:

William Moomaw, Director
International Environmental and
    Resource Policy Program
Fletcher School of Law
    and Diplomacy
Tufts University
Medford, MA 02155

Phone: 617-628-7071

ADMISSIONS CONTACT:

Paul Bauer, Director of Admissions
International Environmental and
    Resource Policy Program
Fletcher School of Law
    and Diplomacy
Tufts University
Medford, MA 02155

Phone: 617-627-3040

International Environmental and Resource Policy Program Web site:
http://www.tufts.edu/fletcher/ierpp.html

Tufts University Web site: http://www.tufts.edu/

Quick Facts About the International Environmental
and Resource Policy Program

- Year established: 1992
- Enrollment: 300 master's students / 30 doctoral students
- Graduate degrees conferred: Master of Arts in Law and Diplomacy, doctorate
- Master's degree requirements include: required courses, master's thesis
- Doctoral degree requirements include: required courses, dissertation, qualifying exam, oral exam

Areas of Specialization

Environmental Law and Diplomacy (50% of students)
Environmental Economics/Development (40%)
Earth Science (10%)

Special Program Features

This program is best known for its emphasis on the role of science and technology in international environmental policy, environment and development, energy and environment, and global change. Graduate students can cross-register for courses within other departments. Joint degree programs are offered with the Law School, Business School, and School of Veterinary Medicine. International program experiences include research opportunities, internships, and student exchanges in numerous countries. Future program plans include offering courses in international water policy and adding more in development and biological resources.

Admission to the Program

- Admission requirements for master's applicants include: 2 years of work experience strongly preferred; average GRE scores: 680 verbal/660 math; TOEFL for nonnative English speakers; strong international language background
- Master's degree required for doctoral applicants; no direct admission to doctoral program
- Master's students accepted each year (on average): 20% of 1,800 applicants
- Students may matriculate only in the fall; transfer students are not accepted.

About the Students

There are 170 male and 160 female graduate students currently enrolled in this program; all are full-time; 130 are international and 200 domestic; 80% are Caucasian, 8% Black, 8% Hispanic, and 4% Asian. Graduate students range from age 21 to 45, with a median age of 27.

About the Faculty

There are 5 faculty affiliated with this program. The average faculty member teaches 4 courses and advises 15 master's and 5 doctoral students per year. Advisors are assigned to students. Faculty research is currently being conducted internationally. Three faculty specialize in Environmental Law and Diplomacy and two in Environmental and Resource Economics.

Tuition and Financial Aid

Tuition in 1996 was $20,960 per year. Over 60% of the graduate students in this program receive financial aid. Thirty percent of the master's students are awarded scholarships, 18% are awarded teaching or research assistantships. Seventy-five percent of the doctoral students are awarded scholarships, 15% are awarded teaching assistantships.

Facilities

Computer facilities include 30 student terminals within the program (90% are IBM/clones, and 10% Macintoshes), numerous other computers in various locations, and access to Internet and E-mail. Free or low-cost computer training is available. There are 3 buildings, 15 classrooms, and various libraries available to graduate students. Facilities are handicapped accessible.

Career Counseling and Job Placement

This program offers some student internships with local agencies, but mostly with the United Nations and international nongovernmental organizations (NGOs). Career counseling and job placement services include job placement counselors, active alumni contact, on-campus interviews, and other organized contacts and internships.

☛ Urban and Environmental Policy Program

FACULTY CONTACT:

Sheldon Krimsky, Chair
Department of Urban and
   Environmental Policy
Tufts University
Medford, MA 02155

ADMISSIONS CONTACT:

Ann Urosevich
Graduate School of Arts
   and Sciences
Tufts University
Medford, MA 02155

Phone: 617-627-3394
E-mail: aurosevi@tufts.edu

Department of Urban and Environmental Policy Web site:
http://www.tufts.edu/as/gsas/uep.html

Quick Facts About the Urban and Environmental Policy Program

• Year established: 1973

- Enrollment: 70 master's students
- Graduate degrees conferred: Master of Arts; this program also participates in the Tufts Interdisciplinary Doctoral Program
- Master's degree requirements include: required courses, master's thesis, internship experience
- Faculty/Advisee ratio: 1:9

Areas of Specialization

Resource Policy and Planning (75% of students)
Urban and Social Policy (25%)

Special Program Features

This program is best known for its emphasis on resource management and community environmental policy. Students may concentrate in one of two areas: (1) Urban and Social Policy, including community development and housing, social welfare policy, and child and family policy; or (2) Environmental Policy, including natural resource mangement or environmental protection. Students may also design their own area of specialization, i.e., sustainable communities or community ecology. Graduate students can cross-register for courses within other departments and at other Boston-area universities. Joint degree programs are offered with the Fletcher School of Law and Diplomacy, and the Economics, Biology, and Civil and Environmental Engineering departments. International program experiences are not offered.

Admission to the Program

- Admission requirements for master's applicants include: average GRE scores: 650 verbal/600 math
- Master's students accepted each year (on average): 35% of 180–200 applicants
- Students may matriculate at the start of any term; transfer students are sometimes accepted.

About the Faculty

There are 14 faculty affiliated with this program. Students choose faculty advisors in their second year.

Tuition and Financial Aid

Over 60% of the graduate students in this program receive financial aid. 70% of the master's students are awarded scholarships. This program requires summer internships. Career counseling and job placement services include active alumni contact, job books, and an alumni database.

TULANE UNIVERSITY

Established in 1834, Tulane University has a total enrollment of 11,300 and is located on a 100-acre campus in a residential area of New Orleans, Louisiana.

☙ Ecology, Evolution, and Organismal Biology Program

FACULTY CONTACT:

Milton Fingerman, Professor
  and Chair
Department of Ecology, Evolution,
  and Organismal Biology
Tulane University
310 Dinwiddie Hall
New Orleans, LA 70118-5698

Phone: 540-865-5191
Fax: 504-862-8706

ADMISSIONS CONTACT:

Admission Coordinator
The Graduate School
Tulane University
New Orleans, LA 70118-5673

Department of Ecology, Evolution, and Organismal Biology Web site:
http://www.tulane.edu/~eeob/

University Web site: http://www.tulane.edu/

Quick Facts About the Ecology, Evolution, and Organismal Biology Program

- Year established: 1990
- Enrollment: 9 master's students / 17 doctoral students
- Graduate degrees conferred: Master of Science, doctorate

- Doctoral degree requirements include: dissertation, internship experience, qualifying exam, oral exam
- Faculty/Advisee ratio: 1:3

Areas of Specialization

Environmental Science (70% of students)
Environmental Quality and Public Health (10%)
Botany (5%)

Special Program Features

This program is best known for its emphasis on crustacean biology and aquatic biology. Graduate students can cross-register for courses within other departments. Joint degree programs are not offered. International program experiences include research opportunities and student exchanges in Central America.

Admission to the Program

- Average GRE scores: 600 verbal/600 math for all graduate applicants
- A B.S. degree is required for master's applicants; a master's degree is not required for doctoral applicants
- Master's students accepted each year (on average): 30% of 20 applicants
- Students may matriculate at the start of any term; transfer students are accepted.

About the Students

There are 17 male and 9 female graduate students currently enrolled in this program; all 26 are full-time; 3 are international and 23 domestic; 88% are Caucasian, 8% Black, and 4% Hispanic. Graduate students range from age 22 to 47, with a median age of 24.

About the Faculty

There are 9 faculty affiliated with this program. The average faculty member teaches 4 courses and advises 1 master's and 2 doctoral students per

year. Students choose their faculty advisors. Faculty research is currently being conducted both domestically and internationally. One faculty member specializes in Botany and seven in Environmental Science.

Tuition and Financial Aid

Tuition in 1996 was $19,382 per year. Over 60% of the graduate students in this program receive financial aid. Eight percent of the graduate students are awarded fellowships, and 85% are awarded teaching assistantships.

Facilities

There are 2 buildings, computer facilities, and various museum collections available to graduate students. Facilities are handicapped accessible.

Career Counseling and Job Placement

This program does not offer student internships. Career counseling and job placement services include active alumni contact and on-campus interviews. Ten percent of alumni work for private small business, 10% for corporations or industries, and 80% in science or academia. Ninety-five percent of the students find work within six months of graduation.

➤ Environmental Law Program

FACULTY CONTACT:

Susan Krinsky, Associate Dean
Tulane Law School
New Orleans, LA 70118-5670

Phone: 504-865-5930

ADMISSIONS CONTACT:

Admissions
Tulane Law School
New Orleans, LA 70118-5670

Phone: 504-865-5930

Tulane Law School Web site: http://www.law.tulane.edu

Quick Facts About the Environmental Law Program

- Year established: Law School, 1847; LL.M. in Energy and Environment, early 1980s
- Enrollment: 25 master's students
- Graduate degrees conferred: Juris Doctorate, with certificate in environmental law; Master of Laws (LL.M.) in Energy and Environment

- Master's degree requirements include: required courses
- Doctoral degree requirements include: dissertation

Areas of Specialization

Environmental Law (100% of students)

Special Program Features

This program is best known for its emphasis on environmental law. Graduate students can cross-register for courses within other departments. Joint degree programs are offered with the School of Public Health. International program experiences are not offered. Future plans include increased program offerings.

Admission to the Program

- Admission requirements for all graduate applicants include a law degree
- Master's students accepted each year (on average): 60% of 50 applicants
- Students may matriculate only in the fall; transfer students are not accepted.

About the Students

There are approximately 20 male and 5 female graduate students currently enrolled in this program; 12 are full-time and 12 part-time; 7 are international and 17 domestic; 77% are Caucasian, 12% Black, 6% Hispanic, and 4% Asian. Graduate students range from age 25 to 50, with a median age of 30.

About the Faculty

There are 5 faculty affiliated with this program. There is no formal faculty advising system. Faculty research is currently being conducted domestically.

Tuition and Financial Aid

Over 60% of the graduate students in this program receive financial aid. Ten percent of the master's students are awarded scholarships.

Career Counseling and Job Placement

This program does not offer student internships. Career counseling and job placement services include job placement counselors, active alumni contact, on-campus interviews, job books, an alumni database, and job fairs.

UNIVERSITY OF ARIZONA

Established in 1885, the University of Arizona has a total enrollment of 35,130 and is located on a 345-acre campus in the desert city of Tucson (population 750,000). This school belongs to the Hispanic Association of Colleges and Universities.

☛ Ecology and Evolutionary Biology Program

FACULTY CONTACT:

Margaret Kidwell, Head
Department of Ecology and
    Evolutionary Biology
University of Arizona
Room 310, Biological Sciences
    West Bldg.
Tucson, AZ 85721

Phone: 602-621-1165

ADMISSIONS CONTACT:

Graduate Admissions Office
The University of Arizona
Administration Building, Room #322
Tucson, AZ 85721

Phone: 602-621-3132

Department of Ecology and Evolutionary Biology Web site:
http://eebweb.arizona.edu/index.html-ssi

University of Arizona Web site: http://www.arizona.edu/

Quick Facts About the Ecology and Evolutionary Biology Program

- Year established: 1975
- Enrollment: 14 master's students / 42 doctoral students
- Graduate degrees conferred: Master of Science, doctorate
- Doctoral degree requirements include: dissertation, internship experience, qualifying exam, oral exam
- Faculty/Advisee ratio: 1:2

Areas of Specialization

Applied and Quantitative Ecology (50% of students)
Botany (25%)

Special Program Features

This program is best known for its emphasis on phylogenic biology, population ecology, and theoretical and mathematical biology. Graduate students can cross-register for courses within other departments. Joint degree programs are not offered. International program experiences include research opportunities and field stations in Central America.

Admission to the Program

- Admission requirements for master's applicants include: average GRE scores: 630 verbal/610 math
- Admission requirements for doctoral applicants include: average GRE scores: 650 verbal/670 math
- Master's students accepted each year (on average): 19% of 26 applicants
- Doctoral students accepted each year (on average): 12% of 87 applicants
- Students may matriculate only in the fall; transfer students are accepted.

About the Students

There are 23 male and 33 female graduate students currently enrolled in this program; all 56 are full-time; 7 are international and 49 domestic; 90% are Caucasian and 10% Hispanic. Graduate students range from age 28 to 45, with a median age of 31.

About the Faculty

There are 27 faculty affiliated with this program. The average faculty member teaches 2 courses and advises 0–5 doctoral students per year. Students choose their faculty advisors. Faculty research is currently being conducted both domestically and internationally.

Tuition and Financial Aid

Tuition in 1996 was $0 (plus fees) per year for state residents and $4,056 per year for nonresidents. Over 60% of the graduate students in this program receive financial aid. Fourteen percent of the master's students are awarded fellowships, 7% are awarded scholarships, 63% are awarded teaching or research assistantships. Nine percent of the doctoral students are awarded fellowships, 7% are awarded scholarships, 66% are awarded teaching or research assistantships.

Facilities

Computer facilities include many IBM/clones, many Macintoshes, several computer workrooms, a university computer facility, and access to Internet and E-mail. Free or low-cost computer training is available. Various museum collections and all university libraries are available to graduate students. Facilities are handicapped accessible. The school also owns a farm and various field research sites, including open land available for research on water movement and chemical transport.

Career Counseling and Job Placement

This program does not offer student internships, or career counseling and job placement services. Some 7.3% of alumni work within the government sector, 14.7% for private small business, 3.6% for corporations or industries, and 73.5% in science or academia; 42% of alumni work in the Southwest and 1% in Washington, D.C. Seventy-five percent of the students find work within six months of graduation.

☞ School of Renewable Natural Resources

CONTACT:

Mary Soltero, Academic Advisor
School of Renewable Natural Resources
University of Arizona
325 Biological Sciences East Building
Tucson, AZ 85721

Phone: 602-621-7260

Quick Facts About the School of Renewable Natural Resources

- Year established: 1974
- Enrollment: 86 master's students / 59 doctoral students

- Graduate degrees conferred: Master of Science, Master of Landscape Architecture, doctorate
- Master's degree requirements include: required courses, master's thesis
- Doctoral degree requirements include: required courses, dissertation, qualifying exam, oral exam
- Faculty/Advisee ratio: 1:4

Areas of Specialization

Applied and Quantitative Ecology (32% of students)
Resource Policy and Planning (16%)
Geographic Information Systems (15%)
Hydrology (13%)
Agroforestry (12%)
Landscape Architecture (12%)

Special Program Features

This program is best known for its emphasis on renewable natural resources studies/advanced resource technology options. Graduate students can cross-register for courses within other departments. Joint degree programs and international program experiences are not offered.

Admission to the Program

- Average GRE scores for all graduate applicants: 548 verbal/596 math
- Admission requirements for master's applicants include: 2 semesters of chemistry, 2 of biology, 2 of calculus, 2 of economics
- Master's degrees are required for doctoral applicants
- Graduate students accepted each year (on average): 31% of 191 applicants
- Students may matriculate at the start of any term; transfer students are accepted.

About the Students

There are 86 male and 59 female graduate students currently enrolled in this program; 83 are full-time and 62 part-time; 42 are international and 103

domestic. Graduate students range from age 23 to 75, with a median age of 35.5.

About the Faculty

There are 40 faculty affiliated with this program. The average faculty member teaches 3 courses and advises 3 master's and 1 doctoral student per year. Advisors are assigned to students.

Tuition and Financial Aid

Some 41–60% of the graduate students in this program receive financial aid. One percent of the master's students are awarded fellowships, 23% are awarded teaching or research assistantships. Two percent of the doctoral students are awarded fellowships, 14% are awarded teaching or research assistantships.

Career Counseling and Job Placement

This program offers student internships through the National Park Service and U.S. Fish and Wildlife Service. No career counseling and job placement services are offered.

☘ Soil, Water and Environmental Science Program

FACULTY CONTACT:

Mark Brusseau, Associate Professor
Soil, Water and Environmental Science Department
University of Arizona
429 Shantz Building
Tucson, AZ 85721

Phone: 602-621-3244

Quick Facts About the Soil, Water and Environmental Science Program

- Year established: 1990
- Enrollment: 36 master's students / 44 doctoral students

- Graduate degrees conferred: Master of Science, doctorate
- Master's degree requirements include: required courses, master's thesis
- Doctoral degree requirements include: required courses, dissertation, qualifying exam, oral exam
- Faculty/Advisee ratio: 1:5

Special Program Features

This program is best known for its emphasis on contaminant transport and remediation. Graduate students can cross-register for courses within other departments. Joint degree programs are not offered. International program experiences include research opportunities and field stations in Central America, Africa, and China. Future plans include growth in program offerings.

Admission to the Program

- GRE scores are highly recommended for all graduate applicants
- Admission requirements for master's applicants include: 4 semesters of chemistry, 2 of biology, 2 of calculus, 1 of natural science, 2 of physical science, 1 of computer science
- Master's degree not required for doctoral applicants
- Master's students accepted each year (on average): 20% of 50 applicants
- Doctoral students accepted each year (on average): 50% of 30 applicants
- Students may matriculate at the start of any term; transfer students are accepted.

About the Students

There are 60 male and 20 female graduate students currently enrolled in this program; 68 are full-time and 12 part-time; 43 are international and 37 domestic.

About the Faculty

There are 19 faculty affiliated with this program. The average faculty member teaches 2 courses and advises 2.5 master's and 2.5 doctoral students per year. Students choose their faculty advisors.

Tuition and Financial Aid

Over 60% of the graduate students in this program receive financial aid. Ten percent of the master's students are awarded fellowships; 70% are awarded teaching or research assistantships. Twenty percent of the doctoral students are awarded fellowships; 70% are awarded teaching or research assistantships.

Career Counseling and Job Placement

This program does not offer student internships or career counseling and job placement services. Ninety percent of the students find work within six months of graduation.

☛ Other graduate environmental programs at University of Arizona (no profiles available):

Graduate Program in Environment and Behavior. *Contact:* Robert Bechtel, Chair. *Phone:* 602-621-7430.

Arid Lands Resource Sciences Ph.D Program. *Contact:* Carmen Ortiz-Henley, Program Coordinator. *Phone:* 602-621-7896. *Fax:* 602-621-3816.

UNIVERSITY OF CALIFORNIA, BERKELEY

One of nine campuses of the University of California, the University of California, Berkeley (also known as UC-Berkeley) was established in 1868. It has a total enrollment of 31,000 students and is located on a 180-acre campus in a lively, mid-sized city just across the Bay from San Franscisco.

☛ Program in Environmental Law

FACULTY CONTACT:

Joseph L. Sax, Law Professor
Program in Environmental Law
University of California, Berkeley
Boalt Hall, Law School
Berkeley, CA 94720

ADMISSIONS CONTACT:

Graduate Admissions/Fellowship
    Office
Graduate Division
309 Sproul Hall
University of California, Berkeley
Berkeley, CA 94720

Phone: 510-642-2274

Phone: 510-642-7405

University of California at Berkeley Web site: http://www.berkeley.edu/

Quick Facts About the Program in Environmental Law

- Year established: 1990
- Enrollment: 30 law students
- Graduate degree conferred: Juris Doctorate, with certificate in Environmental Law
- Admission requirements include LSAT scores

Special Program Features

All students specialize in Environmental Law; graduate students can cross-register for courses within other departments. Joint degree programs are offered with School of Public Policy, Business School, and School of Public Health. International program experiences include research opportunities, internships, and student exchanges all over the world.

About the Students

No information available.

About the Faculty

There are 7 faculty affiliated with this program. The average faculty member teaches 3–4 courses per year. Five faculty specialize in Environmental Law, 1 in Environmental History, and 1 in Public Policy Studies.

Tuition and Financial Aid

Tuition in 1996 was $0 (plus fees) per year for state residents and $7,700 for nonresidents. Over 60% of the graduate students in this program receive financial aid.

Facilities

Computer facilities include access to Internet and E-mail. Free or low-cost computer training is available. Facilities are handicapped accessible.

Career Counseling and Job Placement

This program offers student internships via a clinic, run by a full-time director and staffed by students, that serves the San Francisco Bay Area com-

mmunity. Career counseling and job placement services include job placement counselors, active alumni contact, on-campus interviews, job books,
an alumni database, and job fairs. Twenty percent of alumni work within the
government sector, 10% for semi-governmental organizations, 20% for nonprofits, and 50% for private law firms. Virtually all students find work within
six months of graduation.

☞ Other graduate environmental programs at University of California, Berkeley (no profiles available):

Department of Environmental Science, Policy & Management. *Contact:*
Sue Jennison, Student Affairs Officer. *Phone:* 510-642-6410.
Energy and Resources Group. *Contact:* Kate Blake, Student Affairs Officer.
Phone: 510-642-1750.
Department of Geography. *Contact:* Luda Requadt. *Phone:* 510-642-3904.

UNIVERSITY OF CALIFORNIA, DAVIS

Established in 1910, the University of California, Davis, has a total enrollment of 22,890 students and is located on a 5,146-acre campus in the
Sacramento Valley.

☞ Graduate Group in Ecology

FACULTY CONTACT:

Paul Craig
Graduate Group in Ecology
228 Walker Hall
University of California, Davis
Davis, CA 95616-8576

Phone: 916-752-1782

ADMISSIONS CONTACT:

Graduate Group in Ecology
Wickson Hall, Room 3122
University of California, Davis
Davis, CA 95616-8576

Phone: 916-752-6751

University of California, Davis, Web site: http://www.ucdavis.edu/

Quick Facts About the Graduate Group in Ecology Program

• Year established: 1968
• Enrollment: 45 master's students / 105 doctoral students

- Graduate degrees conferred: Master of Science, doctorate
- Master's degree requirements include: required courses, master's thesis
- Doctoral degree requirements include: required courses, dissertation, qualifying exam, exit seminar
- Faculty/Advisee ratio: varies

Areas of Specialization (no statistics available)

Applied and Quantitative Ecology
Botany
Conservation Biology
Environmental Science

Special Program Features

This program offers a special emphasis in the area of environmental policy. Graduate students can cross-register for courses within other departments. A joint Ph.D. degree program is offered with San Diego State University. International program experiences are not offered.

Admission to the Program

- Admission requirements for master's applicants include: 2 semesters of chemistry, 2 of biology, 1 of calculus, 1 of ecology, 2 of physics, 1 of statistics; average GRE scores: 598 verbal/593 math
- Master's degrees are not required for doctoral applicants
- Students may matriculate only in the fall; transfer students are not accepted.

About the Students

There are 75 male and 75 female graduate students currently enrolled in this program; 146 are full-time and 4 part-time; 8 are international and 142 domestic.

About the Faculty

There are 110 faculty affiliated with this program. Advisors are assigned to students.

Tuition and Financial Aid

Tuition in 1996 was $0 (plus fees) per year for state residents and $7,690 for nonresidents.

Facilities

Computer facilities are available; free or low-cost computer training is available. Various museum collections are available to graduate students. Some facilities are handicapped accessible.

Career Counseling and Job Placement

Career counseling and job placement services are not offered.

UNIVERSITY OF CALIFORNIA, LOS ANGELES (UCLA)

Situated on an urban campus in Los Angeles, UCLA has a total enrollment of 35,400 students. This school belongs to the Hispanic Association of Colleges and Universities.

☝ Environmental Health Science Program

CONTACT:

Chairperson
Department of Environmental
    Health Science
UCLA School of Public Health
56-070 CHS
Los Angeles, CA 90024-1772

Phone: 310-825-7675
Fax: 310-794-2106

Department of Environmental Health Science Web site:
http://www.ph.ucla.edu/ehs/ehs.html

University of California, Los Angeles, Web site: http://www.ucla.edu/

Quick Facts About the Environmental Health Science Program
• Year established: 1989

- Enrollment: 100 master's students / 20 doctoral students
- Graduate degrees conferred: Master of Science, Master of Public Health (M.PH), doctorate, Doctor of Public Health, Doctor of Environmental Science & Engineering (D.Env.)
- Master's degree requirements include: master's thesis, or comprehensive in lieu of thesis for M.PH and non-thesis M.S. students; master's project; internship experience
- Doctoral degree requirements include: dissertation, internship experience, qualifying exam, oral exam
- Faculty/Advisee ratio: 1:11

Areas of Specialization

Industrial Hygiene and Occupational Health (26% of students)
Earth Science (25%)
Corporate Environmental Management (15%)
Applied and Quantitative Ecology (10%)
Conservation Biology (10%)
Environmental Quality and Public Health (7%)
Environmental Science (5%)
Botany (2%)

Special Program Features

This program is best known for its emphasis on industrial hygiene and environmental science and engineering. Graduate students can cross-register for courses within other departments. Joint degree programs are offered with the departments of Engineering, Urban Planning, Law, and the Environmental Science and Engineering Program. International program experiences include research opportunities, internships, student exchanges, and field stations in Southeast Asia, Africa, and Mexico.

Admission to the Program

- Admission requirements for master's applicants include: 2 semesters of chemistry, 1 of biology, 1 of calculus, 1 of natural science, 1 of physical science (some flexibility allowed for applicants with work experience); average GRE scores: 550 verbal/550 math
- Admission requirements for doctoral applicants include: average GRE scores: 600 verbal/600 math; master's degree not required

- Master's students accepted each year (on average): 50% of 60 applicants
- Doctoral students accepted each year (on average): 25% of 20 applicants
- Students may matriculate at the start of any term; transfer students are accepted.

About the Students

There are 52 male and 48 female graduate students currently enrolled in this program; 95 are full-time and 5 part-time; 35 are international and 65 domestic; 48% are Caucasian, 5% Black, 15% Hispanic, 2% Native American, and 30% Asian. Graduate students range from age 21 to 70, with a median age of 23.

About the Faculty

There are 16 faculty affiliated with this program. The average faculty member teaches 3 courses and advises 3 master's and 1–2 doctoral students per year. Advisors are both assigned to and chosen by students. Faculty research is currently being conducted both domestically and internationally. One faculty member specializes in Applied and Quantitative Ecology, 1 in Botany, 1 in Conservation Biology, 2 in Corporate Environmental Management, 2 in Earth Science, 4 in Environmental Quality and Public Health, 3 in Environmental Science, and 3 in Industrial Hygiene.

Tuition and Financial Aid

Tuition in 1996 was $0 (plus fees) per year for state residents and $7,699 for nonresidents. Some 41–60% of the graduate students in this program receive financial aid. Forty percent of the master's students are awarded fellowships, 30% are awarded teaching or research assistantships, and 30% receive a training grant stipend. Seventy percent of the doctoral students are awarded fellowships, and 30% are awarded teaching or research assistantships.

Facilities

Computer facilities include 40 IBM/clones, one terminal per 15 students, a central university facility, and access to Internet and E-mail. Free or low-cost computer training is available. One building, 50 classrooms, 50 laboratories, and 10 libraries are available to graduate students. Facilities are handicapped accessible. The school also owns many properties, including some in nearby mountains, plus an extensive network within the UC Natural Reserve System, with 30 reserves all over California, including the Channel Islands; all are available for student research.

Career Counseling and Job Placement

This program has long-standing relationships within the local commmunity for student internships. Career counseling and job placement services include active alumni contact, on-campus interviews, job books, an alumni database, and job fairs. Fifteen percent of alumni work within the government sector, 5% for semi-governmental organizations, 5% for nonprofits, 20% for private small business, 35% for corporations or industries, and 10% in science or academia; 90% of alumni work in the West, 2% in Washington, D.C., and 8% in international locations. Over 90% of the students find work within six months of graduation.

☜ Geography Program

CONTACT:

Hartmut S. Walter, Professor
Department of Geography
UCLA
Los Angeles, CA 90024-1524

Phone: 310-825-1071

Department of Geography Web site: http://www.geog.ucla.edu/

Quick Facts About the Geography Program

- Year established: 1971
- Enrollment: 30 master's students / 30 doctoral students
- Graduate degrees conferred: Master of Arts, doctorate
- Master's degree requirements include: master's thesis
- Doctoral degree requirements include: dissertation, qualifying exam, oral exam
- Faculty/Advisee ratio: 1:3

Special Program Features

This program is best known for its emphasis on biogeography and regional biodiversity studies. Graduate students can cross-register for courses within other departments. Joint degree programs are not offered. International program experiences include internships, student exchanges, and field stations in numerous countries.

Admission to the Program

- GRE scores are required for all graduate applicants
- Master's degrees are required for doctoral applicants
- Master's students accepted each year (on average): 30% of 30 applicants
- Doctoral students accepted each year (on average): 40% of 25 applicants
- Students may matriculate at the start of any term; transfer students are sometimes accepted.

About the Students

There are 45 male and 15 female graduate students currently enrolled in this program; all 60 are full-time; 10 are international and 50 domestic; 70% are Caucasian, 10% Black, 10% Hispanic, and 10% Asian. Graduate students range from age 22 to 45, with a median age of 28.

About the Faculty

There are 20 faculty affiliated with this program. The average faculty member teaches 5 courses and advises 3 master's and 2–4 doctoral students per year. Advisors are assigned to students.

Tuition and Financial Aid

Fifty percent of the master's students are awarded teaching or research assistantships. Twenty percent of the doctoral students are awarded fellowships, 10% are awarded scholarships, and 70% are awarded teaching or research assistantships.

Career Counseling and Job Placement

This program does not offer student internships at the graduate level. Career counseling and job placement services include active alumni contact, on-campus interviews, an alumni database, and job fairs. Thirty percent of alumni work within the government sector, 10% for nonprofits, 10% for private small business, 10% for corporations or industries, and 40% in science or academia; 60% of alumni work in California and 20% in Washington, D.C. All students find work within six months of graduation.

☜ Environmental Science and Engineering Program

CONTACT:

Arthur Winer, Director
Environmental Science and Engineering Program
UCLA
10833 Le Conte Avenue
Room 46-081 CHS
Los Angeles, CA 90024-1772

Phone: 310-206-1278

Quick Facts About the Environmental Science and Engineering Program

- Year established: 1973
- Enrollment: 48 doctoral students
- Graduate degree conferred: Doctor of Environmental Science & Engineering (D.Env.)
- Doctoral degree requirements include: required courses, dissertation, internship experience, qualifying exam, oral exam
- Faculty/Advisee ratio: 1:10

Areas of Specialization

Environmental Science (45% of students)
Atmospheric Science (35%)
Environmental Quality and Public Health (10%)
Ecosystem Management (5%)
Public Policy Studies (5%)

Special Program Features

This program is best known for its emphasis on air and water quality issues. Graduate students can cross-register for courses within other departments. Joint degree programs are available; the program is interdepartmental. International program experiences are not offered.

Admission to the Program

- Admission requirements for doctoral applicants include: master's degree; average GRE scores: 650 verbal/710 math
- Doctoral students accepted each year (on average): 25% of 40 applicants
- Students may matriculate at the start of any term; transfer students are accepted.

About the Students

There are 25 male and 23 female graduate students currently enrolled in this program; 45 are full-time and 3 part-time; 8 are foreign and 40 domestic. Graduate students range from age 25 to 67.

About the Faculty

There are 27 faculty affiliated with this program. The average faculty member teaches 3 courses and advises 1–2 master's and 5–10 doctoral students per year. Advisors are both assigned to and chosen by students. Faculty research is currently being conducted domestically.

Tuition and Financial Aid

Over 60% of the graduate students in this program receive financial aid. All doctoral students are awarded fellowships.

Facilities

Computer facilities include 8 IBM/clones, 1 Macintosh, 2 GIS computers, and access to Internet and E-mail. Free or low-cost computer training is available.

Career Counseling and Job Placement

All program students conduct their dissertation reseach during student internships. Career counseling and job placement services include active alumni contact, on-campus interviews, and an alumni database. Fifty percent of alumni work within the government sector, 5% for semi-governmental organizations, 5% for nonprofits, 10% for private small business, 10% for corporations or industries, and 10% in science or academia; 70% of alumni work in the West, 10% in Washington, D.C., and 10% in international locations. All students find work within six months of graduation.

UNIVERSITY OF CALIFORNIA, SANTA BARBARA

With a total enrollment of 17,834 students. the University of California, Santa Barbara (UCSB) is located on the Calfornia coast, 100 miles north of Los Angeles. UCSB is consistently ranked among the nation's top universities in the natural and physical sciences.

☛ School of Environmental Science and Management

FACULTY CONTACT:
Jeff Dozier, Dean
School of Environmental Science
and Management
University of California,
Santa Barbara
Santa Barbara, CA 93106-5131

ADMISSIONS CONTACT:
Graduate Division
University of California,
Santa Barbara
Santa Barbara, CA 93106-2070

Phone: 805-893-7363
Fax: 805-893-7612
E-mail: dozier@esm.ucsb.edu

Phone: 805-893-2277

School of Environmental Science and Management Web site:
http://www.esm.ucsb.edu/esm-info.html

Graduate Division Web site: http://graddiv.ucsb.edu

Quick Facts About the School of Environmental Science and Management

- Year established: 1996
- Graduate degree conferred: Master of Environmental Science and Management
- Master's degree requirements: interdisciplinary colloquium, required courses, master's thesis based on group project, written and oral examinations
- Number of students enrolled: 23

Areas of Specialization

Applied Quantitative Ecology
Environmental Biogeochemistry
Earth System Science
Environmental Policy and Resource Management

Special Program Features

Established in the fall of 1996, this program currently offers a Master of Environmental Science and Management degree; future plans include a research-oriented doctoral program and a Mid-Career Associates certificate program.

About the Faculty

The School plans to appoint approximately 17 full-time faculty members by 2001. Seven new faculty, plus the dean, are currently affiliated with the program.

Facilities

The School is currently housed in the Physical Sciences North building on the UCSB campus. A new 40,000-square-foot building is scheduled for completion in 2000.

Tuition and Financial Aid

Tuition in 1996–97 was $0 per year for state residents, plus $4,917 in fees for state residents, and $8,394 for nonresidents (plus fees).

UNIVERSITY OF CALIFORNIA, SANTA CRUZ

Established in 1965, the University of California, Santa Cruz, has a total enrollment of 10,260 students. It is located in a scenic town overlooking Monterey Bay.

☙ Environmental Studies Board

CONTACT:

Juanita Nama, Administrative Assistant
Environmental Studies Graduate Program
University of California, Santa Cruz
Santa Cruz, CA 95064

Phone: 408-459-4837

Environmental Studies Web site: http://zzyx.ucsc.edu/ES/browse.html

University of California, Santa Cruz Web site: http://www.ucsc.edu/

Quick Facts About the Environmental Studies Graduate Program

- Year established: Undergraduate Program, 1970 / Graduate Program, 1994
- Enrollment: 10 doctoral students
- Graduate degree conferred: doctorate
- Doctoral degree requirements include: required courses, dissertation, qualifying exam, oral exam
- Faculty/Advisee ratio: 1:1

Areas of Specialization

Agroecology (30% of students)
Conservation Biology (20%)
Political Economy and Sustainability (20%)
Environmental Geography (10%)
Resource Policy and Planning (10%)
Applied and Quantitative Ecology (10%)

Special Program Features

This program is best known for its emphasis on conservation biology, agroecology, political economy, and sustainability. Graduate students can cross-register for courses within other departments. Joint degree programs and international program experiences are not offered. Two new faculty have recently been hired, and future program plans include hiring two more.

Admission to the Program

- Master's degree not required for doctoral applicants; average GRE scores: 635 verbal/659 math
- Doctoral students accepted each year (on average): 13.3% of 75 applicants
- Transfer students are sometimes accepted.

About the Students

There are 5 male and 5 female graduate students currently enrolled in this program; all 10 are full-time; none are international; 70% are Caucasian and 10% Hispanic. Graduate students range from age 28 to 49, with a median age of 31.

About the Faculty

There are 10 faculty affiliated with this program. The average faculty member teaches 4 courses and advises 1 doctoral student per year. Advisors are assigned to students and work in teams. Faculty research is currently being conducted both domestically and internationally. Five faculty specialize in Applied and Quantitative Ecology, 3 in Conservation Biology, 2 in Environmental Geography, 1 in Environmental Law, 1 in Environmental Studies, 2 in Resource Policy and Planning, and 5 in Agroecology, Political Economy, and Sustainability.

Tuition and Financial Aid

Tuition in 1996 was $0 (plus fees) per year for state residents and $7,699 for nonresidents. Under 20% of the graduate students in this program receive financial aid. Twenty percent of the doctoral students are awarded fellowships, 10% are awarded scholarships, and all are awarded teaching assistantships.

Facilities

Computer facilities include several IBM/clones, many Macintoshes, one terminal per 2 students, 5 GIS computers, university-wide computer labs, and access to Internet and E-mail. Free or low-cost computer training is available. There are campus-wide buildings and classrooms, 7 laboratories, and 2 libraries available to graduate students. Facilities are handicapped accessible. The school also owns about 10 reserves throughout California, plus a 25-acre farm and a 4-acre garden, that are available for student research.

Career Counseling and Job Placement

Student internships are offered as an academic unit within the program. Since this is a new program, the percentage of students that find work within six months of graduation is still unknown.

UNIVERSITY OF COLORADO AT BOULDER

With a total enrollment of 25,090 students (5,000 graduate students), the University of Colorado at Boulder is the largest of the four campuses of the University of Colorado system. It was established in 1875 and is located in a small, cosmopolitan city (population 83,000) not far from Denver and the Front Range of the Rocky Mountains.

School of Law

CENTER CONTACT:

Katherine Taylor, Coordinator
Natural Resources Law Center
University of Colorado School of Law
Campus Box 401
Boulder, CO 80309-0401

Phone: 303-492-1286
Fax: 303-492-1297

ADMISSIONS CONTACT:

Admissions Office
University of Colorado
Campus Box 403
Boulder, CO 80309-0403

Phone: 303-492-7203

School of Law Web site: http://stripe.colorado.edu/~lawadmin/

University of Colorado at Boulder Web site: http://www.colorado.edu/

Quick Facts About the School of Law

• Year established: 1982

• Enrollment: 476 students

• Graduate degree conferred: Juris Doctorate

• Doctoral degree requirements include: required courses for 1st and 2nd year students

Areas of Specialization

Environmental Law (50%)

Special Program Features

This program is best known for its emphasis on environmental law: Indian, water, natural resources, and policy. Graduate students can cross-register for courses within other departments. Joint degree programs are offered with the Business School. International program experiences are not offered, but students may participate through other programs and transfer credit. Future program plans are being formulated.

Admission to the Program

- Admission requirements include LSAT scores in the 94th percentile (165 out of 180)
- Doctoral students accepted each year (on average): 18% of 2,750 applicants
- Students may matriculate only in the fall; transfer students are accepted.

About the Students

There are 262 male and 214 female graduate students currently enrolled in this program; all 476 are full-time; 80% are Caucasian, 4.6% Black, 11.1% Hispanic, 2.9% Native American, and 1.4% Asian. Graduate students range from age 21 to 45, with a median age of 26.

About the Faculty

There are 33 faculty affiliated with this program. The average faculty member teaches 4 courses per year. There is no formal faculty advising system. Faculty research is currently being conducted both domestically and internationally. Three faculty specialize in Environmental Education, 4 in Environmental Law, 2 in Environmental Studies, and 4 in Resource Policy and Planning.

Tuition and Financial Aid

Graduate tuition in 1996 was $3,014 per year for state residents and $13,014 for nonresidents. Over 60% of the graduate students in this program receive financial aid. Sixty percent of the doctoral students are awarded scholarships, and 11% are awarded research assistantships.

Facilities

Computer facilities include 12 IBM/clones, 9 Macintoshes, one terminal per 10 students, aproximately 200 university-wide computers, and access to Internet and E-mail. Free or low-cost computer training is available. One building, 11 classrooms, and 6 libraries are available to graduate students. Some facilities are handicapped accessible.

Career Counseling and Job Placement

This program offers both student externships for credit and internships for money. Many externships are with local government and public interest groups. Career counseling and job placement services include job placement counselors, active alumni contact, on-campus interviews, job books, an alumni database, and job fairs. Thirty percent of alumni work within the government sector, 3% for nonprofits, 46% for private small business, and 2% for industries; 78% of alumni work in the West, 3% in Washington, D.C., and 1% in international locations. Eighty-six percent of the students find work within six months of graduation.

☛ Other graduate environmental programs at University of Colorado at Boulder (no profiles available):

Department of Environmental, Population, and Organismic Biology. *Contact:* Jill Skarstad, Graduate Secretary, Campus Box 334, Department of EPO Biology, University of Colorado, Boulder, CO 80309-0334. *Phone:* 303-492-8982. *Fax:* 303-492-8699. *E-mail:* jill.skarstad@colorado.edu.

Cooperative Institute for Research in Environmental Sciences, a research institute of the Graduate School. *Contact:* Susan K. Avery, Director, Cooperative Institute for Research in Environmental Sciences, University of Colorado at Boulder, Boulder, CO 80309-0216. *E-mail:* cires@cires.colorado.edu.

Interdisciplinary Graduate Certificate Program in Environmental Policy. *Contact:* Environmental Policy Certificate Program, Center for Public Policy Research, University of Colorado at Boulder, Ketchum 126, Campus Box 330, Boulder, CO 80309-0330. *Phone:* 303-492-8586. *Fax:* 303-492-0978.

UNIVERSITY OF COLORADO AT DENVER

Established in 1876, the University of Colorado at Denver has a total enrollment of 11,190 students. Situated on an urban campus in the city of Denver, it is the second largest of the four campuses of the University of Colorado system.

☛ Environmental Sciences Program

PROGRAM CONTACT:

Rosemary Wormington
Administrative Assistant
Environmental Sciences Program
University of Colorado at Denver
Campus Box 136
P.O. Box 173364
Denver, CO 80217-3364

Phone: 303-556-4520
Fax: 303-556-4292

ADMISSIONS CONTACT:

Office of Admissions
University of Colorado at Denver
Campus Box 167
P.O. Box 173364
Denver, CO 80217-3364

Phone: 303-556-2704 or 4841
Fax: 303-556-4838

University of Colorado at Denver Web site: http://www.cudenver.edu/

Quick Facts About the Environmental Sciences Program

- Year established: 1971
- Enrollment: 68 master's students
- Graduate degree conferred: Master of Science
- Master's degree requirements include: required courses, master's project
- Faculty/Advisee ratio: 7:34

Areas of Specialization

Earth Science (25% of students)
Environmental Quality and Public Health (20%)
Environmental Science (20%)
Applied and Quantitative Ecology (15%)
Conservation Biology (5%)
Resource Policy and Planning (5%)

Special Program Features

This program is best known for its emphasis on air pollution chemistry and public health (toxicology, risk assessment, and epidemiology). Graduate students can cross-register for courses within other departments. Joint degree programs and international program experiences are not offered. Future program plans include growth and continual development of courses to enhance the curriculum.

Admission to the Program

- Admission requirements for master's applicants include: 2 semesters of chemistry, 1 of biology, 1 of calculus, 1 of physical science, 1 of statistics; an undergraduate degree in a natural/physical science, or engineering; GRE scores
- Master's students accepted each year (on average): 35% of 85 applicants
- Students may matriculate at the start of any term; transfer students are sometimes accepted.

About the Students

There are 32 male and 36 female graduate students currently enrolled in this program; 38 are full-time and 32 part-time; 2 are international and 66 domestic; 93% are Caucasian, 2% Black, 3% Hispanic, and 2% Asian.

About the Faculty

There are 14 faculty affiliated with this program. The average faculty member teaches 4 courses and advises 5 master's students per year. Students choose their faculty advisors. Faculty research is currently being conducted both domestically and internationally. One faculty member specializes in Conservation Biology, 1 in Environmental Geography, 2 in Environmental Quality and Public Health, and 1 in Resource Policy and Planning.

Tuition and Financial Aid

Tuition in 1996 was $2,846 per year for state residents and $10,720 for nonresidents. Under 20% of the graduate students in this program receive financial aid. Two percent of the master's students are awarded scholarships, and 8% are awarded teaching or research assistantships.

Facilities

Computer facilities include a campus mainframe and access to Internet and E-mail. Free or low-cost computer training is available. Five libraries are available to graduate students. Facilities are handicapped accessible.

Career Counseling and Job Placement

This program offers student internships or educational opportunities within the local commmunity. No career counseling and job placement services are available. Forty percent of alumni work within the government sector, 40% for private small business, and 10% in science or academia.

☞ Program Concentration in Environmental Affairs

FACULTY CONTACT:

Lloyd Burton
Program Concentration in Environmental Affairs
Graduate School of Public Affairs
University of Colorado at Denver
1445 Market Street, Suite 350
Denver, CO 80202

Phone: 303-820-5600
Fax: 303-534-8774

Graduate School of Public Affairs Web site:
http://www.cudenver.edu/~rworming/index.html
http://www.cudenver.edu/public/gspa/menu.html

Quick Facts About the Program Concentration in Environmental Affairs

• Year established: 1975
• Enrollment: 320 master's students / 90 doctoral students
• Graduate degrees conferred: Master of Public Affairs, Master of Criminal Justice, doctorate
• Master's degree requirements include: required courses, master's thesis (optional), qualifying exam
• Doctoral degree requirements include: required courses, dissertation, qualifying exam
• Faculty/Advisee ratio: 1:25

Special Program Features

This program is best known for its emphasis on environmental law and policy, and health policy and administration. Graduate students can cross-register for courses within other departments. Joint degree programs are offered with the Law School and Department of City Planning. International program experiences include student exchanges and conferences in Central America and China.

Admission to the Program

- Admission requirements for doctoral applicants include: average GRE scores of 582 verbal/614 math; no master's degree is required
- Master's students accepted each year (on average): 80% of 150 applicants
- Doctoral students accepted each year (on average): 25% of 65 applicants
- Students may matriculate at the start of any term; transfer students are accepted.

About the Students

There are 250 male and 160 female graduate students currently enrolled in this program; 80 are full-time and 330 part-time; 20 are international and 390 domestic; 80% are Caucasian, 5% Black, and 10% Hispanic. Graduate students range from age 22 to 65, with a median age of 30 to 35.

About the Faculty

There are 17 faculty affiliated with this program. The average faculty member teaches 4 courses and advises 2–3 doctoral students per year. Advisors are both assigned to and chosen by students. Faculty research is currently being conducted both domestically and internationally.

Tuition and Financial Aid

Tuition in 1994 was $3,100 for state residents and $9,936 for nonresidents. Under 20% of the graduate students in this program receive financial aid. Twenty percent of the master's students are awarded scholarships, 10% are awarded research assistantships. Twenty percent of the doctoral students are awarded fellowships, 20% are awarded teaching or research assistantships.

Career Counseling and Job Placement

This program offers student internships or educational opportunities within the local commmunity. Seventy-five percent of alumni work within the government sector, 5% for semi-governmental organizations, 10% for nonprofits, and 10% in science or academia; 90% of alumni work in the Rocky Mountain region. Ninety percent of the students find work within six months of graduation.

☛ Other graduate environmental programs at University of Colorado at Denver (no profiles available):

Program in Environmental and Land Use Planning. *Contact:* Dr. Ray Studer, Urban and Regional Planning Program, School of Architecture and Planning, University of Colorado at Denver, Campus Box 126, P.O. Box 173364, Denver, CO 80217-3364.

Master of Science in Civil Engineering. *Contact:* Dr. N.Y. Chang, Department of Civil Engineering, University of Colorado at Denver, Campus Box 113, P.O. Box 173364, Denver, CO 80217-3364. *Phone:* 303-556-2871.

UNIVERSITY OF CONNECTICUT

Established in 1881, the University of Connecticut has a total enrollment of 24,130 students. It is located in Storrs, in a scenic agricultural area 25 miles from the capital city of Hartford.

☛ Department of Ecology & Evolutionary Biology

FACULTY CONTACT:

John A. Silander, Professor
Department of Ecology &
    Evolutionary Biology
University of Connecticut
Box U-43
75 North Eagleville Road
Storrs, CT 06269-3043

Phone: 203-486-4300

ADMISSIONS CONTACT:

Graduate Admissions Office
University of Connecticut
U-6, Room 108
438 Whitney Road Ext.
Storrs, CT 06269-1006

Phone: 203-486-3617

Department of Ecology and Evolutionary Biology Web site:
http://kottke.eeb.uconn.edu/

University of Connecticut Web site: http://www.uconn.edu/

Quick Facts About the Department of Ecology & Evolutionary Biology

- Year established: 1985
- Enrollment: 11 master's students / 41 doctoral students

- Graduate degrees conferred: Master of Science, doctorate
- Master's degree requirements include: required courses, master's thesis (a few students complete non-thesis degrees)
- Doctoral degree requirements include: required courses, dissertation, oral exam, thesis defense
- Faculty/Advisee ratio: 1:2

Areas of Specialization

Population and Community Ecology (21% of students)
Evolutionary Biology (21%)
Plant Systematics (15%)
Conservation Biology (10%)
Animal Systematics (8%)
Ecosystem Ecology (6%)
Physiological Ecology (6%)
Botany (6%)
Behavioral Biology (4%)
Marine Ecology (2%)

Special Program Features

This program is best known for its emphasis on plant ecology, tropical biology, evolutionary biology, systematics, and animal behavior. Graduate students can cross-register for courses within other departments. Joint degree programs are not offered. International program experiences include research opportunities, internships, and field stations in Central and South America. Future program plans include more students and course offerings in conservation biology.

Admission to the Program

- Admission recommendations for master's applicants include: 4 semesters of chemistry, 6 of biology, 2 of calculus, 2 of physical science, 2 of statistics, 2 of computer science
- Average GRE scores for all graduate students: 680 verbal/720 math
- No master's degree required for doctoral applicants
- Master's students accepted each year (on average): 20% of 10 applicants
- Doctoral students accepted each year (on average): 18% of 90 applicants

• Students may matriculate at the start of any term; transfer students are accepted.

About the Students

There are 35 male and 17 female graduate students currently enrolled in this program; 46 are full-time and 6 part-time; 12 are international and 40 domestic. 77% are Caucasian. Graduate students range from age 22 to 56, with a median age of 31.8.

About the Faculty

There are 28 faculty affiliated with this program. The average faculty member teaches 2 courses and advises 0.5 master's and 5 doctoral students per year. Teams of advisors work with students. Faculty research is currently being conducted both domestically and internationally. Seven percent of the faculty specialize in Plant Systematics, 11% in Animal Systematics, 28% in Evolutionary Biology, 7% in Behavioral Biology, 7% in Ecosystem Ecology, 11% in Botany, 21% in Population and Community Ecology, 4% in Physiological Ecology, and 4% in Marine Ecology.

Tuition and Financial Aid

Tuition in 1996 was $4,800 per year for state residents and $12,474 for non-residents. Over 60% of the graduate students in this program receive financial aid. Sixty-four percent of the master's students are awarded teaching or research assistantships, and 36% receive outside support. Twenty-two percent of the doctoral students are awarded fellowships, 12% are awarded scholarships, and 46% are awarded teaching or research assistantships.

Facilities

Computer facilities include 25 IBM/clones, 8 Macintoshes, a university computer center, labs, mainframe, and access to Internet and E-mail. Free or low-cost computer training is available. There are 3 buildings, 4 classrooms, 6 laboratories, various museum collections, and 4 libraries available to graduate students. Some facilities are handicapped accessible. The school also owns research farms and natural areas, woodlands, fields, forests, ponds and streams that are available for student research.

Career Counseling and Job Placement

This program offers student internships, including both regional and international placements with The Nature Conservancy. Career counseling and job placement services include job books, an alumni database, and occasional workshops. Alumni work in all sectors. All students find work within six months of graduation.

UNIVERSITY OF FLORIDA

With a total enrollment of 35,110 students, the University of Florida is located on 2,000 acres in the mid-sized city of Gainesville (population 150,000), which has a mild climate and is situated in close proximity to a series of freshwater lakes, rivers, and beaches. Founded in 1853, this school belongs to the Hispanic Association of Colleges and Universities.

☙ Botany Program

FACULTY CONTACT:

J. Thomas Mullins,
    Graduate Coordinator
Department of Botany
University of Florida
220 Bartram Hall
P.O. Box 118526
Gainesville, FL 32611-8529

Phone: 904-392-1095

ADMISSIONS CONTACT:

Office of Admissions
201 Criser Hall
University of Florida
Gainesville, FL 32611

Phone: 904-392-1365

University of Florida Web site: http://www.ufl.edu/

Quick Facts About the Botany Program

- Year established: 1909
- Enrollment: 19 master's students / 19 doctoral students
- Graduate degrees conferred: Master of Science, doctorate
- Master's degree requirements include: required courses, master's thesis, oral exam on thesis

- Doctoral degree requirements include: required courses, dissertation, qualifying exam, oral exam
- Faculty/Advisee ratio: 7:19

Areas of Specialization

Applied and Quantitative Ecology (46% of students)
Botany (25%)
Conservation Biology (8%)
Paleontology (5%)
Ecological Genetics (5%)

Special Program Features

This program is best known for its emphasis on tropical plant ecology. Graduate students can cross-register for courses within other departments. Joint degree programs are not offered. International program experiences include research opportunities and field stations in Central America.

Admission to the Program

- Admission requirements for all graduate applicants include: average GRE scores: 610 verbal/647 math/671 analytical
- Master's degree not required for doctoral applicants
- Graduate students accepted each year (on average): 60% of 42 applicants
- Students may matriculate at the start of any term; transfer students are sometimes accepted.

About the Students

There are 18 male and 20 female graduate students currently enrolled in this program; 37 are full-time and 1 part-time; 11 are international and 27 domestic; 74% are Caucasian, 10% Hispanic, and 16% Asian. Graduate students range from age 22 to 45.

About the Faculty

There are 14 faculty affiliated with this program. The average faculty member teaches 2.5–3 courses and advises 2 master's and 2 doctoral students per year. Advisors are both assigned to and chosen by students. Faculty research is currently being conducted both domestically and internationally. Six faculty specialize in Applied and Quantitative Ecology and one in Paleobotany.

Tuition and Financial Aid

Tuition in 1996 was $109 per credit hour for state residents and $362 for nonresidents. Over 60% of the graduate students in this program receive financial aid.

Facilities

Computer facilities include a university main frame and access to Internet and E-mail. Free or low-cost computer training is available. There are various museum collections and libraries available to graduate students, as well as a 280-acre wildlife sanctuary and the 57-acre Bivens Arm Nature Park. Facilities are handicapped accessible. The school also has access to state, federal, and private lands that are available for student research.

Career Counseling and Job Placement

This program does not offer student internships. Career counseling and job placement services are unofficial; usually school is contacted directly by employers.

☞ Other graduate environmental programs at University of Florida (no profiles available):

School of Forest Resources & Conservation (Master of Forest Resources and Conservation, Master of Science, Ph.D.). *Contact:* Timothy White, Graduate Coordinator, School of Forest Resources & Conservation, 118 Newins-Ziegler Hall, P.O. Box 110420, University of Florida, Gainesville, FL 32611-0420. *Phone:* 904-392-1791. *Fax:* 904-392-1707.

Department of Environmental Engineering Sciences. *Contact:* J. Delfino, Chair.

Department of Environmental Horticulture. *Contact:* C. Gray, Graduate Coordinator.

Department of Food and Resource Economics. *Contact:* R. Kilmer, Graduate Coordinator.

Department of Geography. *Contact:* T. Fik, Graduate Coordinator.

Department of Geology, Specialty in Environmental Geology. *Contact:* P. Mueller.

Department of Soil and Water Science. *Contact:* J. Sarturn, Graduate Coordinator.

UNIVERSITY OF ILLINOIS AT SPRINGFIELD

Formerly known as Sangamon State University, the University of Illinois at Springfield was established in 1969 and has a total enrollment of 4,540 students. Its setting is a 746-acre campus in a mid-sized, capital city.

☜ Program in Environmental Studies

FACULTY CONTACT:

Malcolm Levin, Chair
Program in Environmental Studies
School of Public Affairs and Administration
University of Illinois at Springfield
Springfield, IL 62794-9243

Phone: 800-252-8533 or 217-786-6720

University of Illinois at Springfield Web site: http://www.uis.edu

Quick Facts About the Program in Environmental Studies

- Year established: 1970
- Enrollment: 109 master's students
- Graduate degree conferred: Master of Arts
- Master's degree requirements include: required courses; master's thesis, or comprehensive exam plus additional course work; master's project; internship experience (optional)
- Faculty/Advisee ratio: 1:20

Areas of Specialization

Resource Policy and Planning (35% of students)
Environmental Quality and Public Health (30%)

Corporate Environmental Management (10%)
Environmental Geography (10%)
Environmental Science (10%)
Environmental Studies (5%)

Special Program Features

This program is best known for its emphasis on environmental planning, environmental administration, and risk assessment. Graduate students can cross-register for courses within other departments. Joint degree programs and international program experiences are not offered.

Admission to the Program

- Admission requirements for master's applicants include: a baccalaureate degree and GPA of 3.0; admission with GPA of 2.5 contingent upon satisfactory completion of core curriculum
- Master's students accepted each year (on average): 50% of 30–50 applicants
- Students may matriculate at the start of any term; transfer students are accepted.

About the Students

There are 60 male and 49 female graduate students currently enrolled in this program; 64 are full-time and 45 part-time; 6 are international and 103 domestic; 90% are Caucasian, 3% Black, and 1% Asian. Graduate students range from age 22 to 55, with a median age of 32.

About the Faculty

There are 13 faculty affiliated with this program. The average faculty member teaches 6 courses and advises 5 master's students per year. Advisors are both assigned to and chosen by students. Faculty research is currently being conducted domestically. One faculty member specializes in Applied and Quantitative Ecology, 1 in Corporate Environmental Management, 2 in Earth Science, 1 in Environmental Education, 1 in Environmental Geography, 1 in Environmental Law, 1 in Environmental Quality and Public Health, and 2 in Resource Policy and Planning.

Tuition and Financial Aid

Tuition in 1996 was $83 per credit hour for state residents and $249 per credit hour for nonresidents. Under 20% of the graduate students in this program receive financial aid. Two percent of the master's students are awarded scholarships, and 2% are awarded administrative assistantships.

Facilities

Computer facilities include 5 IBM/clones, university computer labs with both IBM/clones and Macs, 2 GIS computers, and access to Internet and E-mail. Free or low-cost computer training is available. Various laboratories and libraries are available to graduate students. Facilities are handicapped accessible.

Career Counseling and Job Placement

This program offers student internships or educational opportunities within the local commmunity. Career counseling and job placement services are not offered. Forty-five percent of alumni work within the government sector, 5% for nonprofits, 10% for private small business, 20% for corporations or industries, and 20% in science or academia; 80% of alumni work in Illinois.

THE UNIVERSITY OF IOWA

With a total enrollment of 27,460 students, the University of Iowa was established in 1847. It is located in the small city of Iowa City, on a campus surrounded by rolling countryside.

☜ Department of Preventive Medicine & Environmental Health

FACULTY CONTACT:

James Merchant, Professor
100 Oakdale Campus, 124 AMRF
The University of Iowa
Iowa City, IA 52242-5000

Phone: 319-335-4189

ADMISSIONS CONTACT:

Office of Admissions
The University of Iowa
107 Calvin Hall
Iowa City, IA 52242-1396

Phone: 319-335-3847
            or 800-553-IOWA

Department of Preventive Medicine and Environmental Health Web site:
http://www.pmeh.uiowa.edu/

The University of Iowa Web site: http://www.uiowa.edu/

Quick Facts About the Department of Preventive Medicine & Environmental Health

- Year established: 1921
- Enrollment: 17 master's students / 11 doctoral students
- Graduate degrees conferred: Master of Science, doctorate
- Master's degree requirements include: required courses, master's thesis or master's exam and preceptorship
- Doctoral degree requirements include: required courses, dissertation, internship experience (preceptorship), qualifying exam, written exam
- Faculty/Advisee ratio: 1:2.8

Areas of Specialization (no statistics available)

Urban and Regional Planning
Occupational Health
Environmental Health
Agricultural Health
Industrial Hygiene

Special Program Features

This program is best known for its emphasis on agricultural health, industrial hygiene, environmental health, and occupational health. Graduate students can cross-register for courses within other departments. Joint degree programs are offered with the Department of Urban and Regional Planning. International program experiences are not offered.

Admission to the Program

- Admission requirements for master's applicants include: 2 semesters of chemistry, 1 of calculus, 1 of physical science; average GRE scores: 1120 combined
- Admission requirements for doctoral applicants include: average GRE scores: 1140 combined; master's degree not required

- Master's students accepted each year (on average): 60% of 19 applicants
- Doctoral students accepted each year (on average): 80% of 5 applicants
- Students may matriculate at the start of any term; transfer students are accepted.

About the Students

There are 14 male and 14 female graduate students currently enrolled in this program; 21 are full-time and 7 part-time; 5 are international and 23 domestic; 82% are Caucasian and 18% Asian. Graduate students range from age 23 to 47, with a median age of 31.

About the Faculty

There are 15 faculty affiliated with this program. The average faculty member teaches 1 course and advises 2 master's and 0.5 doctoral students per year. Advisors are assigned, but students may change them. Faculty research is currently being conducted both domestically and internationally. One faculty member specializes in Corporate Environmental Management, 1 in Environmental Quality and Public Health, 1 in Environmental Chemistry, 5 in Agricultural Health, 4 in Occupational Health, 5 in Environmental Health, and 4 in Industrial Hygiene.

Tuition and Financial Aid

Tuition in 1996 was $2,834 per year for state residents and $9,002 for non-residents. Some 41–60% of the graduate students in this program receive financial aid. Forty-seven percent of the master's students are awarded fellowships, 11% are awarded scholarships, 41% are awarded research assistantships. Forty-five percent of the doctoral students are awarded fellowships, 9% are awarded scholarships, and 45% are awarded research assistantships.

Facilities

Computer facilities include a campus computer center and access to Internet and E-mail. Free or low-cost computer training is available. There are 3 buildings, 4 classrooms, 6 laboratories, and 10 libraries available to graduate students. All facilities are handicapped accessible.

Career Counseling and Job Placement

This program offers student preceptorships with local industry, the Public Health Department, and health care organizations. Career counseling and job placement services include job placement counselors, job books, and job fairs. Twenty-eight percent of alumni work within the government sector, 16% for private small business, 28% for corporations or industries, and 12% in science or academia; 16% go for a Ph.D. or to medical school; 60% of alumni work in the Midwest and 12% in international locations. All students find work within six months of graduation.

UNIVERSITY OF LOUISVILLE

Established in 1798, the University of Louisville has a total enrollment of 22,630 students. Its campus is two miles from the downtown area of the large city of Louisville, Kentucky.

☙ Biology Program

FACULTY CONTACT:

William Davis, Graduate Advisor
Department of Biology
University of Louisville
139 Life Sciences Building
Louisville, KY 40292

Phone: 502-852-5490
Fax: 502-852-0725

ADMISSIONS CONTACT:

Office of Admissions, Dept. AO
University of Louisville
Louisville, KY 40292

Phone: 502-588-6531

Department of Biology Web site: http://www.louisville.edu/a-s/biology/

University of Louisville Web site: http://www.louisville.edu/

Quick Facts About the Biology Program

- Year established: 1907
- Enrollment: 40 master's students / 27 doctoral students
- Graduate degrees conferred: Master of Science, doctorate
- Master's degree requirements include: required courses, master's thesis

- Doctoral degree requirements include: required courses, dissertation, qualifying exam, oral exam
- Faculty/Advisee ratio: 1:1

Areas of Specialization

Environmental Science (50% of students)
Applied and Quantitative Ecology (20%)
Water Resource Management (20%)
Microbial Ecology (15%)
Botany (5%)

Special Program Features

This program is best known for its emphasis on aquatic ecology, large river studies, and biological adaptation to environment (microgravity & exercise). Graduate students can cross-register for courses within other departments. Joint degree programs are offered with the School of Education. International program experiences are not offered. Future program plans include expanded offerings due to new faculty positions.

Admission to the Program

- Admission requirements for master's applicants include: 4 semesters of chemistry, 5 of biology, 2 of calculus, 1 of physical science; bachelor's degree with GPA above 3.0; average GRE scores: 500 verbal/560 math
- Admission requirements for doctoral applicants include: average GRE scores: 555 verbal/605 math; master's degree not required
- Graduate students accepted each year (on average): 25% of 40 applicants
- Students may matriculate at the start of any term; transfer students are accepted.

About the Students

There are 37 male and 30 female graduate students currently enrolled in this program; 55 are full-time and 12 part-time; 7 are international and 60 domestic; 92% are Caucasian, 1% Black, and 7% Asian. Graduate students range from age 21 to 55, with a median age of 24.

About the Faculty

There are 22 faculty affiliated with this program. The average faculty member teaches 4 courses and advises 3–4 master's and 2–3 doctoral students per year. Students choose their faculty advisors. Faculty research is currently being conducted both domestically and internationally. Four faculty specialize in Applied and Quantitative Ecology, 5 in Botany, 22 in Environmental Science, and 5 in Molecular Biology, Physiology, and Microbiology.

Tuition and Financial Aid

Tuition in 1996 was $2,480 per year for state residents and $7,440 for nonresidents. Some 41–60% of the graduate students in this program receive financial aid. Forty-three percent of the master's students are awarded teaching assistantships. Six percent of the doctoral students are awarded fellowships, and 65% are awarded teaching or research assistantships.

Facilities

Computer facilities include 40 IBM/clones, 40 Macintoshes, one terminal per 5 students, and access to Internet and E-mail. Free or low-cost computer training is available. There are 2 buildings, 8 classrooms, 21 laboratories, and 4 libraries available to graduate students. Facilities are handicapped accessible. The school also owns Burnheim Forest, which includes streams and ponds and is available for student research. Several nature preserves are within 30 minutes of the school, and the Ohio River is 3 miles from campus.

Career Counseling and Job Placement

This program offers student internships with the EPA, the Louisville Water Company, and local industry. Career counseling and job placement services are not offered. Fifty percent of alumni work within the government sector, 25% for corporations or industries, and 25% in science or academia. All students find work within six months of graduation.

UNIVERSITY OF MAINE

With a total enrollment of 12,500 students, the University of Maine is located on a 3,298-acre campus in the rural town of Orono.

☝ Wildlife Ecology Program

FACULTY CONTACT:

James Gilbert, Chair
Department of Wildlife Ecology
210 Nutting Hall
University of Maine
Orono, ME 04469-5755

Phone: 207-581-2862
Fax: 207-581-3232

ADMISSIONS CONTACT:

Graduate School
5782 Winslow Hall
University of Maine
Orono, ME 04469-5782

Phone: 207-581-3218

Department of Wildlife Ecology Web site:
http://wlm13.umenfa.maine.edu/w4v1.html

University of Maine Web site: http://www.ume.maine.edu/

Quick Facts About the Wildlife Ecology Program

- Year established: 1935
- Enrollment: 16 master's students / 12 doctoral students
- Graduate degrees conferred: Master of Science, Master of Wildlife Conservation, doctorate
- Master's degree requirements include: required courses, master's thesis
- Doctoral degree requirements include: required courses, dissertation, oral exam
- Faculty/Advisee ratio: 2:7

Areas of Specialization

Applied and Quantitative Ecology (65% of students)
Environmental Geography (20%)
Conservation Biology (10%)
Environmental Quality and Public Health (5%)

Special Program Features

This program is best known for its emphasis on applied quantitative ecology, conservation biology, and environmental geography. Graduate students can cross-register for courses within other departments. Joint degree programs are not offered. International program experiences are offered in the Middle East.

Admission to the Program

- Admission requirements for master's applicants include: 2 semesters of chemistry, 4 of biology, 1 of calculus, 2 of natural science; B.S. degree
- Master's degree generally required for doctoral applicants
- Average GRE scores for all graduate students: 650 verbal/650 math
- Graduate students accepted each year (on average): 5% of 120 applicants
- Students may matriculate at the start of any term; transfer students are accepted.

About the Students

There are 16 male and 12 female graduate students currently enrolled in this program; 27 are full-time and 1 part-time; 3 are international and 25 domestic.

About the Faculty

There are 9 faculty affiliated with this program. The average faculty member teaches 3 courses and advises 2 master's and 2 doctoral students per year. Faculty advisors choose their students. Faculty research is currently being conducted both domestically and internationally. Ninety percent of the faculty specialize in Applied and Quantitative Ecology and 10% in Environmental Geography.

Tuition and Financial Aid

Tuition in 1996 was $168 per credit hour for state residents and $476 for nonresidents. All graduate students in this program receive financial aid; 10% are awarded teaching assistantships, and 90% are awarded research assistantships.

Facilities

Computer facilities include 40 IBM/clones, a mainframe, 5 GIS computers, computer clusters in dorms, and access to Internet and E-mail. Free or low-cost computer training is available. The school also owns various plots, including a 2,000-acre forest adjacent to campus and two refuges—one of 200 acres and another about 300 acres; all are available for student research.

Career Counseling and Job Placement

This program does not offer student internships. Career counseling and job placement services include job placement counselors, active alumni contact, on-campus interviews, and an alumni database. Forty percent of alumni work within the government sector, 15% for nonprofits, 5% for private small business, 5% for corporations or industries, and 35% in science or academia. All students find work within six months of graduation.

☛ Forest Management Program

FACULTY CONTACT:
David Field
Graduate Coordinator and Chair
Department of Forest Management
University of Maine
5755 Nutting Hall
Orono, ME 04469-5755

ADMINISTRATIVE CONTACT:
Cindy Paschal
Administrative Assistant
Department of Forest Management
University of Maine
5755 Nutting Hall
Orono, ME 04469-5755

Phone: 207-581-2856
Fax: 207-581-2858
E-mail:
field@apollo.umenfa.maine.edu

Phone: (207)581-2841

E-mail:
paschal@apollo.umenfa.maine.edu

Forest Management Program Web site:
http://www.ume.maine.edu/~nfa/for_mgt/welcome.htm

Quick Facts About the Department of Forest Management

- Enrollment: 61 master's students / 25 doctoral students
- Graduate degrees conferred: Master of Science, Master of Forestry, doctorate
- Master's degree requirements include: master's thesis for M.S., master's project for M.F.
- Doctoral degree requirements include: dissertation, qualifying exam, oral exam
- Faculty/Advisee ratio: 1:5

Special Program Features

Graduate students can cross-register for courses within other departments. Joint degree programs are not offered. International program experiences include research opportunities and student exchanges in Central America.

Admission to the Program

- Admission requirements for master's applicants include: average GRE scores: 550 verbal/680 math
- Admission requirements for doctoral applicants include: average GRE scores: 600 verbal/720 math; master's degree is not required
- Graduate students accepted each year (on average): 50% of 155 applicants
- Students may matriculate at the start of any term; transfer students are accepted.

About the Students

There are 57 full-time and 29 part-time graduate students currently enrolled in this program; 75% are Caucasian, 2% Hispanic, and 14% Asian. Graduate students range from age 25 to 35, with a median age of 30.

About the Faculty

There are 22 faculty affiliated with this program. The average faculty member teaches 2 courses and advises 2 master's and 3 doctoral students per year. Advisors are both assigned to and chosen by students.

Tuition and Financial Aid

Some 21–40% of the graduate students in this program receive financial aid. Five percent of the master's students are awarded fellowships, and 20% are awarded teaching or research assistantships. Five percent of the doctoral students are awarded fellowships, and 72% are awarded teaching or research assistantships.

Career Counseling and Job Placement

This program does not offer student internships. Career counseling and job placement services include active alumni contact and job books. Ten percent of alumni work within the government sector, 10% for semi-governmental organizations, 10% for private small business, 40% for corporations or industries, and 30% in science or academia; 40% of alumni work in Maine and 10% in Washington, D.C. All students find work within six months of graduation.

UNIVERSITY OF MARYLAND AT COLLEGE PARK

Located in the small city of College Park, not far from the Chesapeake Bay, the University of Maryland at College Park has a total enrollment of 32,860 students, 9,000 of whom are graduate students.

☜ Graduate Program in Sustainable Development and Conservation Biology

FACULTY CONTACT:

David Inouye, Director
Graduate Program in
    Sustainable Development and
    Conservation Biology
Zoology–Psychology Bldg.,
    Room 1201
University of Maryland
    at College Park
College Park, MD 20742

Phone: 301-405-7409

ADMISSIONS CONTACT:

Office of Graduate Admissions
University of Maryland
    at College Park
2107 Lee Building
College Park, MD 20742-5121

Phone: 301-405-4198

University of Maryland College Park Web site: http://www.umcp.umd.edu/

Quick Facts About the Graduate Program in Sustainable Development & Conservation Biology

• Year established: 1989

• Enrollment: 30 master's students

• Graduate degree conferred: Master of Science

• Master's degree requirements include: required courses, master's thesis, internship experience

• Faculty/Advisee ratio: 1:5

Areas of Specialization

Conservation Biology (90% of students)
Sustainable Development (10%)

Special Program Features

This program is best known for its emphasis on conservation biology, and problem solving. Graduate students can cross-register for courses within other departments. Joint degree programs are not offered. International program experiences include internships and field stations in South America.

Admission to the Program

- Admission requirements for master's applicants include: average GRE scores: 610 verbal/650 math/660 analytical
- Master's students accepted each year (on average): 25% of 48 applicants
- Students may matriculate only in the fall; transfer students are sometimes accepted.

About the Students

There are 20 male and 10 female graduate students currently enrolled in this program; 28 are full-time and 2 part-time; 7 are international and 23 domestic; 75% are Caucasian, 20% Hispanic, and 5% Asian. Graduate students range from age 21 to 50, with a median age of 25.

About the Faculty

There are 20 faculty affiliated with this program. The average faculty member teaches 3 courses and advises 3 master's students per year. There is group and peer advising of students. Faculty research is currently being conducted both domestically and internationally. Ten faculty specialize in Applied and Quantitative Ecology, 2 in Botany, 3 in Conservation Biology, 1 in Environmental Education, 3 in Environmental Geography, 2 in Environmental Law, 2 in Environmental Quality and Public Health, and 1 in Environmental Studies.

Tuition and Financial Aid

Tuition in 1996 was $3,910 per year for state residents and $6,375 for non-residents. Some 41–60% of the graduate students in this program receive fi-

nancial aid. Fifteen percent of the master's students are awarded fellow-ships, and 55% are awarded teaching or administrative assistantships.

Facilities

Computer facilities include 8 IBM/clones, 4 Macintoshes, 6 GIS comput-ers, and access to Internet and E-mail. Free or low-cost computer training is available. One building, 10 classrooms, 25 laboratories, 3 libraries, and various museum collections are available to graduate students. Facilities are handicapped accessible.

Career Counseling and Job Placement

This program offers student internships as a required part of the program. Job placement services include an alumni database. Twenty percent of alumni work within the government sector, 20% for semi-governmental or-ganizations, 20% for nonprofits, 20% for private small business, and 20% in science or academia; 80% of alumni work in Washington, D.C. and 10% in international locations. Eighty percent of the students find work within six months of graduation.

☜ Program in Plant Ecology

FACULTY CONTACT:

Elisabeth Gantt, Professor
Department of Botany, Program in Plant Ecology
University of Maryland College Park
HJ Patterson Hall, Room 3236
College Park, MD 20742

Phone: 301-405-1624

Quick Facts About the Program in Plant Ecology

- Enrollment: 2 master's students / 48 doctoral students
- Graduate degrees conferred: Master of Science, doctorate
- Master's degree requirements include: required courses, master's thesis (optional)
- Doctoral degree requirements include: dissertation, qualifying exam

Special Program Features

Students specialize in Botany, Systematics, Ecology Physiology, and Development; graduate students can cross-register for courses within other departments. Joint degree programs are not offered. Future program plans include more ecology offerings.

☛ Other graduate environmental programs at University of Maryland College Park (no profiles available):

Graduate Program in Marine, Estuarine & Environmental Sciences. *Contact:* Kenneth Sebens, Director, Department of Natural Sciences. *Phone:* 301-405-7978.
College of Libraries and Information Services. *Contact:* Diane Barlow. *Phone:* 301-405-2033.

UNIVERSITY OF MIAMI

With a total enrollment of 13,160 students, the University of Miami was established in 1925 and is located near Miami, Florida.

☛ Rosenstiel School of Marine and Atmospheric Science

FACULTY CONTACT:

Susan MacMahon
Director of Graduate Studies
Rosenstiel School of Marine
    and Atmospheric Science
University of Miami
4600 Rickenbacker Causeway
Miami, FL 33149-1098

Phone: 305-361-4155

ADMISSIONS CONTACT:

Graduate Studies Office
Rosenstiel School of Marine
    and Atmospheric Science
University of Miami
4600 Rickenbacker Causeway
Miami, FL 33149-1098

Phone: 305-361-4155

Rosenstiel School Web site: http://www.rsmas.miami.edu

University of Miami Web site: http://www.miami.edu/

*Quick Facts About the Rosenstiel School of Marine
and Atmospheric Science*

- Year established: 1943

- Enrollment: 73 master's students / 85 doctoral students

- Graduate degrees conferred: Master of Science, Master of Arts, doctorate

- Master's degree requirements include: required courses, master's thesis, master's project, internship experience, oral comprehensive exam

- Doctoral degree requirements include: required courses, dissertation, qualifying exam

- Faculty/Advisee ratio: 1:2

Areas of Specialization

Marine Biology and Fisheries (32% of students)
Marine Geology and Geophysics (17%)
Meteorology and Physical Oceanography (17%)
Marine Affairs and Policy (15%)
Marine and Atmospheric Chemistry (8%)
Applied Marine Physics (11%)

Special Program Features

This program is known for being one of the top 4 oceanographic institutes in the United States. Graduate students can cross-register for courses within other departments. Joint degree programs and international program experiences are not offered.

Admission to the Program

- Admission requirements for master's applicants include: 5 semesters of chemistry, 5 of biology, 1 of calculus, 3 of physical science (depending upon major)

- Average GRE scores for all graduate students: 550 verbal/700 math

- Master's degree not required for doctoral applicants

- Master's students accepted each year (on average): 19% of 200 applicants

- Doctoral students accepted each year (on average): 18% of 180 applicants

• Students may matriculate only in the fall; transfer students are sometimes accepted.

About the Students

There are 96 male and 62 female graduate students currently enrolled in
this program; 150 are full-time and 8 part-time; 61 are international and 97
domestic; 67% are Caucasian, 2% Black, 12% Hispanic, and 19% Asian.
Graduate students range from age 21 to 35, with a median age of 27.

About the Faculty

There are 68 faculty affiliated with this program. The average faculty member teaches 2 courses and advises 2 master's and 1 doctoral students per
year. Advisors are assigned to students. Faculty research is currently being
conducted internationally. Twenty-five faculty specialize in Applied and
Quantitative Ecology, 34 in Earth Science, 1 in Environmental Law, 13 in
Environmental Science, and 4 in Resource Policy and Planning.

Tuition and Financial Aid

Tuition in 1996 was $706 per credit hour. Almost 100% of all graduate stu-
dents in this program are awarded fellowships, scholarships, teaching assistantships, administrative assistantships, or research assistantships.

Facilities

Computer facilities include access to those on main campus and medical
campus, and access to Internet and E-mail. Free or low-cost computer training is available. There are 9 buildings, 8 classrooms, 120 laboratories, various museum collections, and 3 libraries available to graduate students.
Some facilities are handicapped accessible. The school also owns Bimini Biological Field Station, which is set up for tropical marine biology field research and shark research.

Career Counseling and Job Placement

This program offers student internships with public schools, government
agencies, and other sources. No career counseling and job placement services are available. Thirty percent of alumni work within the government

sector, 5% for semi-governmental organizations, 30% for private small business, and 30% in science or academia.

UNIVERSITY OF MICHIGAN

With a total enrollment of 36,758 students (14,910 of whom are graduate
students), the University of Michigan is located in the cosmopolitan city of
Ann Arbor.

☜ School of Natural Resources and Environment

CONTACT:

School of Natural Resources and Environment
University of Michigan
Dana Building, 430 E. University
Ann Arbor, MI 48109-1115

Phone: 313-764-1404

School of Natural Resources and Environment Web site:
http://www.admins@snre.umich.edu

Quick Facts About the School of Natural Resources and Environment

- Year established: 1950
- Enrollment: 200 graduate students
- Graduate degrees conferred: Master of Science, Master of Landscape Ar-
  chitecture, Master of Forestry
- Doctoral degrees conferred: Ph.D. in Natural Resources and Environ-
  ment, Ph.D. in Landscape Architecture
- Master's degree requirements include: required courses, master's thesis,
  master's project, internship experience, oral comprehensive exam

Areas of Specialization (according to program literature)

Resource Policy and Behavior
Resource Ecology and Management
Landscape Architecture

Special Program Features

This program is known for its comprehensive nature and for its innovative approach to integrating a variety of disciplines. In addition to the three areas of concentration listed above, students specialize in one natural resource area or "sub-field." Joint or dual degree programs are offered in the areas of (1) Law and Natural Resources and Environment, (2) Business School and Natural Resources and Environment, (3) Center for Russian & East European Studies and the School of Natural Resources and Environment, and a variety of additional programs at the University of Michigan.

Tuition and Financial Aid

Tuition in 1996 was $8,878 per year for state residents and $18,038 for non-residents. Seventy-five percent of students receive financial aid, which is available in the form of fellowships, teaching assistantships, and research assistantships.

Facilities

The school operates a microcomputer and geographic information systems laboratory, a remote sensing laboratory, and two landscape architecture studios. The University's graduate library holds over 2 million volumes, and students also have access to the Matthaei Botanical Garden and the Nichols Arboretum.

Career Counseling and Job Placement

Graduates of this program find employment in a wide range of sectors and professions. Examples of recent positions filled include: Media Representative, Sierra Club; Remote Sensing Specialist, ERIM; Director of Public Relations, World Wildlife Fund; Curator, Cincinnati Zoo; and Chairman, New Hampshire Water and Pollution Control Commission.

UNIVERSITY OF MINNESOTA, TWIN CITIES CAMPUS
SCHOOL OF NATURAL RESOURCES

Established in 1851, the University of Minnesota has a total enrollment of 40,000 students. Its setting is an urban campus in the heart of the Minneapolis–St. Paul area.

☜ Forestry Program

FACULTY CONTACT:

Kenneth N. Brooks, Director
Graduate Studies in Forestry
University of Minnesota
School of Natural Resources
235 Natural Resources
   Administration Building
2003 Upper Buford Circle
St. Paul, MN 55108-6146

ADMISSIONS CONTACT:

Office of Student Affairs
College of Natural Resources
135 Natural Resources
   Administration Building
University of Minnesota
2003 Upper Buford Circle
St. Paul, MN 55108-6146

Phone: 612-624-2774
E-mail: CNR-Info@forestry.umn.edu

Phone: (612) 624-6768

School of Natural Resources Web site: http://www.gis.umn.edu/cnr/

University of Minnesota Web site: http://www.umn.edu

Quick Facts About the Forestry Program

- Year established: 1910
- Enrollment: 61 master's students / 65 doctoral students
- Graduate degrees conferred: Master of Science, Master of Forestry, doctorate
- Master's degree requirements include: required courses, master's thesis, master's project
- Doctoral degree requirements include: required courses, dissertation, written preliminary exam, oral preliminary exam, final oral exam
- Faculty/Advisee ratio: 1:4

Areas of Specialization

Forestry (24% of students)
Resource Policy and Planning (23%)
Forest Products (22%)
Parks and Recreation Management (15%)
Environmental Geography (14%)
Applied and Quantitative Ecology (12%)
Earth Science (12%)
Botany (4%)

Special Program Features

This program is best known for its emphasis on biometrics, forest economics/policy, international forestry, and watershed management. Graduate students can cross-register for courses within other departments. Joint degree programs are offered, as approved by Graduate Program. International program experiences include research opportunities, student exchanges, and field stations in numerous countries. Future program plans include curriculum revision to better represent diversity of environmental issues.

Admission to the Program

- Admission requirements for master's applicants include: B.S. degree; average GRE scores: 553 verbal/658 math

- Admission requirements for doctoral applicants include: average GRE scores: 580 verbal/685 math; master's degree is not required

- Master's students accepted each year (on average): 57% of 63 applicants

- Doctoral students accepted each year (on average): 63% of 38 applicants

- Students may matriculate at the start of any term; transfer students are accepted.

About the Students

There are 79 male and 47 female graduate students currently enrolled in this program; 82 are full-time and 44 part-time; 26 are international and 100 domestic; 78.5% are Caucasian, 1.5% Black, 0.7% Native American, and 17% Asian. Graduate students range from age 22 to 51.

About the Faculty

There are 30 faculty affiliated with this program. The average faculty member teaches 3 courses and advises 3 master's and 3 doctoral students per year. Faculty research is currently being conducted both domestically and internationally. Six faculty specialize in Applied and Quantitative Ecology, 5 in Earth Science, 2 in Environmental Geography, 16 in Forestry, 3 in Parks and Recreation Management, 6 in Resource Policy and Planning, and 6 in Natural Resources/Forest Economics.

Tuition and Financial Aid

Tuition in 1996 was $4,350 per year for state residents and $9,390 per year for nonresidents. Over 60% of the graduate students in this program receive financial aid; 5.6% of the master's students are awarded fellowships, 85% are awarded teaching or research assistantships; 5.6% of the doctoral students are awarded fellowships, 82% are awarded teaching or research assistantships.

Facilities

Computer facilities include 25 IBM/clones, 20 Macintoshes, 10 GIS computers, and access to Internet and E-mail. Free or low-cost computer training is available. There are 3 buildings, 6 classrooms, 26 laboratories, and various libraries available to graduate students. Facilities are handicapped accessible. The school also owns a field forestry center, with a laboratory, instructors, and housing, that is available for student research.

Career Counseling and Job Placement

Student internships are available with state and federal agencies but are not initiated by this program. Career counseling and job placement services are not offered. Twenty percent of alumni work within the government sector, 5% for corporations or industries, and 55% in science or academia; 60% of alumni work in Minnesota and 5% in international locations. Eighty percent of the students find work within six months of graduation.

☜ Other graduate environmental programs at University of Minnesota, Twin Cities (no profiles available):

Department of Ecology, Evolution, and Behavior. *Contact:* Edward Cushing, Director of Graduate Studies. *Phone:* 612-625-5713. *Fax:* 612-625-4490.

THE UNIVERSITY OF MONTANA

Located in the small city of Missoula (near Yellowstone National Park), the University of Montana was established in 1893 and has a total enrollment of 10,060 students.

♞ Program in Environmental Studies

FACULTY CONTACT: ADMISSIONS CONTACT:

Tom Roy, Director   Graduate Admissions
Program in Environmental Studies   Graduate School
The University of Montana   The University of Montana
Rankin Hall   Missoula, MT 59812
Missoula, MT 59812

Phone: 406-243-6273

Program in Environmental Studies Web site:
http://www.umt.edu/nss/gradcat/evst.htm

University of Montana Web site: http://www.umt.edu/

Quick Facts About the Program in Environmental Studies

- Year established: 1967
- Enrollment: 80 master's students
- Graduate degree conferred: Master of Science
- Master's degree requirements include: required courses, master's thesis, master's project, internship experience
- Faculty/Advisee ratio: 1:10

Special Program Features

This program is best known for being an interdisciplinary program that em-phasizes environmental science, policy, and ethics equally, and particularly emphasizes advocacy—especially with citizen/public interest groups. Grad-uate students can cross-register for courses within other departments. Joint degree programs are offered with the Law School. International program ex-periences are not offered.

Admission to the Program

- Admission requirements for master's applicants include: 1 semester of bi-ology; average GRE scores: 650 verbal/680 math
- Master's students accepted each year (on average): 35% of 300 applicants
- Students may matriculate only in the fall; transfer students are some-times accepted.

About the Students

There are 40 male and 40 female graduate students currently enrolled in this program; 70 are full-time and 10 part-time; 6 are foreign and 74 domestic; 97% are Caucasian, 1% Black, 1% Hispanic, and 1% Native American. Graduate students range from age 23 to 55, with a median age of 27.

About the Faculty

There are 35 faculty affiliated with this program. The average faculty member teaches 5 courses and advises 10 master's students per year. Advisors are both assigned to and chosen by students. Faculty research is currently being conducted both domestically and internationally. Two faculty specialize in Applied and Quantitative Ecology, 1 in Botany, 2 in Conservation Biology, 1 in Environmental Education, 1 in Environmental Law, 1 in Environmental Quality and Public Health, 1 in Environmental Science, 3 in Environmental Studies, 2 in Resource Policy and Planning, and 1 in Social Ecology.

Tuition and Financial Aid

Tuition in 1996 was $2,237 per year for state residents and $5,565 for nonresidents. Fifty percent of the doctoral students are awarded scholarships and 40% are awarded teaching assistantships.

Facilities

Computer facilities include 5 IBM/clones, 4 Macintoshes, and access to Internet and E-mail. Free or low-cost computer training is available. One building, 3 classrooms, and 1 library are available to graduate students. Facilities are handicapped accessible.

Career Counseling and Job Placement

This program offers student internships. Career counseling and job placement services are not offered. Ten percent of alumni work within the government sector, 10% for semi-governmental organizations, 55% for nonprofits, 5% for private small business, and 10% in science or academia. Ninety percent of the students find work within six months of graduation; 75% find work in their field.

🎓 School of Law

CONTACT:

John Horwich, Associate Dean
School of Law
University of Montana
Missoula, MT 59812

Phone: 406-243-4311
Fax: 406-243-2576

School of Law Web site: http://www.umt.edu/law

Quick Facts About the School of Law

- Year established: 1911
- Enrollment: 226 law students
- Graduate degree conferred: Juris Doctorate
- Tuition in 1994: $9,207 out-of-state / $4,531 in-state

Special Program Features

Fifteen percent of each law class focuses upon Environmental Law; graduate students cannot cross-register for courses within other departments. Future program plans include a joint Juris Doctorate/Master of Environmental Studies degree.

About the Students

Graduate students range from age 22 to 50, with a median age of 29.

About the Faculty

There are 16 faculty affiliated with this program. The average faculty member teaches 4 courses per year. Two faculty specialize in Environmental Law. There is no formal faculty advising system.

Career Counseling and Job Placement

This program does not offer student internships. Career counseling and job placement services include job placement counselors, active alumni contact, on-campus interviews, and job books. Ninety percent of the students find work within six months of graduation.

☀ Other graduate environmental programs at University of Montana (no profiles available):

School of Forestry. *Contact:* Perry Brown, Dean. *Phone:* 406-243-5521. *Fax:* 406-243-4845.

UNIVERSITY OF NEW HAMPSHIRE

Established in 1866, the University of New Hampshire has a total enrollment of 11,500 students and is located on a 200-acre campus in the semirural town of Durham.

☀ Department of Natural Resources

FACULTY CONTACT:

Robert Harter
Graduate Admissions Coordinator
Department of Natural Resources
University of New Hampshire
215 James Hall
56 College Road
Durham, NH 03824

ADMISSIONS CONTACT:

The Graduate School
University of New Hampshire
Thompson Hall, Room 109
105 Main Street
Durham, NH 03824-3547

Phone: 603-862-1020
Fax: 603-862-4976

University of New Hampshire Web site: http://unhinfo.unh.edu/

Quick Facts About the Department of Natural Resources

- Enrollment: 38 master's students / 16 doctoral students
- Graduate degrees conferred: Master of Science, doctorate
- Master's degree requirements include: required courses, master's thesis or master's project, oral exam

- Doctoral degree requirements include: required courses, dissertation, qualifying exam, oral exam
- Faculty/Advisee ratio: 1:3.5

Areas of Specialization

Applied and Quantitative Ecology (50% of students)
Earth Science (15%)
Environmental Science (15%)
Environmental Education (10%)
Resource Policy and Planning (10%)

Special Program Features

Graduate students can cross-register for courses within other departments. Joint degree programs are offered with several other colleges and schools on campus. International program experiences are not offered.

Admission to the Program

- GRE scores not required for master's applicants, but required for doctoral applicants
- Master's students accepted each year (on average): 31% of 44 applicants
- Doctoral students accepted each year (on average): 33% of 24 applicants
- Students may matriculate at the start of any term; transfer students are accepted.

About the Students

There are 32 male and 22 female graduate students currently enrolled in this program; 41 are full-time and 13 part-time; 3 are international and 51 domestic; 96% are Caucasian, 2% Black, and 2% Asian. Graduate students range from age 22 to 60, with a median age of 32.

About the Faculty

There are 27 faculty affiliated with this program. The average faculty member teaches 2.5 courses and advises 1 doctoral and 3–4 master's students per year. Teams of advisors choose students prior to admission. Faculty research is currently being conducted both domestically and internationally. Ten faculty specialize in Applied and Quantitative Ecology, 1 in Conservation Biology, 1 in Environmental Education, 1 in Environmental Geography, 2 in Environmental Studies, and 2 in Resource Policy and Planning.

Tuition and Financial Aid

Tuition in 1996 was $4,170 per year for state residents and $12,840 for nonresidents. Over 60% of the graduate students in this program receive financial aid. Three percent of the master's students are awarded scholarships, 66% are awarded teaching or research assistantships. Six percent of the doctoral students are awarded fellowships, 18% are awarded scholarships, 48% are awarded teaching or research assistantships, and 25% are research associates.

Facilities

Computer facilities include 3 IBM/clones, one terminal per 4 students, 10 GIS computers, several university operated clusters, and access to Internet and E-mail. Free or low-cost computer training is available. There are 3 libraries available to graduate students. Facilities are handicapped accessible. The school also owns 5,000 acres of property that is available for student research.

Career Counseling and Job Placement

This program does not offer student internships. Career counseling and job placement services include job books. Forty percent of alumni work within the government sector, 10% for nonprofits, 20% for private small business, 10% for corporations or industries, and 20% in science or academia. Nearly all of the students find work within six months of graduation.

THE UNIVERSITY OF NORTH CAROLINA AT CHAPEL HILL

The country's oldest state university, the University of North Carolina at Chapel Hill is located on 729 acres in a bucolic town of 40,000 in the research triangle of North Carolina.

☙ Department of City and Regional Planning

FACULTY CONTACT:

Edward Kaiser, Chair
Department of City and
  Regional Planning
Campus Box #3140,
  Room 103, New East
University of North Carolina–
  Chapel Hill
Chapel Hill, NC 27599-3140

Phone: 919-962-3983
Fax: 919-962-5206

ADMISSIONS CONTACT:

Ms. Patricia Coke,
  Student Services Manager
Department of City and
  Regional Planning
Campus Box #3140,
  Room 103, New East
University of North Carolina–
  Chapel Hill
Chapel Hill, NC 27599-3140

Phone: 919-962-4784

Department of City and Regional Planning Web site:
http://www.unc.edu/depts/dcrpweb/

Quick Facts About the Department of City and Regional Planning

- Year established: 1946
- Graduate degrees conferred: Master of Regional Planning, doctorate
- Master's degree requirements include: required courses, master's project
- Doctoral degree requirements include: 30 credits of required courses, dissertation, exam

Areas of Specialization (according to program literature)

Economic Development
Housing, Real Estate, and Community Development
Land Use and Environmental Planning
International Applications

Special Program Features

This program is known for being one of the oldest and most widely recognized programs of graduate planning in the country. Graduate students can cross-register for courses in other departments and schools of the University, as well as at Duke University, North Carolina Central University, and

North Carolina State University. Joint degree programs are offered in the following combinations: (1) Law and Planning, (2) Business and Planning, and (3) Public Administration and Planning. A Ph.D. is offered in the specialization of Public Policy Analysis, which draws from courses in a variety of departments.

About the Faculty

There are 21 faculty affiliated with this program.

Tuition and Financial Aid

Tuition in 1996 was $948 per year for state residents and $9,064 for nonresidents. Incoming master's students receive up to $5,000 in financial assistance, and doctoral candidates receive up to an average of $6,500. A variety of merit-based fellowships and scholarships are available, as well as internships, work study opportunities, and teaching and research assistantships.

Facilities

Two computer labs are operated by the Department of City and Regional Planning, and students have access to all university libraries as well as resources at other area schools.

Career Counseling and Job Placement

While career counseling services are limited, this program provides ample opportunity for interaction with potential employers within the surrounding community. Several faculty members have held positions within local and state planning agencies, and course assignments often require hands-on research and analysis on "real-world" issues. These activities provide students the chance to work closely with local professionals to gain hands-on experience in regional planning.

☛ Other graduate environmental programs at The University of North Carolina at Chapel Hill (no profiles available):

Department of Environmental Sciences and Engineering. *Contact:* Graduate School. *Phone:* 919-966-2611.

UNIVERSITY OF RHODE ISLAND

With a total enrollment of 14,000 students, the University of Rhode Island was established in 1892 and is located in the rural, coastal town of Kingston.

☎ Department of Natural Resources Science

CONTACT:

Peter August, Director of Graduate Studies
Department of Natural Resources Science
University of Rhode Island
Kingston, RI 02881-0804

Phone: 401-792-4794
Fax: 401-792-4561
E-mail: pete@edcserv.edc.uri.edu

Department of Natural Resources Web site:
http://www.edc.uri.edu/rreapage/nrs/index.htm

University of Rhode Island Web site: http://www.uri.edu/

Quick Facts About the Department of Natural Resources Science

- Year established: 1983
- Enrollment: 28 master's students / 2 doctoral students
- Graduate degrees conferred: Master of Science, doctorate
- Master's degree requirements include: required courses, master's thesis
- Doctoral degree requirements include: required courses, dissertation, qualifying exam, oral exam
- Faculty/Advisee ratio: 1:3

Areas of Specialization

Applied and Quantitative Ecology (50% of students)
Earth Science (20%)
Conservation Biology (15%)
Environmental Geography (10%)
Environmental Quality and Public Health (5%)

Special Program Features

This program is best known for its emphasis on landscape scale studies, wetland ecology, and water resources. Graduate students can cross-register for courses within other departments. Joint degree programs and international program experiences are not offered.

Admission to the Program

- Admission requirements for master's applicants include: 2 semesters of chemistry, 1 of biology, 1 of calculus, 1 of physical science; average GRE scores: 75th percentile
- Admission requirements for doctoral applicants include: master's degree; average GRE scores: 80th percentile
- Master's students accepted each year (on average): 10% of 50 applicants
- Doctoral students accepted each year (on average): 10% of 10 applicants
- Students matriculate mainly in the fall; transfer students are sometimes accepted.

About the Students

There are 15 male and 15 female graduate students currently enrolled in this program; 20 are full-time and 10 part-time; 5 are international and 25 domestic; 95% are Caucasian and 5% Asian. Graduate students range from age 21 to 32, with a median age of 25.

About the Faculty

There are 10 faculty affiliated with this program. The average faculty member teaches 2–3 courses and advises 2 master's and less than 1 doctoral student per year. Students choose their faculty advisors. Faculty research is currently being conducted both domestically and internationally. Six faculty specialize in Applied and Quantitative Ecology, 1 in Conservation Biology, 1 in Earth Science, 1 in Environmental Geography, and 1 in Environmental Quality and Public Health.

Tuition and Financial Aid

Tuition in 1996 was $4,132 per year for state residents and $8,136 for non-residents. Over 60% of the graduate students in this program receive financial aid. Eighty percent of the master's students are awarded teaching or research assistantships. Sixty percent of the doctoral students are awarded fellowships, and 40% are awarded teaching or research assistantships.

Facilities

Computer facilities include 30 IBM/clones, 3 Macintoshes, 30 GIS computers, multiple PC clusters, a mainframe, an IBM Risc 6000 server, and access to Internet and E-mail. Free or low-cost computer training is available. There are 2 buildings, 6 classrooms, 10 laboratories, and 2 libraries available to graduate students. Facilities are handicapped accessible. The school also owns the Alton Jones campus research area in West Greenwich, Rhode Island.

Career Counseling and Job Placement

This program offers student internships, consisting of special projects, on a case-by-case basis. Career counseling and job placement services are available. Sixty percent of alumni work within the government sector, 5% for semi-governmental organizations, 10% for nonprofits, 20% for private small business, and 5% in science or academia; 70% of alumni work in the New England region and 5% in international locations. Ninety-five percent of the students find work within six months of graduation.

UNIVERSITY OF TENNESSEE, KNOXVILLE

Established in 1794, the University of Tennessee at Knoxville has a total enrollment of 26,000 students. One of six campuses within the state university system, it is located in a large city near the North Carolina border.

☞ Department of Geography

FACULTY CONTACT:

Carol Harden, Head
Department of Geography
The University of Tennessee,
   Knoxville
408 Geography and
   Geology Building
Knoxville, TN 37901

Phone: 423-974-2418
Fax: 423-974-6025

ADMISSIONS CONTACT:

Graduate Admissions and Records
The University of Tennessee,
   Knoxville
218 Student Services Building
Knoxville, TN 37996-0220

Phone: 423-974-3251

Department of Geography Web site:
http://funnelweb.utcc.utk.edu/~twallin/geohome.html

University of Tennessee, Knoxville Web site: http://www.utk.edu/

Quick Facts About the Department of Geography

- Year established: 1914

- Enrollment: 35 master's students / 20 doctoral students

- Graduate degrees conferred: Master of Science, doctorate

- Master's degree requirements include: required courses, master's thesis

- Doctoral degree requirements include: required courses, dissertation, qualifying exam, oral exam

- Faculty/Advisee ratio: 1:5

Areas of Specialization

Environmental Geography (50% of students)
Earth Science (20%)
Biogeography, Paleoecology, and Geomorphology (20%)

Special Program Features

This program is best known for its emphasis on biogeography, paleoecology, geomorphology, and climatology. Graduate students can cross-register for courses within other departments. Joint degree programs are offered with the Department of Environmental Science. International program experiences include research opportunities and field stations in Central and South America. Future program plans include strengthening the climatology and GIS offerings.

Admission to the Program

- Admission requirements for master's applicants include: average GRE scores: 625 verbal/650 math

- Admission requirements for doctoral applicants include: master's degree; average GRE scores: 650 verbal/650 math

- Master's students accepted each year (on average): 10% of 80 applicants

- Doctoral students accepted each year (on average): 10% of 20 applicants

- Students may matriculate only in the fall; transfer students are sometimes accepted.

About the Students

There are 40 male and 15 female graduate students currently enrolled in this program; 40 are full-time and 15 part-time; 2 are international and 53 domestic; 91% are Caucasian, 1% Black, and 8% Asian. Graduate students range from age 21 to 50, with a median age of 28.

About the Faculty

There are 15 faculty affiliated with this program. The average faculty member teaches 4 courses and advises 3 master's and 2 doctoral students per year. Students choose their faculty advisors. Faculty research is currently being conducted both domestically and internationally. Two faculty specialize in Earth Science and 3 in Environmental Geography.

Tuition and Financial Aid

Tuition in 1996 was $2,338 per year for state residents and $6,468 for nonresidents. Over 60% of the graduate students in this program receive financial aid. Ten percent of the graduate students are awarded fellowships, and 80% are awarded teaching assistantships.

Facilities

Computer facilities include 18 IBM/clones, 5 Macintoshes, 20 GIS computers, various computer labs at other departments, and access to Internet and E-mail. Free or low-cost computer training is available. Various libraries are available to graduate students. Some facilities are handicapped accessible.

Career Counseling and Job Placement

This program offers student internships with local research, planning, and governmental agencies. Career counseling and job placement services include job placement counselors, active alumni contact, and on-campus interviews. Twenty percent of alumni work within the government sector, 5% for semi-governmental organizations, 2% for nonprofits, 10% for private small business, 20% for corporations or industries, and 30% in science or academia.

☞ **Other graduate environmental programs at University of Tennessee at Knoxville (no profiles available):**

Department of Forestry, Wildlife and Fisheries. *Contact:* Paul Winistorfer, Associate Professor. *Phone:* 615-974-7126.

Graduate Program in Ecology. *Contact:* Dewey Bunting, Director. *Phone:* 615-974-3065.

THE UNIVERSITY OF VERMONT

Located on a 425-acre campus in the scenic, lakeside town of Burlington, the University of Vermont was established in 1791 and has a total enrollment of 9,800 students. It is the state's land-grant institution.

☞ Field Naturalist Program

FACULTY CONTACT:

Jeffrey Hughes, Director
Department of Botany,
Field Naturalist Program
The University of Vermont
Marsh Life Science Building
Burlington, VT 05405-0086

Phone: 802-656-2930
Fax: 802-656-8429

ADMISSIONS CONTACT:

The University of Vermont
Graduate College Admissions
332 Waterman Building
Burlington, VT 05405-0160

Phone: 802-656-2699

Department of Botany Web site: http://www.uvm.edu/~plantbio/grad/

University of Vermont Web site: http://www.uvm.edu/

Graduate College Web site: http://www.uvm.edu/~gradcoll/page.html

Quick Facts About the Field Naturalist Program

- Year established: 1982
- Enrollment: 10 master's students
- Graduate degree conferred: Master of Science
- Master's degree requirements include: required courses, master's project, field practicum each semester
- Faculty/Advisee ratio: 1:3

Areas of Specialization (no statistics available)

Applied and Quantitative Ecology
Conservation Biology
Earth Science

Special Program Features

This program is best known for its emphasis on land–water interfaces, integrative field ecology, and environmental problem solving. Graduate students can cross-register for courses within other departments. Joint degree programs and international program experiences are not offered.

Admission to the Program

- Admission requirements for master's applicants include: 1 semester of chemistry, 2 of biology, 1 of natural science, 1 of physical science, 3–4 years of work experience; average GRE scores: 710 verbal/740 math
- Master's students accepted each year (on average): 5–10% of 80 applicants
- Students may matriculate only in the fall; transfer students are not accepted.

About the Students

There are 5 male and 5 female graduate students currently enrolled in this program; all 10 are full-time; all are Caucasian. Graduate students range from age 26 to 36, with a median age of 29.

About the Faculty

There are 14 faculty affiliated with this program. The average faculty member advises 2 master's students per year. Students choose their faculty advisors. Faculty research is currently being conducted both domestically and internationally. Ten faculty specialize in Applied and Quantitative Ecology, 5 in Conservation Biology, 3 in Earth Science, 1 in Environmental Education, 4 in Environmental Science, 1 in Environmental Studies, and 1 in Forestry.

Tuition and Financial Aid

Tuition in 1996 was $3,234 per year for state residents and $8,082 per year for nonresidents. All master's students in this program are awarded fellowships.

Facilities

Computer facilities include 1 IBM/clone, 1 Macintosh, and access to Internet and E-mail. The University has 3 Macintosh labs and 3 IBM labs, totalling over 200 computers. Free or low-cost computer training is available. Two libraries are available to graduate students. All facilities are handicapped accessible. The school also owns natural areas and forest lands that are available for student research.

Career Counseling and Job Placement

This program does not offer student internships. Career counseling and job placement services include active alumni contact, an alumni database, and employer contact. Ten percent of alumni work within the government sector, 10% for semi-governmental organizations, 50% for nonprofits, 10% for private small business, and 20% in science or academia; 80% of alumni work in the Pacific Northwest, Alaska, Colorado, and New England regions; 10% in Washington, D.C.; and 10% in international locations. All students find work within six months of graduation.

☚ School of Natural Resources

FACULTY CONTACT:

Mary Watzin
Graduate Program Coordinator
School of Natural Resources
George D. Aiken Center
University of Vermont
Burlington, VT 05405-0088

Phone: 802-656-2620

ADMISSIONS CONTACT:

The University of Vermont
Graduate College Admissions
332 Waterman Building
Burlington, VT 05405-0160

School of Natural Resources Web site: http://www.uvm.edu/~snrdept/

Quick Facts About the School of Natural Resources

- Year established: 1979
- Enrollment: 60 master's and doctoral students
- Graduate degrees conferred: Master of Science, doctorate
- Master's degree requirements include: required courses; master's thesis for Wildlife/Fisheries Biology, Water Resources, and some Forestry ma-

jors; master's project for Natural Resources Planning and some Forestry majors

- Doctoral degree requirements include: required courses, dissertation, internship experience, qualifying exam, oral exam, international language or cross-cultural experience
- Faculty/Advisee ratio: 1:3

Areas of Specialization

Natural Resources Planning (50% of students)
Wildlife and Fisheries Biology (25%)
Water Resources (15%)
Forestry (10%)

Special Program Features

The School of Natural Resources offers the Master of Science in the following areas: Forestry, Water Resources, Wildlife and Fisheries Biology, and Natural Resource Planning. Graduate students can cross-register for courses within other departments. Joint degree programs are offered with the Geology and Civil Engineering departments. International program experiences are not offered. Recent program changes have included the addition of a new Ph.D. in Natural Resources in the fall of 1994.

Admission to the Program

- GRE scores are required for graduate applicants
- No master's degree is required for doctoral applicants
- Master's students accepted each year (on average): 40% of 110 applicants
- Students may matriculate at the start of any term; transfer students are sometimes accepted.

About the Faculty

There are 24 faculty affiliated with this program. The average faculty member teaches 3–4 courses and advises 1–2 master's students per year. Students choose their faculty advisors. Six faculty specialize Wildlife and Fisheries Biology, 4 in Water Resources, 6 in Forestry, and 8 in Natural Resources Planning.

Tuition and Financial Aid

Some 41–60% of the graduate students in this program receive financial aid. Fifty percent of the master's students are awarded teaching or research assistantships. This program does not offer student internships or career counseling and job placement services.

UNIVERSITY OF VIRGINIA

Founded by Thomas Jefferson in 1819, the University of Virginia has an enrollment of over 18,000 students, about 5,000 of whom are graduate students. It is located in the small city of Charlottesville, about 20 miles east of the Blue Ridge Mountains.

☟ Master of Planning, School of Architecture

FACULTY CONTACT:

Timothy Beatley, Chair
Department of Urban and
    Environmental Planning
Campbell Hall
University of Virginia
School of Architecture
Charlottesville, VA 22903

Phone: 804-924-6459
Fax: 804-982-2678
E-mail: tb6d@virginia. edu

ADMISSIONS CONTACT:

Admissions Secretary
University of Virginia
School of Architecture
202 Campbell Hall
Charlottesville, VA 22903

Phone: 804-924-6442

University of Virginia Web site: http://www.virginia.edu/

Quick Facts About the School of Architecture

- Year established: Early 1900s
- Graduate degrees conferred: Master of Architecture, Master of Landscape Architecture, Master of Architectural History, Master of Planning, Ph.D. in History of Architecture.
- Master of Planning degree requirements include: 2 years (50 credits) of required courses, summer internship

Areas of Specialization (according to program literature)
Urban Development
Environmental Planning
Land Use Planning
Policy Planning

Special Program Features

Under the direction of Dean William McDonough, the University of Virginia School of Architecture is becoming increasingly well known for its cutting-edge instruction in the areas of sustainable architecture and community planning. In 1996, Dr. Timothy Beatley developed an innovative course entitled "Sustainable Communities Forum" that included presentations by well-known guest lecturers from around the country. Joint degree programs are offered with a variety of departments of the Graduate School of Arts & Sciences, as well as with the Law School, the Darden School of Business Administration, and the School of Engineering and Applied Science.

Tuition and Financial Aid

Tuition in 1996 was $4,618 per year for state residents and $14,010 for non-residents. A wide variety of sources of financial aid are available in the form of assistantships, fellowships, grants, and scholarships.

☞ Other graduate environmental programs at University of Virginia (no profiles available):

Department of Environmental Sciences Graduate Program. Web site:
http://atlantic.evsc.virginia.edu/EVSC/evsc.html

UNIVERSITY OF WASHINGTON

Established in 1919, the University of Washington has a total enrollment of 34,600 students and is located on a lakeside campus in the city of Seattle.

☞ School of Fisheries

FACULTY CONTACT:
Dr. Marsha Landolt, Director

ADMISSIONS CONTACT:
School of Fisheries, WH-10

School of Fisheries
University of Washington
Seattle, WA 98195

Graduate Student Services
Box 357980
University of Washington
Seattle, WA, 98195

Phone: 206-543-4270
Fax: 206-685-7471
E-mail: graduate@fish.washington.edu or
      Instruct@fish.washington.edu

Phone: (206) 542-7457
Fax: 206-685-7471

School of Fisheries Web site: http://www.fish.washington.edu/

University of Washington Web site: http://www.washington.edu/

Quick Facts About the School of Fisheries

- Year established: 1919
- Enrollment: 79 master's students / 63 doctoral students
- Graduate degrees conferred: Master of Science, doctorate
- Master's degree requirements include: required courses, master's thesis
- Doctoral degree requirements include: required courses, dissertation, qualifying exam, oral exam
- Faculty/Advisee ratio: 1:4

Special Program Features

This program is best known for its emphasis on quantitative fisheries management. All students specialize in Applied and Quantitative Ecology; graduate students can cross-register for courses within other departments. Joint degree programs are offered with the School of Marine Affairs. International program experiences are not offered.

Admission to the Program

- GRE minimum combined scores of 1100 are required for all graduate applicants
- A master's degree is required for doctoral applicants
- Graduate students accepted each year (on average): 20% of 140 applicants

- Students may matriculate only in the fall; transfer students are sometimes accepted.

About the Students

There are 97 male and 45 female graduate students currently enrolled in this program; 60% are full-time and 40% part-time; 26 are international and 116 domestic; 91% are Caucasian, 1% Black, 3% Hispanic, 2% Native American, and 3% Asian.

About the Faculty

There are 36 faculty affiliated with this program. The average faculty member teaches 2–3 courses and advises 3–4 master's and 1–2 doctoral students per year. Students choose their faculty advisors. Faculty research is currently being conducted both domestically and internationally.

Tuition and Financial Aid

Tuition in 1996 was $4,746 per year for state residents and $11,889 for non-residents. Over 60% of the graduate students in this program receive financial aid. Five percent of the graduate students are awarded scholarships, 5% teaching assistantships, and 90% research assistantships.

Facilities

Computer facilities include IBM/clones, Macintoshes, an academic computing center, and access to Internet and E-mail. Free or low-cost computer training is available. Various museum collections and libraries are available to graduate students. Facilities are handicapped accessible. The school also owns a field station on the Olympic Peninsula and 4 field stations in Alaska that are available for student research.

Career Counseling and Job Placement

This program offers student internships or educational opportunities within the local commmunity. Career counseling and job placement services include job placement counselors, on-campus interviews, job books, job fairs, and a weekly job list. Over 90% of the students find work within six months of graduation.

🐦 Other graduate environmental programs at University of Washington (no profiles available):

Institute of Forest Resources. Anderson Hall, AR-10, University of Washington, Seattle, WA 98195.

Institute for Environmental Studies. Engineering Annex FM-12, University of Washington, Seattle, WA 98195. *Phone:* 206-543-1812

UNIVERSITY OF WISCONSIN–GREEN BAY

With a total enrollment of 5,500 students, the University of Wisconsin–Green Bay was established in 1970 and is located on an urban campus in the mid-sized city of Green Bay.

🐦 Environmental Science and Policy Graduate Program

FACULTY CONTACT:

John Stoll, Coordinator
Department of Environmental
   Science and Policy Graduate
   Program
University of Wisconsin–
   Green Bay
2420 Nicolet Drive
Green Bay, WI 54311-7001

Phone: 414-465-2358
Fax: 414-465-2718

ADMISSIONS CONTACT:

Graduate Studies Office
University of Wisconsin–
   Green Bay
2420 Nicolet Drive
Green Bay, WI 54311-7001

Phone: 414-465-2484

University of Wisconsin–Green Bay Web site: http://www.uwgb.edu/

Quick Facts About the Environmental Science and Policy Graduate Program

- Year established: 1974
- Enrollment: 273 master's students
- Graduate degree conferred: Master of Science
- Master's degree requirements include: required courses, master's thesis
- Faculty/Advisee ratio: 1:5

Areas of Specialization

Resource Policy and Planning (30% of students)
Applied and Quantitative Ecology (25%)
Conservation Biology (10%)
Earth Science (10%)
Environmental Quality and Public Health (10%)
Environmental Science (10%)
Botany (5%)

Special Program Features

This program is best known for its emphasis on freshwater ecosystems and wetlands, and public policy analysis. Graduate students can cross-register for courses within other departments. Joint degree programs and international program experiences are not offered.

Admission to the Program

- Admission requirements for master's applicants include: average GRE scores: 550 verbal/550 math
- Master's students accepted each year (on average): 50% of 60 applicants
- Students may matriculate at the start of any term; transfer students are accepted.

About the Students

There are 144 male and 129 female graduate students currently enrolled in this program; 148 are full-time and 125 part-time; 8 are international and 265 domestic; 97% are Caucasian, 0.3% Black, 0.3% Hispanic, 0.3% Native American, and 2% Asian. Graduate students range from age 22 to 63, with a median age of 35.

About the Faculty

There are 26 faculty affiliated with this program. The average faculty member teaches 7 courses and advises 2–4 master's students per year. Initially advisors are assigned; students then choose their advisors. Faculty research is currently being conducted both domestically and internationally. Six faculty specialize in Applied and Quantitative Ecology, 1 in Botany, 1 in Conservation Biology, 2 in Corporate Environmental Management, 1 in Environmental Geography, 2 in Environmental Quality and Public Health, 3 in Environmental Science, and 4 in Resource Policy and Planning.

Tuition and Financial Aid

Tuition in 1996 was $3,122 per year for state residents and $9,350 for non-residents.

Facilities

The school owns the 270-acre Cofrin Arboretum on campus, the Toft Point Conservancy, Peninsula Center Conservancy, and Kingfish Farm; all are available for student research.

Career Counseling and Job Placement

This program offers student internships, arranged with local and state agencies, industry, and private consulting firms. Career counseling and job placement services include active alumni contact, and job books. 45% of alumni work within the government sector, 5% for nonprofits, 30% for private small business, 10% for corporations or industries, and 5% in science or academia. 70% of alumni work in the Midwest; and 5% work in international locations. Over 90% of the students find work within six months of graduation.

UNIVERSITY OF WISCONSIN–MADISION

Established in 1849, the University of Wisconsin–Madison has a total enrollment of 41,950 students and is located on a lakeside campus in the state's capital city. This school belongs to the Hispanic Association of Colleges and Universities.

☛ Department of Agricultural Journalism

CONTACT:

John Fett, Professor
Department of Agricultural Journalism
University of Wisconsin–Madison

440 Henry Mall
Madison, WI 53706

Phone: 608-262-1464

University of Wisconsin–Madison Web site: http://www.wisc.edu/

Quick Facts About the Department of Agricultural Journalism

- Year established: 1908
- Enrollment: 23 master's students / 13 doctoral students
- Graduate degrees conferred: Master of Science, doctorate
- Master's degree requirements include: required courses, master's thesis, and at least one course in communication theory, research methodology, and statistics
- Doctoral degree requirements include: required courses, dissertation, qualifying exam, oral exam, program approval by Ph.D. in Mass Communications committee
- Faculty/Advisee ratio: 1:4

Areas of Specialization

Environmental Education and Communications (25% of students)

Special Program Features

This program is best known for its emphasis on environmental communication. Graduate students can cross-register for courses within other departments. Joint degree programs are offered with the School of Journalism and Mass Communication. International program experiences are not offered.

Admission to the Program

- GRE scores of 590 verbal/560 math are required for graduate applicants
- A master's degree is required for doctoral applicants
- Master's students accepted each year (on average): 60% of 25 applicants
- Doctoral students accepted each year (on average): 65% of 10 applicants
- Students may matriculate at the start of any term; transfer students are accepted.

About the Students

There are 8 male and 28 female graduate students currently enrolled in this program; 25 are full-time and 11 part-time; 9 are international and 27 domestic; 64% are Caucasian, 6% Black, 5% Hispanic, and 20% Asian. Graduate students range from age 22 to 50, with a median age of 28.

About the Faculty

There are 10 faculty affiliated with this program. The average faculty member teaches 3 courses and advises 3 master's and 2 doctoral students per year. Advisors are assigned to students. Faculty research is currently being conducted both domestically and internationally. Three faculty specialize in Environmental Education.

Tuition and Financial Aid

Tuition in 1996 was $4,136 per year for state residents and $12,574 for non-residents. Some 41–60% of the graduate students in this program receive financial aid. Five percent of the master's students are awarded scholarships, 30% are awarded teaching or research assistantships, and 10% receive project assistantships. Five percent of the doctoral students are awarded fellowships, and 60% are awarded teaching or research assistantships.

Facilities

Computer facilities include 30 IBM/clones, 4 Macintoshes, numerous computer labs, and access to Internet and E-mail. Free or low-cost computer training is available. One building, 1 classroom, 1 laboratory, and 37 libraries are available to graduate students. Facilities are handicapped accessible.

Career Counseling and Job Placement

This program offers occasional student internships or educational opportunities within the local commmunity. Career counseling and job placement services include job placement counselors, active alumni contact, and job books. Thirty percent of alumni work within the government sector, 5% for semi-governmental organizations, 5% for nonprofits, 5% for private small business, 25% for corporations or industries, and 30% in science or academia; 60% of alumni work in the Midwest, 3% in Washington, D.C., and 20% in international locations. Ninety-five percent of the students find work within six months of graduation.

🎓 Department of Forestry

CONTACT:

Ronald Giese, Chair
Department of Forestry
University of Wisconsin–Madison
1630 Linden Drive
120 Russell Labs
Madison, WI 53706-1598

Phone: 608-262-3073

Quick Facts About the Department of Forestry

- Year established: 1962
- Enrollment: 33 master's students / 29 doctoral students
- Graduate degrees conferred: Master of Science, doctorate
- Master's degree requirements include: individually designed plans of study; joint programs have a prescribed curriculum
- Doctoral degree requirements include: dissertation, qualifying exam, oral exam
- Faculty/Advisee ratio: 8:31

Areas of Specialization

Forestry (44% of students)

Special Program Features

This program is best known for its emphasis on forest biology/ecology; management/economics; fiber science/wood chemistry. Graduate students can cross-register for courses within other departments. Joint degree programs are offered with the departments of Conservation Biology, Plant Breeding, and Plant Genetics. International program experiences include research opportunities and student exchanges in Central and South America.

Admission to the Program

- GRE scores are required for all graduate applicants
- Master's degree is not required for doctoral applicants
- Students may matriculate at the start of any term; transfer students are accepted.

About the Students

There are 41 male and 21 female graduate students currently enrolled in this program; 57 are full-time and 5 part-time; 24 are international and 38 domestic; 95% are Caucasian and 5% Black.

About the Faculty

There are 16 faculty affiliated with this program. The average faculty member teaches 2 courses and advises 2 master's and 2 doctoral students per year. Students and advisors choose one another by mutual agreement.

Tuition and Financial Aid

Tuition in 1994 was $3,700 for state residents and $11,000 for nonresidents. Over 60% of the graduate students in this program receive financial aid. Five percent of the master's students are awarded fellowships, 68% are awarded research assistantships, and 12% (international students) receive home government support. Five percent of the doctoral students are awarded fellowships, 80% are awarded research assistantships and 15% receive home government support.

Career Counseling and Financial Aid

This program does not offer student internships. Career counseling and job placement services include job placement counselors. Twenty percent of alumni work within the government sector, 5% for semi-governmental organizations, 10% for nonprofits, 10% for private small business, 10% for corporations or industries, and 45% in science or academia. Eighty-five percent of the students find work within six months of graduation.

🐦 Institute for Environmental Studies (IES)

CONTACT:

Barbara Borns
Senior Student Services Coordinator
Institute for Environmental Studies (IES)
University of Wisconsin–Madison
70 Science Hall, 550 North Park Street
Madison, WI 53706-1491

Phone: 608-262-0651
Fax: 608-262-2273

Please note: The Institute of Environmental Studies offers concentration options in the areas of (1) Conservation Biology & Sustainable Development, (2) Environmental Monitoring, (3) Land Resources, and (4) Water Resources. Because we received such detailed information on each of these ares, we are treating them as separate programs under the "umbrella" of the Institute for Environmental Studies

⚘ Conservation Biology & Sustainable Development Program

Quick Facts About the Conservation Biology & Sustainable Development Program

- Year established: 1990

- Enrollment: 33 master's students

- Graduate degree conferred: Master of Science

- Master's degree requirements include: required courses, master's thesis or master's project

Admission to the Program

- Admission requirements for master's applicants include: course work in biology, economics, natural science, physical science, genetics/evolution, statistics; average GRE scores: 70th percentile

- Master's students accepted each year (on average): 23% of 132 applicants

- Students may matriculate at the start of any term; transfer students are accepted.

Special Program Features

This program is best known for its emphasis on combining conservation biology and sustainable development. Graduate students can cross-register for courses within other departments. Joint degree programs are offered with the Law School, the Geography Department, and other graduate programs. International program experiences are offered in Guelph, Guadalajara, and Canada (for all IES programs).

About the Students

There are 18 male and 15 female graduate students currently enrolled in this program; 26 are full-time and 7 part-time; 8 are international and 25 domestic. Graduate students range from age 22 to 50.

About the Faculty

There are 155 combined IES faculty. The average faculty member teaches 3–4 courses. Students choose their faculty advisors. IES faculty research is currently being conducted both domestically and internationally.

Tuition and Financial Aid

Tuition in 1994 was $5,852 (all IES programs). Some 41–60% of the graduate students in this program receive financial aid.

Facilities

IES computer facilities include 23 IBM/clones, 3 Macintoshes, 8 GIS computers, university computer labs, and access to Internet and E-mail. Older computers are placed in graduate student offices. Free or low-cost computer training is available. IES programs have 485 buildings, 614 classrooms, 3,453 laboratories, and 29 libraries available to graduate students. All facilities are handicapped accessible.

Career Counseling and Job Placement

All IES programs coordinate a number of student internships with the Wisconsin Department of Natural Resources, especially with their Bureau of Air Management. IES's career counseling and job placement services include job placement counselors, active alumni contact, job books, and an alumni database. Thirty percent of alumni work within the government sector, 45% for nonprofits, 10% for private small business, and 10% for corporations or industries. Eighty percent of the students find work within six months of graduation.

☛ Environmental Monitoring Program

Quick Facts About the Environmental Monitoring Program
- Year established: 1976

- Enrollment: 15 master's students / 4 doctoral students
- Graduate degrees conferred: Master of Science, doctorate
- Master's degree requirements include: required courses, master's thesis
- Doctoral degree requirements include: required courses, dissertation, qualifying exam, oral exam

Admission to the Program

- Average GRE scores: 70th percentile for all graduate applicants
- Admission requirements for master's applicants include: 2 semesters of calculus, 2 of statistics, some computer science
- Master's degree is required for doctoral applicants
- Master's students accepted each year (on average): 50% of 24 applicants
- Doctoral students accepted each year (on average): 20% of 21 applicants
- Students may matriculate at the start of any term; transfer students are accepted.

Special Program Features

This program is best known for its emphasis on use of remote sensing data and GIS. Graduate students can cross-register for courses within other departments. Joint degree programs are offered with the Law School and other departments, including forestry.

About the Students

There are 15 male and 4 female graduate students currently enrolled in this program; 14 are full-time and 5 part-time; 1 is international and 14 domestic; all are Caucasian. Graduate students range from age 20 to 50.

About the Faculty

Faculty advisors are assigned to students.

Tuition and Financial Aid

Over 60% of the graduate students in this program receive financial aid subsequent to admission.

Career Counseling and Job Placement

Thirty percent of alumni work within the government sector, 25% for private small business, 25% for corporations or industries, and 20% in science or academia. Eighty percent of the students find work within six months of graduation.

☚ Land Resources Program

Quick Facts About the Land Resources Program

- Year established: 1975
- Enrollment: 96 master's students / 65 doctoral students
- Graduate degrees conferred: Master of Science, doctorate
- Master's degree requirements include: required courses, master's thesis
- Doctoral degree requirements include: required courses, dissertation, qualifying exam, oral exam

Admission to the Program

- Average GRE scores: 70th percentile for all graduate applicants
- A master's degree is required for doctoral applicants
- Master's students accepted each year (on average): 28% of 89 applicants
- Doctoral students accepted each year (on average): 18% of 42 applicants
- Students may matriculate at the start of any term; transfer students are accepted.

Special Program Features

This program is best known for its emphasis on special curricula in energy analysis and policy, and air resources management. Graduate students can cross-register for courses within other departments. Joint degree programs are offered with the Law School and other departments, including civil and environmental engineering, forestry, and education.

About the Students

There are 107 male and 54 female graduate students currently enrolled in this program; 96 are full-time and 65 part-time; 21 are international and 140 domestic; 92% are Caucasian, 2% Black, 4% Hispanic, 1% Native American, and 1% Asian. Graduate students range from age 22 to 50.

About the Faculty

Faculty advisors are both assigned to and chosen by students.

Tuition and Financial Aid

Some 41–60% of the graduate students in this program receive financial aid subsequent to admission.

Career Counseling and Job Placement

Forty-five percent of alumni work within the government sector, 10% for nonprofits, 9% for private small business, 9% for corporations or industries, and 17% in science or academia. Eighty percent of the students find work within six months of graduation.

☛ Water Resources Management Program

Quick Facts About the Water Resources Management Program

- Year established: 1965
- Enrollment: 27 master's students
- Graduate degree conferred: Master of Science
- Master's degree requirements include: required courses, master's project

Admission to the Program

- Average GRE scores: 70th percentile for master's applicants
- Master's students accepted each year (on average): 38% of 47 applicants
- Students may matriculate at the start of any term; transfer students are accepted.

Special Program Features

This program is best known for its emphasis on hydrology, water chemistry, geology and hydrogeology, water law, policy institutions, and environmental education. Graduate students can cross-register for courses within other departments. Joint degree programs are offered with the Law School and other departments, including civil and environmental engineering, and geology.

About the Students

There are 27 male and 22 female graduate students currently enrolled in this program; 31 are full-time and 18 part-time; 2 are international and 47 domestic. Graduate students range from age 22 to 50.

About the Faculty

Students choose their faculty advisors.

Tuition and Financial Aid

Some 41–60% of the graduate students in this program receive financial aid subsequent to admission.

Career Counseling and Job Placement

Fifty-three percent of alumni work within the government sector, 2% for nonprofits, 18% for private small business, 19% for corporations or industries, 6% in science or academia, and 2% for utilities. Eighty percent of the students find work within six months of graduation.

☎ Other graduate environmental programs at University of Wisconsin–Madison (no profiles available):

Department of Agricultural Economics. *Contact:* Philip Harris, Chair. *Phone:* 608-263-4472.

Department of Continuing and Vocational Education. *Contact:* Robert Ray, Chair. *Phone:* 608-263-2422.

Center for Environmental Toxicology. *Contact:* Colin Jefcoate, Director. *Phone:* 608-263-4580.

Department of Landscape Architecture. *Contact:* Evelyn Howell, Chair. *Phone:* 608-263-7300.

Department of Oceanography & Limnology. *Contact:* Linda Graham, Chair. *Phone:* 608-263-3264.

Department of Rural Sociology. *Contact:* William Freudenberg. *Phone:* 608-263-4893.

Department of Soil Science. *Contact:* James Bockheim. *Phone:* 608-262-2633.

Department of Wildlife Ecology. *Contact:* Robert Ruff, Chair. *Phone:* 608-262-2671.

Energy Analysis & Policy Curriculum & Certificate. *Contact:* Rodney Stevenson, Chair. *Phone:* 608-262-0651.

UNIVERSITY OF WISCONSIN–STEVENS POINT

The University of Wisconsin–Stevens Point has a total enrollment of 8,620 students and is located in a rural town in the geographic center of Wisconsin.

☜ College of Natural Resources

FACULTY/ADMISSIONS CONTACT:

Richard Wilke, Graduate Program Coordinator
University of Wisconsin–Stevens Point
College of Natural Resources
Room 107
Stevens Point, WI 54481-3897

Phone: 715-346-2853
Fax: 715-346-3624

Web site: http://www.uwsp.edu/acad/cnr/cnr.htm

University Web site: http://www.uwsp.edu/

Quick Facts About the College of Natural Resources

• Year established: 1945
• Enrollment: 95 master's students
• Graduate degree conferred: Master of Science
• Master's degree requirements include: required courses, master's thesis, master's project
• Faculty/Advisee ratio: 1:2

Areas of Specialization

Applied and Quantitative Ecology (43%)
Environmental Education (13%)

Resource Policy and Planning (8%)
Earth Science (8%)
Forestry (6%)
Environmental Quality and Public Health (6%)
Botany (4%)
Conservation Biology (2%)
Corporate Environmental Management (2%)
Environmental Geography (2%)
Environmental Law (2%)
Environmental Science (2%)
Parks and Recreation Management (2%)

Special Program Features

This program is best known for its emphasis on water resources, environmental education, and wildlife. Graduate students can cross-register for courses within other departments. Joint degree programs are not offered. International program experiences include study tours of 1–4 months in Western Europe, Australia/New Zealand, and Central America.

Admission to the Program

- Admission requirements for master's applicants include: average GRE scores: 525 verbal/525 math
- Master's students accepted each year (on average): 19% of 116 applicants
- Students may matriculate at the start of any term; transfer students are accepted.

About the Students

There are 55 male and 40 female graduate students currently enrolled in this program; 52 are full-time and 43 part-time; all 95 are domestic; 97% are Caucasian, 1% Black, and 1% Native American. Graduate students range from age 23 to 52, with a median age of 27.

About the Faculty

There are 46 faculty affiliated with this program. The average faculty member teaches 7 courses and advises 2 master's students per year. Advisors choose students from applicant pool. Faculty research is currently being conducted both domestically and internationally. Twenty faculty specialize in Applied and Quantitative Ecology, 2 in Botany, 1 in Conservation Biology, 1 in Corporate Environmental Management, 4 in Earth Science, 5 in Environmental Education, 1 in Environmental Geography, 1 in Environmental Law, 3 in Environmental Quality and Public Health, 1 in Environmental Science, 3 in Forestry, and 4 in Parks and Recreation Management.

Tuition and Financial Aid

Tuition in 1996 was $3,107 per year for state residents and $9,335 for non-residents. All graduate students in this program receive financial aid. Five percent of the master's students are awarded fellowships, and 95% are awarded teaching or research assistantships.

Facilities

Computer facilities include 28 IBM/clones, 2 Macintoshes, 5 GIS computers, five computer labs, a GIS lab, and access to Internet and E-mail. Free or low-cost computer training is available. There are 3 buildings, 75 classrooms, 18 laboratories, various museum collections, and 1 library available to graduate students. Facilities are handicapped accessible. The school also owns a residential environmental education center, community nature center and preserve, residential natural resources field station, prairie chicken research area, and several forested tracts ranging from 40 to 200 acres; all are available for student research.

Career Counseling and Job Placement

This program offers student internships with federal agencies nationwide, but few locally. Career counseling and job placement services include job placement counselors, on-campus interviews, Internet job hunts, vacancy bulletins, and posted lists from subscription services. Thirty percent of alumni work within the government sector, 20% for nonprofits, 40% for private small business, and 10% in science or academia; 70% of alumni work in the Midwest (lake states region). Ninety percent of the students find work within six months of graduation.

UNIVERSITY OF WYOMING

Established in 1886, the University of Wyoming has a total enrollment of 12,500 students and is located in the small, sunny city of Laramie.

☚ Department of Zoology and Physiology

FACULTY CONTACT:

Dr. Steven Buskirk, Head
Wildlife and Fisheries Biology
   & Management
University of Wyoming
Laramie, WY 82071-3166

Phone: 307-766-4207
Fax: 307-766-5625

ADMISSIONS CONTACT:

Graduate School
P.O. Box 3108
Room #108, Knight Hall
University of Wyoming
Laramie, WY 82071-3108

Phone: 307-766-6858

Department of Zoology and Physiology Web site:
http://www.uwyo.edu/a&s/zoology/zohmpage.htm

University of Wyoming Web site: http://www.uwyo.edu/

Quick Facts About the Department of Zoology and Physiology

- Year established: 1930
- Enrollment: 60 master's students / 15 doctoral students
- Graduate degrees conferred: Master of Science, doctorate
- Master's degree requirements include: required courses, master's thesis, master's project
- Doctoral degree requirements include: required courses, dissertation, internship experience, qualifying exam, oral exam, research experience
- Faculty/Advisee ratio: 1:2.5

Areas of Specialization

Applied and Quantitative Ecology (25%)
Environmental Quality and Public Health (20%)
Conservation Biology (10%)
Environmental Science (5%)

Special Program Features

This program is best known for its emphasis on aquatic toxicology and steppe ecology. Graduate students can cross-register for courses within other departments. Joint degree programs are offered with the Department of Water Research. International program experiences are not offered.

Admission to the Program

- GRE scores are required for all graduate applicants
- A master's degree is not required for doctoral applicants
- Graduate students accepted each year (on average): 10% of 150 applicants
- Students may matriculate at the start of any term; transfer students are sometimes accepted.

About the Students

There are 70 full-time and 5 part-time graduate students currently enrolled in this program; 3 are international and 72 domestic; 90% are Caucasian, 5% Hispanic, and 5% Asian. Graduate students range from age 21 to 45, with a median age of 24.

About the Faculty

There are 23 faculty affiliated with this program. The average faculty member teaches 2.5 courses and advises 2 master's and 1 doctoral student per year. Advisors are assigned to students. Faculty research is currently being conducted both domestically and internationally. Six faculty specialize in Applied and Quantitative Ecology, 1 in Conservation Biology, 3 in Environmental Quality and Public Health, and 1 in Environmental Science.

Tuition and Financial Aid

Tuition in 1996 was $2,106 per year for state residents and $6,498 for non-residents. Over 60% of the graduate students in this program receive financial aid. Thirty percent of the graduate students are awarded teaching assistantships, and 70% research assistantships.

Facilities

Computer facilities include 25 IBM/clones, 2 GIS computers, and access to Internet and E-mail. Free or low-cost computer training is available. Various museum collections are available to graduate students. All facilities are handicapped accessible. The school also owns the Red Buttes Environmental Biology Laboratory, which is available for student research.

Career Counseling and Job Placement

This program does not offer student internships. Career counseling and job placement services include job placement counselors. Eighty-five percent of the students find work within six months of graduation.

UTAH STATE UNIVERSITY

With a total enrollment of 17,500 students, Utah State University was established in 1888. Its setting is a 332-acre campus in the small city of Logan near the mountains.

☜ Department of Forest Resources

FACULTY CONTACT:

Michael Jenkins, Professor
Department of Forest Resources
College of Natural Resources
Utah State University
Logan, UT 84322-5215

Phone: 801-797-2531

ADMISSIONS CONTACT:

School of Graduate Studies
Office of the Dean
Utah State University
Logan, UT 84322-0900

Phone: 801-750-1189
Fax: 801-750-1192

College of Natural Resources Web site: http://www.nr.usu.edu

Utah State University Web site: http://www.usu.edu/

Quick Facts About the Department of Forest Resources

- Year established: 1937
- Enrollment: 26 master's students / 4 doctoral students
- Graduate degrees conferred: Master of Science, Master of Forestry, doctorate
- Master's degree requirements include: required courses, master's thesis
- Doctoral degree requirements include: required courses, dissertation, qualifying exam, oral exam
- Faculty/Advisee ratio: 1:3

Areas of Specialization

Applied and Quantitative Ecology (66%)
Resource Policy and Planning (15%)
Earth Science (10%)
Environmental Geography (5%)

Special Program Features

This program is best known for its emphasis on recreation. Graduate students can cross-register for courses within other departments. Joint degree programs are offered with the Ecology Center. International program experiences include research opportunities, student exchanges, and field stations in Africa.

Admission to the Program

- Admission requirements for master's applicants include: average GRE scores: 550 verbal/550 math
- Admission requirements for doctoral applicants include: master's degree; average GRE scores: 650 verbal/650 math
- Master's students accepted each year (on average): 51% of 37 applicants
- Doctoral students accepted each year (on average): 40% of 5 applicants
- Students may matriculate at the start of any term; transfer students are accepted.

About the Students

There are 16 male and 14 female graduate students currently enrolled in this program; 25 are full-time and 5 part-time; 4 are international and 26 domestic; 97% are Caucasian and 3% Asian. Graduate students range from age 23 to 45, with a median age of 28.

About the Faculty

There are 14 faculty affiliated with this program. The average faculty member teaches 3 courses and advises 2.5 master's and 1.5 doctoral students per year. Faculty advisors choose their students. Faculty research is currently being conducted both domestically and internationally. Three faculty specialize in Applied and Quantitative Ecology, 2 in Botany, 2 in Forestry, 2 in

Parks and Recreation Management, 2 in Resource Policy and Planning, and 3 in Silviculture, Computer Modeling, and Fire and Avalanche Studies.

Tuition and Financial Aid

Tuition in 1996 was $2,036 per year for state residents and $6,180 for non-residents. Over 60% of the graduate students in this program receive financial aid. Five percent of the master's students are awarded fellowships, 95% are awarded teaching or research assistantships. Ten percent of the doctoral students are awarded fellowships, 90% are awarded teaching or research assistantships.

Facilities

All computers are in open-lab arrangements and available to all university students; facilities include 427 IBM/clones, 112 Macintoshes, 5 GIS computers, one terminal per 30 students, and access to Internet and E-mail. Free or low-cost computer training is available. There are various museum collections and 2 libraries available to graduate students. All facilities are handicapped accessible. The school also owns a forest that is available for student research.

Career Counseling and Job Placement

This program does not offer student internships. Career counseling and job placement services include job placement counselors, active alumni contact, and on-campus interviews. Seventy-five percent of alumni work within the government sector and 25% in science or academia; 65% of alumni work in the Rocky Mountain region and 20% in international locations. Fifty percent of the students find work within six months of graduation.

🐾 Other graduate environmental programs at Utah State University (no profiles available):

Department of Biology. *Contact:* Edmund D. Brodie, Jr., Dean. *Phone:* 801-797-0068.

College of Natural Resources. *Contact:* John Kadlec, Assistant Dean of Academic Affairs. *Phone:* 801-797-2460.

VERMONT LAW SCHOOL

With one of the top environmental law programs in the nation, Vermont Law School has a total enrollment of 530 and is located on a rural campus in the small town of South Royalton.

☜ Environmental Law Center

FACULTY CONTACT:

Craig Wells, Assistant Director
Environmental Law Center
Vermont Law School
P.O. Box 96
South Royalton, VT 05068

Phone: 800-227-1395
E-mail: elcinfo@vermontlaw.edu

ADMISSIONS CONTACT:

Admissions
Environmental Law Center
Vermont Law School
P.O. Box 96
South Royalton, VT 05068

Phone: 800-227-1395

Environmental Law Center Web site: http://www.vermontlaw.edu/elc.htm

Vermont Law School Web site: http://www.vermontlaw.edu/

Quick Facts About the Environmental Law Center

- Year established: 1978
- Enrollment: 30 master's students / 60 joint J.D./M.S.L. students
- Graduate degrees conferred: Master of Studies in Law (M.S.L.), Juris Doctorate (J.D.)
- Master's degree requirements include: required courses
- Faculty/Advisee ratio: 1:12

Areas of Specialization

Environmental Law
Resource Policy and Planning

Special Program Features

Joint degree programs are offered with the Law School. International program experiences are not offered.

Admission to the Program

- Admission requirements for master's applicants include: LSAT or GREs; average GRE scores: 540 verbal/580 math/670 analytical (analytical particularly important)
- Master's students accepted each year (on average): 40% of 120 applicants
- Joint J.D./M.S.L. students accepted each year (on average): 63% of 95 applicants
- Students may matriculate only in the fall; summer entry for post-J.D. applicants; transfer students are not accepted.

About the Students

Of the master's students, 81% are Caucasian, 16% Hispanic, and 3% Native American. Graduate students range from age 22 to 55, with a median age of 32.

About the Faculty

There are 44 faculty affiliated with this program. The average faculty member teaches 4 courses. Faculty advisors are assigned to students. Faculty specialize in Environmental Law and in Resource Policy and Planning.

Tuition and Financial Aid

Tuition in 1996 was $17,250 per year. One master's student is awarded a fellowship and 2–3 are awarded research assistantships.

Facilities

Computer facilities include 4 IBM/clones, 1 Macintosh, 9 Westlaw terminals and 9 Lexis/Nexis terminals, and access to Internet and E-mail. Free or low-cost computer training is available (Lexis and Westlaw). There are 13 buildings, 10 classrooms, and various libraries available to graduate students. Facilities are handicapped accessible.

Career Counseling and Job Placement

This program offers part-time or full semester internships, ranging from local to international. Career counseling and job placement services include job placement counselors, active alumni contact, on-campus interviews, job books, and job fairs. Thirty-six percent of alumni work within the government and semi-governmental sectors, 3% for nonprofits, 7% for private small business, 7% for corporations or industries, 7% in science or academia, and 39% in law firms (joint J.D./M.S.L. alumni); 46% of alumni work in the New England region, 20% in Washington, D.C., and 5% in international locations. Seventy-four percent of the students find work within six months of graduation.

VIRGINIA POLYTECHNIC INSTITUTE AND STATE UNIVERSITY

Located in the mountainside town of Blacksburg, Virginia, Virginia Tech has an enrollment of over 24,000 students, 3,700 of whom are graduate students.

☚ Department of Fisheries and Wildlife

PROGRAM CONTACT:
Department of Fisheries and
  Wildlife Sciences
Virginia Polytechnic Institute
  and State University
Blacksburg, VA 24061-0321

Phone: 540-231-5573

ADMISSIONS CONTACT:
Graduate School
Virginia Polytechnic Institute
  and State University
100 Sandy Hall
Blacksburg, VA 24061-0325

Phone: 540-231-3714

Department of Fisheries and Wildlife Web site:
http://www.fiw.vt.edu/fisheries/

Quick Facts and Special Program Features

Tuition at Virginia Tech in 1996 was $4,709 per year for state residents and $6,941 per year for nonresidents. We did not receive a completed survey from Virginia Tech; because the array of graduate environmental opportunities at this school is so widespread, we recommend that interested applicants access the school's abundant Web site at http://www.vt.edu/ and obtain a copy of the graduate bulletin from the address listed above under "Admissions Contact."

The Graduate School offers a variety of additional programs in such departments as Environmental Engineering, Crop & Soil Environmental Sciences, Environmental Design & Planning, Forestry, and Urban and Regional Planning. Contact the Graduate School for a comprehensive bulletin.

WASHINGTON STATE UNIVERSITY

With a total enrollment of 16,700 students, Washington State University was established in 1890 and is located on a 415-acre campus in the small, semi-rural town of Pullman.

☞ Program in Environmental Science & Regional Planning

FACULTY CONTACT:

George Hinman, Chair
Program in Environmental Science
  & Regional Planning
Washington State University
Pullman, WA 99164-4430

Phone: 509-335-8536
Fax: 509-335-7636

ADMISSIONS CONTACT:

Graduate School
French Administration Bldg.,
  Room 324
Washington State University
Pullman, WA 99164-1030

Phone: 509-335-3535

Program in Environmental Science & Regional Planning Web site:
http://www.wsu.edu:8080/~franz/

Washington State University Web site: http://www.wsu.edu/

Quick Facts About the Program in Environmental Science
& Regional Planning

- Year established: 1968
- Enrollment: 116 master's students / 4 doctoral students
- Graduate degrees conferred: Master of Science, Master of Regional Planning, doctorate
- Master's degree requirements include: required courses, master's thesis or master's project
- Doctoral degree requirements include: required courses, dissertation, qualifying exam, oral exam
- Faculty/Advisee ratio: 1:3
- Doctoral program is too new to have acquired many statistics

Areas of Specialization

Environmental Quality and Public Health (30% of students)
Resource Policy and Planning (25%)
Earth Science (13%)
Corporate Environmental Management (10%)
Parks and Recreation Management (10%)
Applied and Quantitative Ecology (5%)
Environmental Geography (5%)
Social Ecology (2%)

Special Program Features

This program is best known for its emphasis on waste management, GIS, energy, systems, and human ecology. Future program plans include more emphasis on environmental health. Graduate students can cross-register for courses within other departments. Joint degree programs are offered with the College of Agriculture and Home Economics. International program experiences include student exchanges in Russia.

Admission to the Program

- Admission requirements for master's applicants include: 2 semesters of biology, 1 of calculus, 3 of chemistry or physics, 1 of social science; average GRE scores: 546 verbal/622 math
- No master's degree required for doctoral applicants
- Master's students accepted each year (on average): 80% of 130 applicants
- Students may matriculate at the start of any term; transfer students are accepted.

About the Students

There are 60 male and 60 female graduate students currently enrolled in this program; 60 are full-time and 60 part-time; 10 are international and 110 domestic; 90% are Caucasian, 5% Black, and 5% Asian. Graduate students range from age 22 to 50, with a median age of 28.

About the Faculty

There are 44 faculty affiliated with this program. The average faculty member teaches 4 courses and advises 2 master's students per year. Advisors are both assigned to and chosen by students. Faculty research is currently being

conducted both domestically and internationally. Ten faculty specialize in
Applied and Quantitative Ecology, 7 in Earth Science, 3 in Environmental
Geography, 8 in Environmental Quality and Public Health, 13 in Resource
Policy and Planning, and 2 in Social Ecology.

Tuition and Financial Aid

Tuition in 1996 was $4,748 for state residents and $11,892 for nonresidents. Some 21–40% of the graduate students in this program receive financial aid. One percent of the master's students are awarded fellowships,
and 25% are awarded teaching or research assistantships.

Facilities

Computer facilities include 9 IBM/clones, 3 Macintoshes, 25 GIS computers, several large university computer collections, and access to Internet and
E-mail. Free or low-cost computer training is available. There are two libraries available to graduate students. Facilities are handicapped accessible.

Career Counseling and Job Placement

This program offers student internships or educational opportunities within
the local commmunity. Career counseling and job placement services include job placement counselors, on-campus interviews, and job books. Forty
percent of alumni work within the government sector, 30% for private small
business, and 30% for corporations or industries; 80% of alumni work in the
Pacific Northwest, 10% in Washington, D.C., and 10% in international locations. Ninety percent of the students find work within six months of graduation.

WEST VIRGINIA UNIVERSITY

West Virginia University was established in 1867 and has a total enrollment
of 22,000 students. Its setting is the small city of Morgantown, in the Ap-
palachian Mountains of northern West Virginia.

🎓 Division of Resource Management

FACULTY CONTACT:

Peter Schaeffer, Director
Division of Resource Management
West Virginia University
P.O. Box 6108
Morgantown, WV 26506-6108

Phone: 304-293-4832

Fax: 304-293-3740

ADMISSIONS CONTACT:

West Virginia University
Office of Admissions and Records
P.O. Box 6009
Morgantown, WV 26506-6009

Phone: 304-293-2121
or 800-344-WVU1

West Virginia University Web site: http://www.wvu.edu/

Quick Facts About the Division of Resource Management

- Year established: 1970
- Enrollment: 32 master's students / 19 doctoral students
- Graduate degrees conferred: Master of Science, doctorate
- Master's degree requirements include: required courses
- Doctoral degree requirements include: required courses, dissertation, qualifying exam, oral exam
- Faculty/Advisee ratio: 1:6

Special Program Features

This program is best known for its emphasis on environmental and natural resource economics. All students specialize in Resource Policy and Planning; graduate students can cross-register for courses within other departments. Joint degree programs and international program experiences are not offered. An international program with Egypt is in the planning stages.

Admission to the Program

- Admission requirements for master's applicants include: recommended average GRE scores: 400 verbal/400 math
- Admission requirements for doctoral applicants include: master's degree; average GRE scores: 600 verbal/600 math

- Students may matriculate at the start of any term (fall preferred); transfer students are sometimes accepted.

About the Students

There are 37 male and 14 female graduate students currently enrolled in this program; all 51 are full-time; 28 are international and 23 domestic.

About the Faculty

There are 18 faculty affiliated with this program. The average faculty member teaches 2–3 courses and advises 3 master's and 1–2 doctoral students per year. Advisors are initially assigned; students may subsequently choose them. One faculty member specializes in Environmental Law, 1.5 in Environmental Geography, 1 in Environmental Quality and Public Health, and 9 in Resource Policy and Planning.

Tuition and Financial Aid

Tuition in 1996 was $1,744 per year for state residents and $6,422 for non-residents.

Facilities

Computer facilities include 80 IBM/clones, 2 Macintoshes, other university computer labs (including mainframe), and access to Internet and E-mail. Free or low-cost computer training is available. There are 2 buildings, 9 classrooms, 3 laboratories, and 2 libraries available to graduate students. All facilities are handicapped accessible.

Career Counseling and Job Placement

This program offers student internships and career counseling and job placement services only on an informal basis.

☎ Other graduate environmental programs at West Virginia University (no profiles available):

Division of Plant and Soil Sciences. *Contact:* Barton Baker, Chair. *Phone:* 304-293-4817.

Division of Forestry. *Contact:* James Armstrong, Interim Director. *Phone:* 304-293-4411

YALE UNIVERSITY

Established in 1701, Yale University has a total enrollment of 11,500 students and is located on an urban campus in New Haven, Connecticut, a large city on Long Island Sound.

☜ School of Forestry and Environmental Studies

FACULTY CONTACT:

Nancy Rabbott
Director of Student and
  Academic Affairs
Yale School of Forestry and
  Environmental Studies
Yale University
205 Prospect Street
New Haven, CT 06511

ADMISSIONS CONTACT:

Registrar
Yale School of Forestry and
  Environmental Studies
Yale University
205 Prospect Street
New Haven, CT 06511

Phone: 203-432-5100

University Web site: http://www.yale.edu/

School of Forestry and Environmental Studies Web site: http://www.yale.edu/forestry

Quick Facts About the School of Forestry and Environmental Studies

- Year established: 1900

- Enrollment: 200 master's students / 60 doctoral students

- Graduate degrees conferred: Master of Science, Master of Environmental Science, Master of Forestry, Master of Forest Science, doctorate, Doctor of Forestry and Environmental Studies

- Master's degree requirements include: required courses, master's project, internship experience

- Doctoral degree requirements include: dissertation, qualifying exam

Areas of Specialization (according to program literature)

Ecosystem Science and Management
Conservation Biology
Coastal and Watershed Systems
Environmental Policy and Management
Social Ecology and Community Development

Special Program Features

Graduate students can cross-register for courses within other departments. Joint degree programs are offered with the Law School, School of International Relations, Business School, School of Public Health, and Economics Department.

About the Students

There are 100 male and 100 female graduate students currently enrolled in this program; 200 are full-time and 3 part-time; 40 are international and 220 domestic. Graduate students range from age 21 to 60, with a median age of 28.

Tuition and Financial Aid

Tuition in 1996–97 was $16,900 per year for master's candidates and $20,300 for doctoral candidates. A limited amount of financial aid is available in the form of scholarships, loans, and assistantships.

Career Counseling and Job Placement

This program offers student internships or educational opportunities within the local commmunity. Career counseling and job placement services include job placement counselors, active alumni contact, on-campus interviews, job books, an alumni database, and job fairs. Ninety percent of the students find work within six months of graduation.

PART III

APPENDIXES

APPENDIX A

ADDITIONAL PROGRAMS NOT PROFILED IN THIS VOLUME

Case Western Reserve University
10900 Euclid Avenue
Cleveland, OH 44106-7080
Contact: Norman Rushforth, Chair, Department of Biology
　　　　Phone: 216-368-3556

Chicago State University
Chicago, IL 60628
Contact: Caroll Henry, Chair, Department of
　　　　Biological Sciences, Environmental Bio Track
　　　　Phone: 312-995-2183

Clarkson University
Rowley Labs
Potsdam, NY 13676-5625
Contact: Suzanne Liberty, Dean, Environmental Science
　　　　& Engineering Graduate Programs
　　　　Phone: 315-268-6442 / *Fax:* 315-268-7994

College of Staten Island—City University of New York
2800 Victory Boulevard
Staten Island, NY 10314-6600

Contact: John Oppenheimer,
Director, Environmental Science Master's Program
Phone: 718-982-3921

Colorado School of Mines
1500 Illinois Street
Golden, CO 80401
Contact: Arthur Kidnay, Dean of Graduate Studies & Research
Division of Environmental Science and Engineering
Phone: 800-446-9488

East Tennessee State
P.O. Box 22960A
Johnson City, TN 37614
Contact: Monroe Morgan, Chair, Department of Environmental Health
Phone: 615-929-6146

Eastern Illinois University
Charleston, IL 61920
Contact: Andrew Methven, Chair, Biological Sciences Graduate Program
Phone: 217-581-6241

Emory University
1518 Clifton Road, NE
Atlanta, GA 30322
Contact: Suzanne Mason, Academic Services Coordinator
Department of Environmental and Occupational Health
Phone: 404-727-7905

Florida State University
B142 Tallahassee, FL 32306-2043
Contact: Thomas Roberts, Associate Chair, Department of Biological
Science, Program in Ecology and Environmental Science
Phone: 904-644-3023 / *Fax:* 904-644-9829

George Mason University
Fairfax, VA 22030-4444
Contact: Geoffrey Birchard, Coordinator of Master's Programs
Department of Biology (Master's and Ph.D. in
Environmental Science and Public Policy)
Phone: 703-993-1065

Governors State University
University Park, IL 60466
Contact: Edwin Cehelnik, Chair, Program in Environmental Biology
     Phone: 708-534-5000, ext. 2402

Hood College
Frederick, MD 21701-8575
Contact: John Commito, Program in Environmental Biology
     Phone: 301-696-3649

Hunter College (CUNY)
695 Park Avenue
New York, NY 10021
Contact: Anthony Grande, Assistant to Dean, Department of
     Geology and Geography
     Phone: 212-772-5412

Indiana State University
Terre Haute, IN 47809
Contact: William Dando, Chair, Department of Geography and Geology
     Phone: 317-237-2400
Contact: William Brett, Chair, Life Sciences Department
     Phone: 317-237-2261

Long Island University, C.W. Post Campus
Brookville, NY 11548
Contact: Lillian Hess, Environmental Studies Program
     Phone: 516-299-2428

Massachusetts Institute of Technology (MIT)
50 Ames Street
Cambridge, MA 02142-1308
Contact: William Thilly, Center for Environmental Health Sciences
     Phone: 617-253-6220

Massachusetts Institute of Technology (MIT), continued
77 Massachusetts Avenue
Cambridge, MA 02139
Contact: Beth Tuths, Admissions Coordinator,
     Department of Ocean Engineering
     Phone: 617-258-6157

McGill University
Campus MacDonald; 21,111 Lakeshore
St-Anne-de Bellevue, Montreal
PQ H9X 3V9 Canada
Contact: E. Donald, Graduate Services,
            Department of Natural Resource Sciences
            Phone: 514-398-7890

Michigan State University
East Lansing, MI 48824-1222
Contact: R. Ben Peyton, Chair, Department of Fisheries and Wildlife
            Phone: 517-353-0647
Contact: Daniel Keathley, Chair, Department of Forestry
            Phone: 517-355-0090 / *Fax*: 517-336-1143
Contact: Charles Nelson, Chair of Graduate Committee
            Department of Park and Recreation Resources
            Phone: 517-353-5190

New Mexico State University
P.O. Box 30003, Campus Box 4901
Las Cruces, NM 88003
Contact: Charles Davis, Department Head,
            Department of Fishery and Wildlife Sciences
            Phone: 505-646-1544, ext. 3718

New York Institute of Technology
Center for Energy Policy and Research
Old Westbury, NY 11568
Contact: Robert Amundsen, Chair, School of Management,
            M.S. in Energy Management/Advanced Certificate in
            Environmental Management Programs
            Phone: 516-686-7578

Northern Michigan University
1401 Presque Isle
Marquette, MN 49855-5341
Contact: Martin Kopenski, Chair, Graduate Committee,
            Department of Biology
            Phone: 906-227-1000

Penn State University
University Park, PA 16802

Contact: Richard Unz, Chair, Environmental Pollution Control Program
  Phone: 814-865-1417
Contact: Richard Yahner, Chair, Graduate Degree Program in Ecology
  Phone: 814-863-3201
Contact: Alan Graefe, Professor in Charge, Leisure Studies
  Graduate Program
  Phone: 814-865-1851 / *Fax:* 814-863-4257

San Francisco State University
1600 Holloway Avenue
San Francisco, CA 94132
Contact: Barbara Holzman, Assistant Professor, Masters of
  Geography/Resource Management & Environmental Planning
  Phone: 415-338-7506

Seton Hall University
One Newark Center
Newark, NJ 07102-5210
Contact: Ronald Riccio, Dean, Environmental Law Program
  Phone: 201-642-8747

Slippery Rock University of Pennsylvania
208 Eisenberg Building
Slippery Rock, PA 16057
Contact: Boliver, Graduate Coordinator
  Department of Parks, Recreation & Environmental Education
  Phone: 412-738-2068

Southern Connecticut State University
501 Crescent Street, Jennings 309
New Haven, CT 06515
Contact: Harris Stone, Director, Center for the Environment
  Program in Environmental Education
  Phone: 203-392-6600

Southern Illinois University at Edwardsville
Box 1099 SIUE
Edwardsville, IL 62026
Contact: Frank Kulfinski, Director, M.S. in Environmental Studies
  Phone: 618-692-3311

Southern Methodist University
Dallas, TX 75275-0240

Contact: C. Paul Rogers, Dean, Environmental Law Program
  Phone: 214-768-2618

Texas A & M University–Kingsville

Campus Box 156
Kingsville, TX 78363
Contact: Fred Guthery, Chair, Department of Animal
  and Wildlife Sciences
  Phone: 512-595-3711 / *Fax:* 512-595-3713

University of Alabama–Huntsville

Huntsville, AL 35899
Contact: S.Q. Kidder, Chair, Environmental Science Graduate Program
  Phone: 205-895-6257

University of Alaska–Fairbanks

Fairbanks, AK 99775-0180
Contact: Mark Oswood, Department Head, Department of
  Biology and Wildlife
  Phone: 907-474-7671
Contact: Al Tyler, Department Head, Department of Fisheries
Contact: Barbara Pierson, Recruitment Coordinator, Department of
  Natural Resources Management
Contact: Robert Carlson, Department Head, Department of
  Civil Engineering, Program in Environmental Quality Science
Contact: Robert Logan, Department Head, Department of Economics,
  Program in Resource Economics
Contact: Susan Henrichs, Program Head, Program in Marine Sciences
  and Limnology

University of British Columbia

Room 436E, 2206 East Mall
Vancouver, BC Canada V6T1Z3
Contact: L. Lavkulich, Chair, Resource Management
  & Environmental Studies
  Phone: 604-822-9249

University of Calgary

2500 University Drive, NW
Calgary, Canada, ALB T2N 1N4
Contact: Richard Revel, Chairperson, Committee on Resources
  and the Environment
  Phone: 403-220-7209

University of California, Irvine
Irvine, CA 92717-5150
Contact: Kay Helwig, Concentration in Environmental Analysis & Design
    Phone: 714-856-5918

University of California, Riverside
Riverside, CA 92521-0424
Contact: Walter Farmer, Chair, Department of Soil
    & Environmental Sciences
    Phone: 714-787-5103 / *Fax:* 714-787-3993
Contact: Sarjeet Gill, Chair, Environmental Toxicology Graduate Program
    Phone: 714-787-4164

University of Hawaii at Manoa
Honolulu, HI 96822
Contact: Jeremy Harrison, Dean, Environmental Law Program
    Phone: 808-956-7966

University of Maryland at Baltimore
Baltimore, MD 21228
Contact: Robert Percival, Director, Environmental Law Program
    Phone: 410-706-7214

University of Massachusetts–Amherst
Amherst, MA 01003
Contact: Brayton Wilson, Graduate Program Director,
    Department of Forestry and Wildlife Management
    Phone: 413-545-2665 / *Fax:* 413-545-4358
Contact: Cleve Willis, Chair, Department of Resource Economics
    Phone: 413-545-1501

University of Nebraska–Lincoln
101 Plant Industry
P.O. Box 830814
Lincoln, NE 68583-0814
Contact: Kyle Hoagland, Chair, Graduate Committee
    Department of Forestry, Fisheries and Wildlife
    Phone: 402-472-2944

University of Nevada–Las Vegas
4505 Maryland Parkway, Box 454004
Las Vegas, NV 89154-4004

Contact: Peter Starkweather, Chair, Department of Biological Sciences
Program in Environmental Biology
Phone: 702-895-3399 / *Fax:* 702-895-3956

University of Nevada–Reno
1000 Valley Road
Reno, NV 89512-0013
Contact: G. Fred Gifford, Chair, Department of Environmental
and Resource Sciences
Phone: 702-784-6763 / *Fax:* 702-784-4583

University of Nevada–Reno, continued
Reno, NV 89557
Contact: L. Oring
Interdisciplinary Program in Ecology, Evolution
& Conservation Biology
Phone: 702-784-4439

University of New Haven
300 Orange Avenue
West Haven, CT 06516
Contact: R. Laurence Davis, Acting Program Coordinator
Program in Environmental Science
Phone: 203-932-7108

University of Oklahoma
730 Van Vleet Oval, Room 314
Norman, OK 73019-0235
Contact: William Shelton, Chair, Graduate Selections Committee,
Department of Zoology
Phone: 405-325-6195 / *Fax:* 405-325-7560

University of Oklahoma, continued
200 Felgar St., Room 127
Norman, OK 73019-0470
Contact: Larry Canter, Director, Environment
and Ground Water Institute
Phone: 405-325-5202 / *Fax:* 405-325-7596

University of Oregon
104 Condon Hall
Eugene, OR 97403

Contact: Alvin Urquhart, Director of Environmental Studies,
        Environmental Studies Center
        Phone: 503-346-5006

University of Pennsylvania
Philadelphia, PA 19104
Contact: Anne Spirn, Chair, Department of Landscape Architecture
        & Regional Planning
        Phone: 215-898-6591

University of Pittsburgh
260 Kappa Drive
Pittsburgh, PA 15260
Contact: Nancy McIntyre, Student Affairs, Environmental
        and Occupational Health
        Phone: 412-967-6500

University of Toronto
Earth Sciences Center
33 Willcocks Street
Toronto, Canada, ON M5S 3B3
Contact: D. Martell, Coordinator of Graduate Studies, Faculty of Forestry
        Phone: 416-978-5480

Washington University in St. Louis
Campus Box 8226
660 S. Euclid Avenue
St. Louis, MO 63310-1093
Contact: Alan Templeton, Coordinator, Department of Biology
        & Biomedical Sciences
        Phone: 800-852-9047

Wayne State University
1109 Biology Sciences Building
Detroit, MI 48202
Contact: Miriam Greenberg, Environmental, Evolutionary
        & Systematic Biology
        Phone: 313-577-2902 / *Fax:* 313-577-6891

West Virginia Graduate College
Institute, WV 25112-1003

Contact: F. Kroesser, Program Director, Environmental Science Program
            Phone: 304-766-2042

Wilkes University
Wilkes-Barre, PA 18766
Contact: Wagiha Taylor, Dean of Graduate Studies
            Department of Earth and Environmental Sciences
            Phone: 717-831-4415

SAMPLE SURVEY FORM

Name of School/Program _____

Graduate School Survey

Name and Title of person completing the survey: _____

General Program

1. University name and address (to whom would one address correspondence?)
   _____
   _____

2. What is the name of your program or department? _____
   _____

3. When was your program established? _____

4. What degrees do you confer? (please circle those that apply)

   MA MS PhD DF JD MBA MEn MES MF MFS MPP MPPM ScD
   Other _____

5. Please indicate the approximate percentage of students in your program or department that specialize in each area of study listed below (Feel free to adapt this list as necessary).

   ___Applied and Quantitative Ecology
      ___Ecosystem Management   ___Fisheries Science   ___Forest Ecology   ___Population Ecology
      ___Marine and Coastal Studies   ___Range Management   ___Restoration Ecology   ___Soils Sciences
      ___Tropical Studies   ___Wetlands Ecology &/or Management   ___Wildlife Ecology
      ___Wildlife Science &/or Management

   ___Botany
      ___Plant Pathology   ___Plant Physiology

   ___Conservation Biology

   ___Corporate or Industrial Environmental Management

   ___Earth Systems Sciences
      ___Atmospheric Science   ___Energy Studies/Sciences   ___Geology   ___Oceanography
      ___Hydrology and Water Resource Management   ___Meteorology and Climate Studies

   ___Environmental Education and Communications
      ___Environmental Advocacy   ___Environmental Journalism

   ___Environmental Geography
      ___Geographic Information Systems   ___Remote Sensing

   ___Environmental Law and Diplomacy
      ___Environmental Law   ___International Relations

   ___Environmental Quality and Public Health
      ___Toxicology   ___Hazardous Waste Management   ___Solid Waste Management   ___Risk Assessment

   ___Environmental Science
      ___Environmental Biology   ___Environmental Chemistry (Aquatic Chemistry)

1

Name of School/Program _____

___**Environmental Studies**
   ___Environmental Ethics   ___Environmental History   ___Environmental Literature

___**Forestry**
   ___Agroforestry   ___Tropical Forestry ___Urban Forestry

___**Parks, Recreation Management and Leisure Studies**

___**Resource Policy, Administration and Planning**
   ___Natural Resource Policy and Administration   ___Public Policy Studies   ___Resource Economics
   ___Urban and Regional Planning

___**Social Ecology**

___**Other**

6. Are there any particular areas of specialization that your program emphasizes or is well known for? Please specify: _____

7. a. Do you anticipate any changes in your program offerings in the next several years?
     Yes   No
   b. If yes, please comment _____
     _____

   c. Does your program have a strategic plan for the next several years? YES   NO
     If yes please send it with this survey.

8. a. Do you offer any joint degree programs?   YES   NO
   b. If yes, with which of the following:
     ___Law School   ___Business School
     ___School of Public Policy   ___School of Education
     ___School of International Relations ___School of Public Health
     Other _____

9. a. Can graduate students cross-register for courses in other departments?   YES   NO
   b. If yes, what percentage of student classes are taken outside your department?
     ___ Less than 25%   ___ 51-75%
     ___ 25-50%   ___ Over 75%

10. How is your program's advising system organized?
   ___ Advisors are assigned to students   ___ No formal advising system
   ___ Students choose faculty advisors   ___ Teams of advisors
   ___ Other _____

11. Do prospective students need faculty sponsorship as a condition of application?
   ___ Unnecessary   ___ Highly Recommended
   ___ Recommended   ___ Necessary

Name of School/Program _____

12. What degree requirements, if any, exist for master's degree students?
    ___ Course distribution requirements
    ___ Master's thesis
    ___ Master's project
    ___ Experiential requirement (e.g., internship)
    ___ Other (please describe) _____
    _____
    (please attach any descriptions you have of student degree requirements)

13. What degree requirements, if any, exist for doctoral students?
    ___ Course distribution requirements
    ___ Dissertation
    ___ Experiential requirement (e.g., internship)
    ___ Qualifying Examination
    ___ Oral Examination
    ___ Other (please describe) _____
    _____

Student Enrollment

14. How many students are enrolled in your graduate program?_____
    _____# Masters   _____# Doctoral
    _____# Men   _____# Women
    _____# Full time   _____# Part-time
    _____# International   _____# Domestic citizens

15. What is the regional distribution of your domestic students?
    _____% Mid-Atlantic States   _____% Great Lakes States
    _____% New England   _____% Southeast
    _____% Southcentral   _____% Pacific northwest
    _____% Southwest   _____% Rocky Mountain States
    _____% West Coast   _____% Other _____

16. What regions do your international students represent?
    _____% Africa   _____% Western Europe
    _____% Central and Eastern Europe _____% SE Asia
    _____% Middle East   _____% China
    _____% South America   _____% Japan
    _____% Central America   _____% India
    _____% Australia/New Zealand   _____% Other _____

17. a. What is the median age of your students?   _____
    b. What is the age range of your students?   _____

18. What is the ethnic/racial distribution of your student body?
    _____% Caucasian   _____% Native American
    _____% Black   _____% Other
    _____% Hispanic   _____% Unknown
    _____% Asian

Name of School/Program _____

Career Counseling & Job Placement

19 a. Does your graduate program offer career counseling and/or job placement services?
      YES   NO

   b. If yes, what services do you provide?
      ___Job placement counselors   ___Job books
      ___Active alumni contact   ___ Alumni database
      ___On campus interviews   ___Job fairs/conferences
      ___Other _____

20. a. Does your graduate program offer students internships or cooperative education
       opportunities in the local community?   YES   NO
    b. If yes, please elaborate._____
       _____

21. What percentage of your students find work within six months of graduation?_____

22. What percentage of your alumni work within the following sectors?
    ___ Government
    ___ Quasi-government (e.g., World Bank, UNDP)
    ___ Non-profit
    ___ Private (small business or consulting)
    ___ Corporate/ Industrial
    ___ Science/Academic
    ___ Other

23. Please indicate the percentage of your alumni working in the following locations:
    a. A particular state   _____%   Which state? _____
    b. A particular region   _____%   Which region? _____
    c. Washington DC   _____%
    d. International locations   _____%

24. Employment opportunities for doctoral students
    ____ % Teaching appointments   ____ % Corporate or industry placement
    ____ % Research appointments   ____ % Science/Academic
    ____ % Post-doctorate appointments   ____ % Other

(Please attach, if available, specific job related information on your alumni)

International Program Affiliation

25. a. Does your program sponsor any international programs?   YES   NO

    b. If yes in which of the following regions?
       _____ South America   _____ Central America   _____ Africa
       _____ SE Asia   _____ Central and Eastern Europe _____ China
       _____ Western Europe   _____ Japan   _____ Middle East
       _____ Australia/New Zealand _____ India   _____ Other _____

4

Name of School/Program _____

c. If yes what type of international experience do you provide?
___ Research opportunities   ___ Internships   ___ Education exchange
___ Field stations/research opportunities   ___ Other _____

Faculty

26. How many of the following are affiliated with your graduate program:
____ # Full-time faculty   ____ # Lecturers
____ # Part-time faculty   ____ # Adjuncts
____ # Full professors   ____ # Guest/special appts.
____ # Associate professors   ____ # Research staff
____ # Assistant professors   ____ # Other

27. a. How many faculty members have their primary appointment with your program?_____

    b. How many faculty members hold joint appointments with other departments?_____

    c. Of those faculty affiliated with other programs, roughly what percent of their time is spent at your program?
    ____ Less than 20%   ____20-50%   ____51-75%   ____More than 75%

28. What is the faculty/advisee ratio?_____

29. How many master's theses or projects does an average faculty member advise in a given year?
_____

30. How many doctoral students does an average faculty member advise?   _____

31. How many courses does the average full-time faculty member teach a year? _____

32. Please indicate the approximate number of faculty in your program that specialize in each area of study listed below (Feel free to adapt this list as necessary).

___Applied and Quantitative Ecology
___Ecosystem Management ___Fisheries Science ___Forest Ecology ___Population Ecology
___Marine and Coastal Studies ___Range Management ___Restoration Ecology ___Soils Sciences
___Tropical Studies ___Wetlands Ecology &/or Management ___Wildlife Ecology
___Wildlife Science &/or Management
___Botany
___Plant Pathology ___Plant Physiology
___Conservation Biology
___Corporate or Industrial Environmental Management
___Earth Systems Sciences
___Atmospheric Science ___Energy Studies/Sciences ___Geology ___Oceanography
___Hydrology and Water Resource Management ___Meteorology and Climate Studies
___Environmental Education and Communications
___Environmental Advocacy ___Environmental Journalism
___Environmental Geography
___Geographic Information Systems ___Remote Sensing
___Environmental Law and Diplomacy
___Environmental Law ___International Relations
___Environmental Quality and Public Health
___Toxicology ___Hazardous Waste Management ___Solid Waste Management ___Risk Assessment
___Environmental Science

5

Name of School/Program _____

___Environmental Biology   ___Environmental Chemistry (Aquatic Chemistry)
___**Environmental Studies**
___Environmental Ethics ___Environmental History   ___Environmental Literature
___**Forestry**
___Agroforestry   ___Tropical Forestry ___Urban Forestry
___**Parks, Recreation Management and Leisure Studies**
___**Resource Policy, Administration and Planning**
___Natural Resource Policy and Administration   ___Public Policy Studies   ___Resource Economics
___Urban and Regional Planning
___**Social Ecology**
___**Other**

33. a. In what domestic regions do faculty conduct research?
____Mid-Atlantic States   ____ Great Lakes States   ____New England
____Southeast   ____Southcentral   ____Pacific northwest
____Southwest   ____Rocky Mountain States ____West Coast
____Other _____

b. In what international regions do faculty conduct research?
____ South America   ____ Central America   ____ Africa
____ SE Asia   ____ Central and Eastern Europe   ____ China
____ Western Europe   ____ Japan   ____ Middle East
____ Australia/New Zealand   ____ India   ____ Other _____

(Please attach faculty research profiles or, if appropriate, curriculum vitae)

Administration

34. How many of the following administrative staff does your program have:
____# Deans, directors, chairs   ____# Librarians
____# Financial aid staff   ____# Administrative
____# Computer staff   ____# Career counseling staff
____# Other administrative staff (please describe) _____

35. What is the tctal annual budget of your program? _____

36. Sources of annual revenue:
_____ $ tuition and fees
_____ $ government contribution
_____ $ government grants and contracts
_____ $ private grants and contracts
_____ $ endowment income
_____ $ investment income
_____ $ other (please elaborate) _____

37. How are your expenditures allocated?
_____ $ Instructional
_____ $ Staff
_____ $ Administration (includes materials and supplies)
_____ $ Facilities (Operation and Maintenance of Physical Plant)
_____ $ Student Services
_____ $ Library
_____ $ Financial Aid
_____ $ Other (please elaborate) _____

6

Name of School/Program _____

Admissions

38. Which of the following are prerequisites or requirements for admission into your master's program?
    ____ #Semesters of chemistry   ____ #Semesters of natural science
    ____ #Semesters of biology   ____ #Semesters of physical science
    ____ #Semesters of calculus   ____ #Semesters of social science
    ____ #Semesters of economics   ____ #Years work experience
    ____ Other (please describe) _____

39. Do you require that applicants for your doctoral program hold a master's or other advanced degree?   YES   NO

40. a. Are GRE scores required?   YES   NO

    b. If yes, what are the average GRE scores of master's degree applicants who are accepted?
           Verbal   _____
           Math   _____

    c. What are the average GRE scores of doctoral degree applicants who are accepted?
           Verbal   _____
           Math   _____

    d. Have you noticed a significant change in GRE scores in the last five years?
       YES   NO

    e. If yes to part d, please explain: _____
       _____
       _____

41. How many master's students apply a year? _____ % accepted _____

42. How many doctoral students apply a year? _____ % accepted _____

43. What is the average duration of funding for doctoral students? _____

44. When may students matriculate: ____Fall only ___Any term ____ Special circumstances

45. Do you accept transfer students?   YES   NO   SOMETIMES

46. a. Have you noticed a change in the size of your *master's* degree applicant pool over the last 5 years?   YES   NO
    b. If yes, what is the percentage increase or decrease? _____% increase _____% decrease

47. a. Have you noticed a change in the size of your *doctoral* degree applicant pool over the last 5 years? YES   NO
    b. If yes, what is the percentage increase or decrease? _____% increase _____% decrease

48. Please indicate the number of doctoral degrees conferred over the last 5 years: _____

7

Name of School/Program _____

Financial Aid

49. a. What are your projected 1994-1995 tuition and fees? (out of state students)
    Tuition $_____   Health Insurance $_____
    Books $_____   Other $_____
    Living Expenses $_____

    b. What is your projected 1994-1995 tuition for in state students if different from above?
    _____

50. What % of your graduate students receive financial aid?
    ___ 0 - 20%
    ___ 21 - 40%
    ___ 41 - 60%
    ___ over 60%

51. To what percentage of master's degree candidates do you award the following:
    _____ Fellowships   _____ Administrative assistantships
    _____ Teaching assistantships _____ Research assistantships
    _____ Scholarships
    _____ Other (please specify) _____

52. To what percentage of your doctoral candidates do you award the following:
    _____ Fellowships   _____ Administrative assistantships
    _____ Teaching assistantships _____ Research assistantships
    _____ Scholarships
    _____ Other (please specify) _____

Facilities

53. Please provide us information on the following facilities:
    #Buildings _____   #Classrooms_____   # Laboratories _____

54. Number of libraries to which students at your program have access _____
        # volumes _____
        # professional journals in environmental and natural resources _____

55. Are these facilities handicapped accessible?   YES: some all   NO

56. Are any natural history or other museums affiliated with your program?   YES NO
    If yes, do students have access to these museum collections?   YES   NO

57. Are there computer facilities at your program?   YES   NO
    a. Number IBM/clone   _____   b. % IBM/ clone   _____
    c. Number Macintosh   _____   d. % Macintosh   _____
    e. Total number of terminals _____   f. #terminal/student ratio _____
    g. Number of Computers for GIS _____
    h. Do you have access to the INTERNET and E-mail?   YES   NO
    i. Is computer training available at your school either free of charge or at low cost?
        YES NO

8

Name of School/Program _____

58. Are there other computer facilities at the university students can use?   YES   NO
    If yes, please describe: _____
    _____

59. Please indicate the percentage of *master's* students that have personal desks or offices in your
    buildings: _____%

60. Please indicate the percentage of *doctoral* students that have personal desks or offices in your
    buildings: _____%

61. Does your program own property that can be used for student research?   YES   NO
    #acres _____
    distance from school # miles_____   #hours _____

62. If you answered yes to number 61, please describe the nature of these facilitites _____
    _____
    _____
    _____

If you have not already done so, please send us information on the following:

•   Employers of recent graduates

•   Titles of representative student research projects, papers, or publications

•   Your program's strategic plan
        Programs in development

•   Research opportunities for students

•   Internships and summer employment opportunities

•   Student clubs and organizations

•   Faculty profiles, Curricula vitae, Publications, External appointments (e.g. Journal editor,
        Board member...), Awards and honors

•   Institutes, research centers, or non-profits organizations affiliated with your program

9

APPENDIX C

RESOURCES

Browstein, Samuel C., Mitchell Weiner, and Sharon Weiner Green. 1994. *Barron's How to Prepare for the GRE*. Hauppauge, NY: Barron's Educational Series, Inc.

Cohn, Susan. 1995. *Green At Work: Finding a Business Career That Works for the Environment (Revised and Expanded Edition)*. Washington, DC: Island Press.

The Environmental Careers Organization. 1995. *The New Complete Guide to Environmental Careers*. Washington, DC: Island Press.

Ferreira, José, Gretchen Van Esselstyn, et al. 1996. *Kaplan GRE All-in-One*. New York: Bantam Doubleday Dell.

Peterson's. 1996. *Graduate and Professional Programs: An Overview 1996*. Princeton, NJ: Peterson's.

Robinson, Adam, and John Katzman. 1996. *The Princeton Review: Cracking the GRE 1997 Edition*. New York: Random House, Inc.

The Student Conservation Association. *Earth Work* (a monthly periodical on environmental careers that includes job listings). Charlestown, NH: The Student Conservation Association.

The Student Conservation Association. 1994. *Earth Work: Resource Guide to Nationwide Green Jobs*. San Francisco: HarperCollins West.

Student Financial Services. 1996. *The Financial Aid Book: The Insider's Guide to Private Scholarships, Grants, and Fellowships*. Seattle, WA: Perpetual Press.

PART IV

INDEXES

SURVEYED UNIVERSITIES WITH GRADUATE ENVIRONMENTAL PROGRAMS BY STATE

ALABAMA

Alabama A&M University (page 41)
Normal, AL 35762

Auburn University (page 52)
Auburn, AL 36849

University of Alabama–Huntsville (see Appendix A)
Huntsville, AL 35899

ALASKA

University of Alaska–Fairbanks (see Appendix A)
Fairbanks, AK 99775

ARIZONA

Arizona State University (page 46)
Tempe, AZ 85287

Prescott College (page 232)
Prescott, AZ 86301

University of Arizona (page 284)
Tucson, AZ 85721

CALIFORNIA

California Polytechnic State University, San Luis Obispo (page 79)
San Luis Obispo, CA 93407

California State University, Chico (page 83)
Chico, CA 95929

California State University, Fullerton (page 87)
Fullerton, CA 92634

California State University, Hayward (page 89)
Hayward, CA 94542

California State University, Long Beach (page 93)
Long Beach, CA 90840

California State University, Northridge (page 95)
Northridge, CA 91330

California State University, Sacramento (page 97)
Sacramento, CA 95819

California State University, Stanislaus (page 101)
Turlock, CA 95382

Humboldt State University (page 150)
Arcata, CA 95521

Moss Landing Marine Labs (page 189)
Moss Landing, CA 95039

San Francisco State University (see Appendix A)
San Francisco, CA 94132

Sonoma State University (page 254)
Rohnert Park, CA 94928

Stanford University (page 262)
Stanford, CA 94305

University of California, Berkeley (page 290)
Berkeley, CA 94720

University of California, Davis (page 292)
Davis, CA 95616

University of California, Irvine (see Appendix A)
Irvine, CA 92717

University of California, Los Angeles (UCLA) (page 294)
Los Angeles, CA 90024

University of California, Riverside (see Appendix A)
Riverside, CA 92521

University of California, Santa Barbara (page 301)
Santa Barbara, CA 93106

University of California, Santa Cruz (page 302)
Santa Cruz, CA 95064

COLORADO

Colorado School of Mines (see Appendix A)
Golden, CO 80401

Colorado State University (page 118)
Fort Collins, CO 80523

University of Colorado at Boulder, School of Law (page 305)
Boulder, CO 80309

University of Colorado at Denver (page 307)
Denver, CO 80217

CONNECTICUT

University of Connecticut (page 312)
Storrs, CT 06269

Southern Connecticut State University (see Appendix A)
New Haven, CT 06515

University of New Haven (see Appendix A)
West Haven, CT 06516

Yale University (page 391)
New Haven, CT 06511

FLORIDA

Florida Institute of Technology (page 140)
Melbourne, FL 32901

Florida State University (see Appendix A)
Tallahassee, FL 32306

Nova Southeastern University (page 205)
Dania, FL 33004

University of Florida (page 315)
Gainesville, FL 32611

University of Miami (page 333)
Miami, FL 33149

GEORGIA

Emory University (see Appendix A)
Atlanta, GA 30322

HAWAII

University of Hawaii at Manoa (see Appendix A)
Honolulu, HI 96822

IDAHO

Idaho State University (page 153)
Pocatello, ID 83209

ILLINOIS

Chicago–Kent College of Law, Illinois Institute of Technology (page 103)
Chicago, IL 60661

Chicago State University (see Appendix A)
Chicago, IL 60628

Eastern Illinois University (see Appendix A)
Charleston, IL 61920

Governors State University (see Appendix A)
University Park, IL 60466

Southern Illinois University at Carbondale (page 256)
Carbondale, IL 62901

Southern Illinois University at Edwardsville (see Appendix A)
Edwardsville, IL 62026

University of Illinois at Springfield (Sangamon State University) (page 318)
Springfield, IL 62794

INDIANA

Ball State University (page 59)
Muncie, IN 47306

Indiana State University (see Appendix A)
Terre Haute, IN 47809

Indiana University (page 156)
Bloomington, IN 47405

Purdue University (page 236)
West Lafayette, IN 47907

IOWA

Iowa State University (page 158)
Ames, IA 50011

University of Iowa (page 320)
Iowa City, IA 52242

KENTUCKY

Eastern Kentucky University (page 135)
Richmond, KY 40475

University of Louisville (page 323)
Louisville, KY 40292

LOUISIANA

McNeese State University (page 172)
Lake Charles, LA 70609

Southern University (page 260)
Baton Rouge, LA 70813

Tulane University (page 280)
New Orleans, LA 70118

MAINE

Audubon Expedition Institute (page 56)
Belfast, ME 04915

College of the Atlantic (page 116)
Bar Harbor, ME 04609

University of Maine (page 325)
Orono, ME 04469

MARYLAND

Frostburg State University (page 142)
Frostburg, MD 21532

Hood College (see Appendix A)
Frederick, MD 21701

Johns Hopkins University (page 162)
Baltimore, MD 21218

University of Maryland at Baltimore (see Appendix A)
Baltimore, MD 21228

University of Maryland at College Park (page 330)
College Park, MD 20742

MASSACHUSETTS

Boston University (page 71)
Boston, MA 02215

Clark University (page 108)
Worcester, MA 01610

Harvard University (page 148)
Cambridge, MA 02138

Massachusetts Institute of Technology (MIT) (see Appendix A)
Cambridge, MA 02139

Tufts University (page 276)
Medford, MA 02155

University of Massachusetts–Amherst (see Appendix A)
Amherst, MA 01003

MICHIGAN

Michigan Technological University (page 177)
Houghton, MI 49931

Michigan State University (see Appendix A)
East Lansing, MI 48824

Northern Michigan University (see Appendix A)
Marquette, MI 49855

University of Michigan (page 336)
Ann Arbor, MI 48109

Wayne State University (see Appendix A)
Detroit, MI 48202

MINNESOTA

Bemidji State University (page 68)
Bemidji, MN 56601

Mankato State University (page 169)
Mankato, MN 56001

University of Minnesota (page 337)
St. Paul, MN 55108

MISSISSIPPI

Jackson State University (page 160)
Jackson, MS 39217

Mississippi State University (page 179)
Mississippi State, MS 39762

MISSOURI

Washington University (see Appendix A)
St. Louis, MO 63310

MONTANA

Montana State University (page 183)
Bozeman, MT 59717

University of Montana (page 340)
Missoula, MT 59812

NEBRASKA

University of Nebraska–Lincoln (see Appendix A)
Lincoln, NE 68583

NEVADA

University of Nevada–Las Vegas (see Appendix A)
Las Vegas, NV 89154

University of Nevada–Reno (see Appendix A)
Reno, NV 89557

NEW HAMPSHIRE

Antioch New England Graduate School (page 43)
Keene, NH 03431

Dartmouth College (page 130)
Hanover, NH 03755

University of New Hampshire (page 344)
Durham, NH 03824

NEW JERSEY

Montclair State University, New Jersey School of Conservation (page 187)
Upper Montclair, NJ 07043

New Jersey Institute of Technology (page 191)
Newark, NJ 07102

Princeton University (page 234)
Princeton, NJ 08544

Rowan College of New Jersey (Glassboro State College) (page 246)
Glassboro, NJ 08028

Rutgers University (page 248)
New Brunswick, NJ 08903

Seton Hall University (see Appendix A)
Newark, NJ 07102

NEW MEXICO

New Mexico State University (see Appendix A)
Las Cruces, NM 88003

NEW YORK

Bard College (page 62)
Annandale-on-Hudson, NY 12504

City University of New York (CUNY) Graduate School
    and University Center (page 105)
New York, NY 10036

Clarkson University (see Appendix A)
Potsdam, NY 13676

College of Staten Island (City University of New York) (see Appendix A)
Staten Island, NY 10314

Columbia University (page 123)
New York, NY 10032

Cornell University (page 125)
Ithaca, NY 14853

Hunter College (City University of New York) (see Appendix A)
New York, NY 10021

Lehman College at the City University of New York (page 167)
Bronx, NY 10468

Long Island University, C.W. Post Campus (see Appendix A)
Brookville, NY 11548

New York Institute of Technology (see Appendix A)
Old Westbury, NY 11568

New York University (page 193)
New York, NY 10003

Pace University School of Law (page 228)
White Plains, NY 10603

Rensselaer Polytechnic Institute (page 239)
Troy, NY 12180

State University of New York (SUNY)
College of Environmental Science and Forestry (page 266)
Syracuse, NY 13210

NORTH CAROLINA

Duke University (page 132)
Durham, NC 27708

North Carolina State University (page 196)
Raleigh, NC 27695

University of North Carolina at Chapel Hill (page 346)
Chapel Hill, NC 27599

OHIO

Case Western Reserve University (see Appendix A)
Cleveland, OH 44106

Miami University (page 174)
Oxford, OH 45056

Ohio State University (page 207)
Columbus, OH 43210

Ohio University (page 212)
Athens, OH 45701

OKLAHOMA

Oklahoma State University (page 214)
Stillwater, OK 74078

University of Oklahoma (see Appendix A)
Norman, OK 73019

OREGON

Northwestern School of Law, Lewis and Clark College (page 203)
Portland, OR 97219

Oregon Graduate Institute of Science & Technology (page 217)
Beaverton, OR 97006

Oregon State University (page 219)
Corvallis, OR 97331

Portland State University (page 230)
Portland, OR 97207

Southern Oregon State College (page 258)
Ashland, OR 97520

University of Oregon (see Appendix A)
Eugene, OR 97403

PENNSYLVANIA

Lehigh University (page 164)
Bethlehem, PA 18015

Penn State University (see Appendix A)
University Park, PA 16802

UTAH

Brigham Young University (page 74)
Provo, UT 84602

Utah State University (page 380)
Logan, UT 84322

VERMONT

Goddard College (page 146)
Plainfield, VT 05667

University of Vermont (page 354)
Burlington, VT 05405

Vermont Law School (page 383)
South Royalton, VT 05068

VIRGINIA

George Mason University (see Appendix A)
Fairfax, VA 22030

University of Virginia (page 358)
Charlottesville, VA 22906

Virginia Polytechnic Institute and State University (page 385)
Blacksburg, VA 24061

West Virginia Graduate College (see Appendix A)
Institute, WV 25112

WASHINGTON

The Evergreen State College (page 137)
Olympia, WA 98505

University of Washington (page 359)
Seattle, WA 98195

Washington State University (page 386)
Pullman, WA 99164

WASHINGTON, DC

George Washington University (page 144)
Washington, DC 20052

WEST VIRGINIA

West Virginia University (page 388)
Morgantown, WV 26506

WISCONSIN

University of Wisconsin–Green Bay (page 362)
Green Bay, WI 54311

University of Wisconsin–Madison (page 364)
Madison, WI 53706

University of Wisconsin–Stevens Point (page 375)
Stevens Point, WI 54481

WYOMING

University of Wyoming (page 377)
Laramie, WY 82071

CANADA

Dalhousie University (page 128)
Halifax, Nova Scotia, Canada B3H 3E2

McGill University (see Appendix A)
St-Anne-de Bellevue, Montreal, Canada PQ H9X 3V9

University of British Columbia (see Appendix A)
Vancouver, BC Canada V6T1Z3

University of Calgary (see Appendix A)
Calgary, Canada, ALB T2N 1N4

University of Toronto (see Appendix A)
Toronto, Canada, ON M5S 3B3

SURVEYED UNIVERSITIES WITH GRADUATE ENVIRONMENTAL PROGRAMS BY SPECIALIZATION

BOTANY

CONSERVATION BIOLOGY / SUSTAINABLE DEVELOPMENT

ENERGY STUDIES

ENVIRONMENTAL ARCHITECTURE
& DESIGN / LANDSCAPE ARCHITECTURE

ENVIRONMENTAL EDUCATION

ENVIRONMENTAL ENGINEERING

ENVIRONMENTAL HEALTH / TOXICOLOGY

Massachusetts Institute of Technology / Center for Environmental Health Sciences (see Appendix A)

New York University / Nelson Institute of Environmental Medicine (page 195)

Penn State University / Environmental Pollution Control Program (see Appendix A)

University of Alaska–Fairbanks / Department of Civil Engineering (see Appendix A)

University of California, Los Angeles / Department of Environmental Health Science (page 294)

University of California, Riverside / Environmental Toxicology Grad Program (see Appendix A)

University of Iowa / Department of Preventive Medicine & Environmental Health (page 320)

University of Pittsburgh / Environmental and Occupational Health (see Appendix A)

University of Wisconsin–Madison / Center for Environmental Toxicology (page 374)

ENVIRONMENTAL JOURNALISM

New York University / Science & Environmental Reporting Program (page 196)

University of Wisconsin–Madison / Program in Environment and Resource Communication, Department of Agricultural Jounalism (page 364)

ENVIRONMENTAL LAW

Chicago–Kent College of Law, Illinois Institute of Technology / Program in Environmental and Energy Law (page 103)

George Washington University / The Environmental Law Program (page 144)

Northwestern School of Law, Lewis and Clark College / Natural Resources Law Institute (page 203)

Pace University School of Law / Environmental Law Program (page 229)

Tulane University Law School / Environmental Law (page 282)

Seton Hall University / Environmental Law Program (see Appendix A)

Southern Methodist University / Environmental Law Program (see Appendix A)

University of California, Berkeley / Program in Environmental Law (page 290)

University of Colorado at Boulder, School of Law / Natural Resources Law Center (page 305)

University of Hawaii at Manoa / Environmental Law Program (see Appendix A)

University of Maryland at Baltimore / Environmental Law Program (see Appendix A)

University of Montana / School of Law (page 343)

Vermont Law School / Environmental Law Center (page 383)

ENVIRONMENTAL STUDIES

FISHERIES SCIENCE

GEOLOGY

HYDROLOGY / WATER RESOURCE MANAGEMENT

NATURAL RESOURCE MANAGEMENT

Ball State University / Department of Natural Resources & Environmental Management (page 59)

Colorado State University / Department of Earth Resources (page 121)

Cornell University / Graduate Field of Natural Resources (page 126)

Duke University / Nicholas School of the Environment (page 132)

Humbolt State University / Natural Resources Graduate Program (page 153)

McGill University / Department of Natural Resource Sciences (see Appendix A)

Purdue University / Department of Forestry and Natural Resources (page 237)

Rensselaer Polytechnic Institute / Environmental Management & Policy Program (page 239)

University of Alaska–Fairbanks / Department of Natural Resources Management (see Appendix A)

University of Arizona / School of Renewable Natural Resources (page 286)

University of California, Berkeley / Department of Environmental Science, Policy & Management (page 292)

University of Calgary / Committee on Resources and the Environment (see Appendix A)

University of Michigan / School of Natural Resources and Environment (page 336)

University of Minnesota / College of Natural Resources (page 337)

University of New Hampshire / Department of Natural Resources (page 344)

University of Rhode Island / Department of Natural Resources Science (page 349)

University of Vermont / School of Natural Resources (page 356)

University of Wisconsin–Stevens Point / College of Natural Resources (page 375)

Utah State University / College of Natural Resources (page 382)

West Virginia University / Division of Resource Management (page 389)

Yale University / School of Forestry and Environmental Studies (page 391)

RANGE SCIENCE

Brigham Young University / Department of Botany & Range Science (page 74)

Colorado State University / Department of Range Science (page 122)

Texas Tech University / Department of Range and Wildlife Management (page 273)

ZOOLOGY